TRIUMPH OF THE
STRAIGHT DOPE

Also by Cecil Adams
The Straight Dope
More of the Straight Dope
Return of the Straight Dope
The Straight Dope Tells All

Also by Ed Zotti
Know It All!

TRIUMPH OF THE STRAIGHT DOPE

Cecil Adams

Edited and with an Introduction by
Ed Zotti

Illustrated by Slug Signorino

Ballantine Books • New York

A Ballantine Book
Published by The Ballantine Publishing Group

http://www.randomhouse.com/BB/

Library of Congress Cataloging-in-Publication Data
Adams, Cecil.
Triumph of the straight dope / Cecil Adams : edited and with an introduction by Ed Zotti : illustrated by Slug Signorino.
p. cm.
ISBN 0-345-42008-X (trade : alk. paper)
1. Questions and answers. 2. Curiosities and wonders. I. Zotti, Ed. II. Title.
AG195.A395 1999
031.02—dc21
98-54615
CIP

Cover and interior illustrations by Slug Signorino

Manufactured in the United States of America

First Edition: February 1999

10 9 8 7 6 5 4 3

To Little Ed, in hopes that someday we'll be able to figure out what it is with him, bratwurst, and rain.

Introduction

Well, here we are, a little sooner than expected, the last Straight Dope book having appeared barely a year ago. The folks at Ballantine were in a big hurry to get this one out, no doubt fearing that the Year 2000 Bug would bring world commerce to a halt, leaving them stuck for the advance. We have now published books at intervals of two years, two years, six years, four years, and one year—a whimsical schedule, some may think, but certainly in keeping with the overall character of the enterprise. We hope at some point to settle into the biennial schedule previously contemplated, but time will tell.

Speaking of the Year 2000 Bug, we note that this book will be appearing in early 1999, mere months before whatever happens at millennium's end in fact happens. Our friend Deborah, more attuned to the moment than we are, suggests we should have taken the opportunity to call this volume *Straight Dope Apocalypse*. Probably we should have, but we had just persuaded Ballantine to let us use the title *Triumph of the Straight Dope*, the first time we have ever gotten a title *we* wanted, mainly by threatening to throw a hissy fit right there in the lobby. So we were not really in a position to come in four weeks later and say we had changed our minds. Whatever may be said for *Apocalypse*, we do feel *Triumph* is a pretty good title, and we urge the Teeming Millions to buy as many copies as they can, since this will significantly enhance our future negotiating position and make us a couple bucks besides.

In this book we continue the practice of including choice excerpts from the Straight Dope Message Board on America Online. We have also included several contributions by the Straight Dope Science Advisory Board, Cecil's raffish but occasionally brilliant online auxiliary. The volume of questions we receive has greatly increased since we went online, and while in one respect this merely means we get thousands of additional iterations of the "gry" question and the like, we also get some genuinely interesting queries that Cecil simply does not have time to address. The Science Advisory Board happily has stepped up to the plate, answering a new question each weekday in the Mailbag section of our AOL site. Cecil is greatly indebted to the SDSAB, although he trembles lest they awaken one day and realize, "By God, we're not getting *paid* for this." But we won't tell them if you won't.

We were going to conclude with some deep thought, but on further consideration have decided to chuck it, since what with the coming of the big 2-triple-zero you're probably getting enough of that kind of thing already. So if we tell you just to go ahead and start reading, don't hold it against us. We are doing the best we can.

—ED ZOTTI

Questions, comments, Pulitzer prize notifications to:

Cecil Adams
c/o Chicago Reader
11 E. Illinois
Chicago, IL 60611
E-mail: cecil@chireader.com
Web site: www.straightdope.com
America Online site at keyword: Straight Dope

Chapter **1**

In The Spotlight

Just what does "colitis" mean? In the song "Hotel California" by the Eagles the first lines are, "On a dark desert highway, cool wind in my hair, warm smell of colitis rising up through the air." I remember I tried looking it up at a university library years ago and couldn't find the answer. I know songwriters sometimes make up words, but I didn't see a Dr. Seuss credit on the album.—Wendy Martin, via the Internet

Uh, Wendy. It's colitas, not colitis. Colitis (pronounced *koe-LIE-tis*) is an inflammation of the large intestine. You're probably thinking of that famous Beatles lyric, "the girl with colitis goes by."

As for "Hotel California," you realize a lot of people aren't troubled

so much by colitas as by the meaning of the whole damn song. Figuring that we should start with the general and move to the particular, I provide the following commonly heard theories:

1. The Hotel California is a real hotel located in (pick one) Baja California on the coastal highway between Cabo San Lucas and La Paz or else near Santa Barbara. In other words, the song is a hard look at the modern hospitality industry, which is plagued by guests who "check out any time [they] like" but then "never leave."

2. The Hotel California is a mental hospital. I see one guy on the Web has identified it as "Camarillo State Hospital in Ventura County between L.A. and Santa Barbara."

3. It's about satanism. Isn't everything?

4. Hotel California is a metaphor for cocaine addiction. See "You can check out any time you like but you can never leave." This comes from the published comments of Glenn Frey, one of the coauthors.

5. It's about the pitfalls of living in southern California in the 1970s, my interpretation since first listen. Makes perfect sense, and goddammit, who you going to believe, some ignorant rock star or me?

6. My fave, posted to the Usenet by Thomas Dzubin of Vancouver, British Columbia: "There was this fireworks factory just three blocks from the Hotel California . . . and it blew up! Big tragedy. One of the workers was named Wurn Snell and he was from the town of Colitas in Greece. One of the workers who escaped the explosion talked to another guy . . . I think it was probably Don Henley . . . and Don asked what the guy saw. The worker said, "Wurn Snell of Colitas . . . rising up through the air."

   He's also got this bit about "on a dark dessert highway, Cool Whip in my hair." Well, *I* thought it was funny.

OK, back to colitas. Personally, I had the idea colitas was a type of desert flower. Apparently not. Type "colitas" into a Web search engine and you get about 50 song-lyric hits plus, curiously, a bunch of citations from Mexican and Spanish restaurant menus. Hmm, one thinks, were the Eagles rhapsodizing about the smell of some good carryout? We asked some native Spanish speakers and learned that colitas is the diminutive feminine plural of the Spanish *cola*, tail. Little tail. Looking for a little . . . we suddenly recalled a (male) friend's guess that colitas referred to a certain feature of the female anatomy. We paused. Naah. Back to those menus. "Colitas de langosta enchiladas" was baby lobster tails simmered in hot sauce with Spanish rice. One thinks: You know, I could write a love song around a phrase like that.

Enough of these distractions. By and by, a denizen of soc.culture. spain wrote: "Colitas is little tails, but here the author is referring to 'colas,' the tip of a marijuana branch, where it is more potent and with more sap (said to be the best part of the leaves)." We knew with an instant shock of certainty that this was the correct interpretation. The Eagles, with the prescience given only to true artists, were touting the virtues of high-quality industrial hemp! (See page 129.) And to think some people thought this song was about drugs.

Our Suspicions Confirmed

This E-mail just in from Eagles management honcho Irving Azoff: "In response to your [recent] memo, in 1976, during the writing of the song 'Hotel California' by Messrs. Henley and Frey, the word 'colitas' was translated for them by their Mexican-American road manager as 'little buds.' You have obviously already done the necessary extrapolation. Thank you for your inquiry."

I knew it.

Why did Charles Manson believe that the Beatles song "Helter Skelter" was about the upcoming race war? Are there any documents that you own that say why in hell he would think this, other than the fact that he is crazy?—J.C. from MI

I'd say the fact that he's crazy pretty well covers it. "Helter Skelter," which appeared on the Beatles' White Album, was Paul McCartney's attempt to outrock Pete Townshend of the Who. Some Beatles fans describe the song as heavy metal, which is putting it a bit strongly. But it had more energy than most McCartney compositions of the period, and the descending refrain "helter skelter" lent it an edginess that made it stick in the mind.

The song's musical qualities had very little to do with its subject matter, however. "In England, home of the Beatles, 'helter skelter' is

another name for a slide in an amusement park," Manson prosecutor Vincent Bugliosi tells us in his book about the case, *Helter Skelter.* The *Oxford English Dictionary* further clarifies that a helter skelter is "a towerlike structure used in funfairs and pleasure grounds, with an external spiral passage for sliding down on a mat." Recall the opening line: "When I get to the bottom I go back to the top of the slide / Where I stop and I turn and I go for a ride." It's a joke, get it? The Rolling Stones might do this faux bad-guy thing about putting a knife right down your throat, but the ever-whimsical McCartney figured he'd rock the house singing about playground equipment.

All this went over the head of Charles Manson. He thought Helter Skelter was the coming race war and the White Album was a call to arms. If you're in a certain frame of mind you can understand some of this—e.g., the "piggies" in the tune of the same name, who need a "damn good whacking," and the sounds of gunfire in "Revolution 9." But to think that the line "you were only waiting for this moment to arise" in the song "Blackbird" was an invitation to black people to start an insurrection . . . sure, Charlie. Whatever you say. Now put down that gun.

In your book The Straight Dope *you were asked whether John Wayne had ever served in the military. You said no—that though*

Wayne as a youth had wanted to become a naval officer, "during World War II, he was rejected for military service." However, it may be more interesting than that. According to a recent Wayne bio, for all his vaunted patriotism, Wayne may actually have tried to stay out of the service.—Virgiejo, via AOL

John Wayne, draft dodger? Oh, what delicious (if cheap) irony! But that judgment is a little harsh. As Garry Wills tells the story in his book *John Wayne's America: The Politics of Celebrity* (1997), the Duke faced a tough choice at the outset of World War II. If he wimped out, don't be so sure a lot of us wouldn't have done the same.

At the time of Pearl Harbor, Wayne was 34 years old. His marriage was on the rocks, but he still had four kids to support. His career was taking off, in large part on the strength of his work in the classic Western *Stagecoach* (1939). But he wasn't rich. Should he chuck it all and enlist? Many of Hollywood's big names, such as Henry Fonda, Jimmy Stewart, and Clark Gable, did just that. (Fonda, Wills points out, was 37 at the time and had a wife and three kids.) But these were established stars. Wayne knew that if he took a few years off for military service, there was a good chance that by the time he got back he'd be over the hill.

Besides, he specialized in the kind of movies a nation at war wanted to see, in which a rugged American hero overcame great odds. Recognizing that Hollywood was an important part of the war effort, Washington had told California draft boards to go easy on actors. Perhaps rationalizing that he could do more good at home, Wayne obtained 3-A status, "deferred for [family] dependency reasons." He told friends he'd enlist after he made just one or two more movies.

The real question is why he never did so. Wayne cranked out thirteen movies during the war, many with war-related themes. Most of the films were enormously successful, and within a short time the Duke was one of America's most popular stars. His bankability now firmly established, he could have joined the military, secure in the knowledge that Hollywood would welcome him back later. He even made a halfhearted effort to sign up, sending in the paperwork to enlist in the naval photography unit commanded by a good friend, director John Ford.

But he didn't follow through. Nobody really knows why; Wayne didn't like to talk about it. A guy who prided himself on doing his own stunts, he doesn't seem to have lacked physical courage. One suspects he just found it was a lot more fun being a Hollywood hero than the real kind. Many movie-star soldiers had enlisted in the first flush of patriotism after Pearl Harbor. As the war ground on, slogging it out in the trenches seemed a lot less exciting. The movies, on the other hand, had put Wayne well on the way to becoming a legend. "Wayne increasingly came to embody the American fighting man," Wills writes. In late 1943 and early 1944 he entertained the troops in the Pacific theater as part of a USO tour. An intelligence big shot asked him to give his impression of Douglas MacArthur. He was fawned over by the press when he got back. Meanwhile, he was having a torrid affair with a beautiful Mexican woman. How could military service compare with *that*?

In 1944 Wayne received a 2-A classification, "deferred in support of [the] national . . . interest." A month later the Selective Service decided to revoke many previous deferments and reclassified him 1-A. But Wayne's studio appealed and got his 2-A status reinstated until after the war ended.

People who knew Wayne say he felt bad about not having served. Some think his guilty conscience was one reason he became such a superpatriot later. The fact remains that the man who came to symbolize American patriotism and pride had a chance to do more than just act the part, and he let it pass.

Some Warner Brothers cartoons are called Looney Tunes; some are called Merrie Melodies. What's the difference between the two?
—*Arnold Wright Blan, Sugar Hill, Georgia*

My initial idea was to tell you that Looney Tunes and Merrie Melodies reflected the dichotomy between the Apollonian and Dionysian impulses or, if you will, the classical and romantic modes of creative expression. However, even I couldn't keep up a crock like that. Then I figured, This is Hollywood, there's gotta be some mercenary angle to it. Sure enough. While there were differences between Tunes and Melodies, the main reason for having two separate series was that's the way they'd structured the deal.

At the outset, the two series were made under separate agreements between Warner Brothers and producer Leon Schlesinger, using different production teams. The Looney Tunes series, created by Hugh Harman and Rudolph Ising, was introduced in 1930. A blatant rip-off of Disney's Silly Symphonies series, each Looney Tune was required to have one full chorus from a song from a Warner feature film. The cartoons typically were run prior to the main feature at theaters, and the idea was that they would promote WB product. (Among other things, the company had various music-publishing concerns.) The schedule called for a new cartoon approximately once a month.

The Tunes were immediately popular, and the following year Warner commissioned Schlesinger to produce a sister series called Merrie Melodies, which also appeared monthly. (The volume of cartoons fluctuated in later years, but the two series were always produced in roughly equal numbers.) At this point Harman and Ising divided responsibilities, with Harman in charge of Looney Tunes and Ising handling the Melodies. Merrie Melodies also featured Warner songs, but where Tunes had regular characters, Melodies for the most part were one-shots, without continuing characters. Another difference was that Melodies were shot in color starting in 1934, while Tunes stayed black-and-white.

In my younger days I would have stopped right there. However, if there's one thing I've learned in this business it's that you can never overestimate the anality of film and animation buffs. Someone would inevitably have made the following observations:

1. By the late 1930s regular characters started appearing in Merrie Melodies, and by the 1940s the same characters were appearing interchangeably in both series.
2. Some of Schlesinger's production people switched freely back and forth between series.
3. Looney Tunes were shot in color after 1943.
4. Leon Schlesinger retired in 1944 and Warner Brothers began doing cartoon production in-house, after which time (and probably long before which time) there was no reason to maintain any distinction between Looney Tunes and Merrie Melodies. The two separate series titles persisted because, you know, there'd always been two separate series titles, and they had different theme music, and why rock the boat?
5. Nyaah nyaah nyaah nyaah.

So childish. Nonetheless, the fact remains that the difference between Looney Tunes and Merrie Melodies was pretty much an existential thing. On a practical level it prepares us to deal with the many meaningless distinctions of life—e.g., Pepsi versus Coke, MasterCard versus Visa, and the Democrats versus the GOP. The Saturday-morning 'toons just a way to kill time? Please. They're Introduction to Reality 101.

While leafing through my Rolling Stone Illustrated History of Rock N' Roll, *I came upon the horrifying fact that Chuck Berry's "Johnny B. Goode," the song that started rock, peaked at #8 in 1958. What seven forgettable songs were deemed better than this classic?—Tim Ring, Montreal, Quebec*

Cecil loves the classics as much as the next guy, but let's not get carried away. "Johnny B. Goode" did not start rock. Even "Maybellene," Chuck Berry's first hit (#5 in 1955), did not start rock, although it was one of the earliest rock tunes to make it big. If you've got to pick one tune that put rock 'n' roll over the top, I still say it's got to be Bill Haley's "Rock Around the Clock," which became—admittedly not right away—a monster hit, selling 22 million copies. And let's not forget the righteous contribution of Alan Freed, the Cleveland DJ who attached the term "rock 'n' roll" to the emerging new sound in 1954.

"Johnny B. Goode" peaked at #8 on the *Billboard* charts on May 5, 1958. My assistant Little Ed, in his ceaseless drive to muck up my holy work, threw out all my old *Billboards* last spring, but I still have the monthly composite chart for May 1958 compiled by Dave McAleer, on which "Johnny B. Goode" ranks #11. It got beaten out by the following tunes, some of which, God help me, I cannot remember, and some of which, God help me, I can't forget: 1) "All I Have to Do Is Dream," Everly Brothers; 2) "Witch Doctor," David Seville; 3) "Wear My Ring Around Your Neck," Elvis Presley; 4) "Twilight Time," Platters; 5) "He's Got the Whole World (In His Hands)," Laurie London; 6) "Return to Me," Dean Martin; 7) "Book of Love," Monotones; 8) "Looking Back/Do I Like It," Nat "King" Cole; 9) "Tequila," Champs; 10) "Oh Lonesome Me/I Can't Stop Lovin' You," Don Gibson.

Don't feel sorry for Chuck Berry, though. He had two other Top 40 hits in 1958, "Sweet Little Sixteen" (peaked at #2) and "Carol" (#18), plus several others that made it into the Top 100. And he definitely had the last laugh. In a career that included such gems as "Roll Over Beethoven" (#29, 1956) and "No Particular Place to Go" (#10, 1964), his only #1 hit was the inane "My Ding-a-Ling," which held the top spot for two weeks in 1972.

There was a news story a few years back about a jazz musician who died and was found to be a woman after living her life as a man. She was married and had three grown children who refused to believe their father was a woman. No one I ask remembers this. Do you?
—SMENGI, *via AOL*

You think I could forget the story of Billy Tipton? Yes, she lived as a man from age 21 till the day she died at age 74. Yes, her three sons (all adopted) never suspected a thing. But that's not the bizarre part. She lived with five women in succession, all of them attractive, a couple of them knockouts. She had intercourse with at least two of them and, who knows, maybe all five. But of the three we know about in detail, none tumbled to the fact that her husband was a woman (one figured it out later). At first you might think: Man, I thought *my* spouse was oblivious. But the more charitable view is that they were taken in by one of the great performances of all time.

We know as much as we know about Billy thanks to a newly published biography by Diane Wood Middlebrook, *Suits Me: The Double Life of Billy Tipton.* Middlebrook reports that Dorothy Lucille Tipton decided to become Billy Tipton in 1935, ostensibly because it was the only way an aspiring jazz musician could get work in an almost exclusively male business. The transformation wasn't all that tough. Billy's face was boyish, and her figure was more Coke can than Coke bottle. (She had sizable breasts but no waist.) A sheet wrapped around her chest, men's clothes, and a bit of padding in the crotch, and she easily passed. In fact, Billy was positively handsome; women thought he was a doll. A talented pianist, horn player, and tenor, he quickly found a gig with a band.

At first Billy was strictly a cross-dresser, making no great effort to conceal her femaleness during her off hours. She lived with a woman with the unusual name of Non Earl Harrell, in what other musicians assumed was a lesbian relationship. Initially they were based in Oklahoma City, but by 1940 they had moved to Joplin, Missouri, then an entertainment center. There Billy began to masquerade as a male full-time, a pose he would adopt for the rest of his life.

Billy and Non Earl broke up in 1942. After a liaison of some years with a singer named June, Billy took up with Betty Cox, a pretty 19-year-old with a striking figure. The two stayed together for seven years, during which time they had what Betty recalled as a passionate heterosexual relationship, including intercourse. She even thought she'd had a miscarriage once. How could you share a bed with someone for seven years and not realize he was a she? Breathtaking naïveté had to be part of it, plus the fact that, as an accomplished entertainer who was 13 years Betty's senior, Billy called the shots. They made love only in the dark. Billy never removed his underwear and wore a jockstrap that Betty later speculated was fitted with a "prosthesis." He wore massive chest bindings at all times, supposedly for an old injury. He would not let himself be touched below the waist or disturbed in the bathroom. Betty also may have been a bit distracted. Acquaintances said she went out with other men while she was with Billy, and while she appears to have been genuinely fond of him, in some ways this may have been a marriage of convenience for both.

A turning point in Billy's life came in 1958. He had his own trio and a growing reputation, and a new hotel in Reno wanted to hire his group as its house band. He seemed on the verge of, if not the big time, at least a fairly high-profile career. But Billy declined. Instead he took a job as a booking agent in Spokane, Washington, playing music on the side. Middlebrook thinks he feared fame would lead to discovery and decided he'd gone as far as he dared.

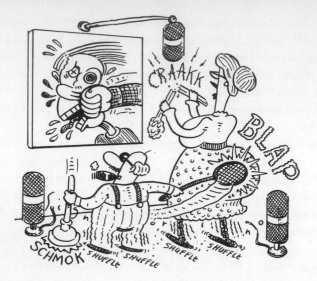

At this point Billy was living with a sometime call girl, but in the early '60s he left her for a beautiful but troubled stripper named Kitty Kelly. She claimed she and Billy never had sex, but in other respects they lived a stereotypical suburban life. They adopted three boys, but neither could handle the kids during adolescence, and after a bitter quarrel in 1980 Billy moved into a trailer with his sons. From there it was all downhill. The boys split, his income dried up, and he spent his last years broke. Refusing to see a doctor despite failing health, he collapsed and died in 1989. The paramedics who were trying to revive him uncovered the truth. Death must have come as a relief; he had been on stage nearly 54 years.

In movies, when someone lands a punch there's this nifty slappy sound that real punches just don't make. What is that sound?
—*Adam S., New Haven, Connecticut*

Welcome to the world of "Foley artists," the unsung geniuses who create the larger-than-life sound effects that make a flick come alive. For a good face punch, a Foley artist might hit a piece of raw meat with his fist, maybe wearing a tight leather glove for enhanced smackiness. I'm told rib cuts are particularly good to use because they have bones to give a crunchy effect. Then again, maybe the Foley artist will just punch himself—hard. The beauty of Foley—named after Jack Foley, chief sound effects guru at Universal for many years—is that nobody's telling you exactly what you have to do. All that counts is that it works on-screen.

Foley art is made necessary by the fact that 1) you need "action noise" (i.e., more than just the actors talking) to make a movie scene seem real, and 2) miking the entire stage or location during shooting just isn't practical. Even if it were, real-life sounds often don't have the oomph the big screen demands. In addition, dubs for foreign markets often require that a sound track be created completely from scratch. So Foley artists add sound in postproduction. The most basic type of Foley consists of one or more people walking around in a well-miked "Foley pit" filled with gravel, sand, loose audiotape (to mimic the sound of crunching leaves), etc., to re-create the sounds of the actors in motion. They do this while watching the movie with the sound off, synchronizing their movements with the action on the screen. This requires a good sense of timing and rhythm, and maybe for that reason a lot of Foley artists are also musicians.

Some Foley effects have been around since the dawn of the talkies—for example, walking on cornstarch in a burlap bag to create the sound of crunching snow. Another time-tested technique is drawing a paddle full of nails across a piece of glass to create the sound of branches scratching on a windowpane.

Other sound effects are of more recent vintage. Foley artist Greg Mauer told us he was recently working on a vampire flick that had a scene in which a character's guts get pulled out. Greg used raw chicken, which he likes because you get a nice moist sound he describes as "slimy." For a simple broken bone there's nothing like the crisp sound of snapping a stalk of celery or a chicken bone.

Not all Foley is fake. If a scene calls for somebody falling, a lot of Foley artists figure there's no substitute for actually falling. Same with walking on sand. But if you need the sound of 150 people running around, no way you're actually going to cram 150 people into the Foley pit. Instead you have maybe three Foley artists laying down a half-dozen tracks. Mix 'em together and voilà—crowd noise.

As you might surmise in this age of high-tech special effects, cinema sound can involve lots of fancy enhancements you'd need a degree in computer science to understand. But it's good to know there's still a place in the movie business for guts and red meat.

While watching a recent interview with Emmylou Harris, I was horrified when a member of the audience asked a rather personal question about Gram Parsons ("Why did Gram Parsons kill himself at such a young age?"). Ms. Harris handled the question gracefully and moved on to other, more pertinent topics (the sad state of commercial country music), but the question got me thinking. I've been a fan of Parsons's music but don't really know all that much about him as a person, other than that he died young and there was some controversy surrounding his death. Can you fill me in?—Jamie D., East Lansing, Michigan

Glad to. Some guys lead weird lives, some guys have weird deaths. Not everybody has a weird cremation.

Gram Parsons has become something of a cult figure in the music business. He never hit it big, and few outside a small circle remember him now. But people who ought to know say he was one of the pioneers behind the country-rock phenomenon of the late 1960s and early '70s. A member of the Byrds for a short time, Parsons was the creative force behind their 1968 country album, *Sweetheart of the Rodeo*, which many consider a classic. He went on to form the Flying Burrito Brothers and later invited then unknown Emmylou Harris out to L.A. to sing on his solo album, *GP* (1973), helping to launch her career. He hung out with the Rolling Stones (his influence can be heard on several cuts from *Exile on Main Street*) and had a big impact on Elvis Costello, Linda Ronstadt, Tom Petty, and the Eagles. Remember New Riders of the Purple Sage and Pure Prairie League? They owed a lot to Parsons. He's received many posthumous honors and musical tributes; Emmylou Harris is working on a tribute album now, 25 years after his death. Best of all, he was born Ingram Cecil Connor III (Parsons came from his stepfather), and you gotta love a guy with a name like that.

Parsons wasn't a suicide, but he killed himself, all right. Blessed with charm and cash (his mother's family had made a pile in the citrus business), he got into booze and drugs early. In September 1973 he finished recording an album and went with some friends to an inn at

Joshua Tree National Monument, one of his favorite places. The group spent much of the day by the pool getting tanked. By evening Gram looked like hell and went to his room to sleep. Later, on their way out for some food, his friends were unable to rouse him, so they left, returning a little before midnight. By that time Parsons was pretty far gone. Taken to a hospital, he was pronounced dead shortly after midnight on September 19. A lab analysis found large amounts of alcohol and morphine in his system; apparently the combination killed him. News coverage of his demise was eclipsed by the death of Jim Croce around the same time. Parsons was 26 years old.

So far, your typical live-fast-die-young story. Then it gets strange. Before his death Parsons had said that he wanted to be cremated at Joshua Tree and have his ashes spread over Cap Rock, a prominent natural feature there. But after his death his stepfather arranged to have the body shipped home for a private funeral, to which none of his music buddies were invited. Said buddies would have none of it. Fortified by beer and vodka, they decided to steal Parsons's body and conduct their own last rites.

Having ferreted out the shipping arrangements, Phil Kaufman

(Parsons's road manager) and another man drove out to the airport in a borrowed hearse, fed the poor schmuck in charge of the body a load of baloney about a last-minute change of plans, signed the release "Jeremy Nobody," and made off with Parsons's remains. They bought five gallons of gas, drove 150 miles to Joshua Tree, and by moonlight dragged the coffin as close to Cap Rock as they could. Kaufman pried open the lid to reveal Parsons's naked cadaver, poured in the gas, and tossed in a match. A massive fireball erupted. The authorities gave chase but, as one account puts it, "were encumbered by sobriety," and the desperadoes escaped.

The men were tracked down a few days later, but there was no law against stealing a body, so they were charged with stealing the coffin or, as one cop put it, "Gram Theft Parsons." (Cops are such a riot.) Convicted, they were ordered to pay $750, the cost of the coffin. What was left of Parsons was buried in New Orleans.

So, youthful high jinks or breathless stupidity? All I know is, I'd want my friends to show a little more enterprise keeping me alive than torching my corpse.

A friend pointed out a haunting secret tucked away in the depths of The Wizard of Oz. *Way in the background at the end of the scene where the angry trees shake apples onto Dorothy, the Tin Man, and the Scarecrow, you can see a man who is supposedly hanging himself. As the trio dances off on the Yellow Brick Road singing "We're Off to See the Wizard," you can catch a glimpse of this man supposedly setting out a block, hanging himself, and lastly kicking the block out with his foot. Although this image is real enough to give you chills, it could conceivably be a fake. Is it? If it is real, then why did the director keep it in the movie? What is the story of this man?—James Leary, via the Internet*

You may say: Cecil, why are you spending time on this obviously brain-damaged question? Come on, tell me *you* wouldn't jump at a chance to call up Munchkins. Besides, I looked at the movie, and you know what? There *is* something strange going on.

The alleged suicide comes not at the end of the apple-tossing scene (at which point the Tin Woodsman hasn't yet appeared) but roughly eight minutes later, after the Wicked Witch has made a surprise visit

and then vanished in a cloud of orange smoke. Resolving to be brave, Dorothy, the Scarecrow, and the now-present Tin Man link arms, march out to the Yellow Brick Road, and dance around a bit. In the background at this point, in about the center of the frame, one can see a dimly lit stand of trees. Something is moving near these trees, but it's hard to make out what. The trio sashays off toward the rear of the set, in the general direction of the trees, then veers and exits stage right. Just as they leave the frame, a limblike thing near the trees swings up briefly into a horizontal position, then drops again. A suicide kicking the ladder out from beneath himself? Or—you have to consider all the possibilities—the leg of a naked woman in the throes of a passionate embrace?

You can guess what I saw. However, the most common version of the legend has it that this is the on-camera suicide of a despairing Munchkin. (Runner-up: a despairing, or just accident-prone, stagehand. Some claim the victim had recently been fired.)

The Straight Dope research department, known for its dogged investigative skills, tracked down Stephen Cox, author of an entertaining volume titled *The Munchkins of Oz* (1996). Cox, who interviewed more than 30 Munchkins to collect stories about the making of the movie, dismissed the suicide story and hinted at an alternative theory, which we'll get to in a moment. He also put us in touch with Mickey Carroll, 78, one of 13 Munchkins still alive today (out of an original 124). Carroll said he'd first heard the story about five years before but also thought it was bunk. "We were on the set for two months," he said. "I think I would have known if someone committed suicide." (Incidentally, several Munchkins did get fired—one for threatening his wife with a gun—but apparently none was the suicidal type.)

Well, OK. But then what are we seeing? Cox points out that if you look closely during the eight or nine minutes preceding the "suicide," i.e., from just before Dorothy and the Scarecrow encounter the apple-tossing trees, you can spot a large bird strolling around the set—maybe a crane or a stork. (For much of the time it appears to be tethered near the house on which the Wicked Witch perches.) Presumably the bird is supposed to provide atmosphere, but basically all it does is pop into the frame at odd moments. Reviewing the "suicide" with this in mind, we instantly realize: it's the stupid bird pecking the ground and then flapping its wings! Though, this being Hollywood Babylon and all, a naked woman's leg can't be entirely ruled out. But the adult in us knows the truth.

Recently on your America Online site you posted your old column about Rock'n Rollen Stewart, the guy who used to hold up those "John 3:16" signs at sports events. You may be interested to know that Stewart is now serving a life sentence in jail.—Name withheld, via AOL

Yowsah. I lost track of Rollen after talking to him in 1987. At the time he struck me, and I'd say most people, as a harmless if obsessed flake. Shows how wrong you can be. A few years later Stewart went completely off his nut, staged a series of bombings, and wound up in prison after a bizarre kidnapping stunt. The whole story is told in *The Rainbow Man/John 3:16*, a documentary by San Francisco filmmaker Sam Green. If you doubt that too much TV is bad for you, you won't after seeing this flick.

Stewart's problems started during his childhood in Spokane, Washington. His parents were alcoholics. His father died when Rollen was

seven. His mother was killed in a house fire when he was 15. That same year his sister was strangled by her boyfriend. A shy kid, Rollen got into drag racing in high school, married his first love, and opened a speed shop. But his wife soon left him. Crushed, he sold the shop and moved to a mountain ranch, where he became a marijuana farmer, tried to grow the world's longest mustache, and watched a lot of TV.

In 1976, looking for a way to make his mark, Rollen conceived the idea of becoming famous by constantly popping up in the background of televised sporting events. Wearing a multicolored Afro wig (hence the nickname "Rainbow Man"), he'd carry a battery-powered TV to keep track of the cameras, wait for his moment, then jump into the frame, giving the thumbs-up and grinning. Rollen figured he'd be able to parlay his underground (OK, background) celebrity into a few lucrative TV gigs and retire rich. But except for one Budweiser commercial, it didn't happen.

Feeling depressed after the 1980 Super Bowl, he began watching a preacher on the TV in his hotel room and found Jesus. He began showing up at TV events wearing T-shirts emblazoned with "Jesus Saves" and various Bible citations, most frequently John 3:16 ("For God so loved the world, that he gave his only begotten Son," etc.). Later accompanied by his wife, a fellow Christian he married in the mid-80s, he spent all his time traveling to sports events around the country, lived in his car, and subsisted on savings and donations. He guesses he was seen at more than a thousand events all told.

This brings us to the late '80s. By now Rollen had gotten his 15 minutes of fame and was the target of increasing harassment by TV and stadium officials. His wife left him, saying he had choked her because she held up a sign in the wrong location. His car was totaled by a drunk driver, his money ran out, and he wound up homeless in L.A. Increasingly convinced that the end was near, Rollen decided to create a radically different media character. He set off a string of bombs in a church, a Christian bookstore, a newspaper office, and several other locations. Meanwhile, he sent out apocalyptic letters that included a hit list of preachers, signing the letters "the Antichrist." Rollen says he wanted to call attention to the Christian message, and while this may seem like a sick way to go about it, it wasn't much weirder than waving signs in the end zone at football games. In any case, no one was hurt in the bombings, which mostly involved stink bombs.

On September 22, 1992, believing the Rapture was only six days away and having prepared himself by watching TV for 18 hours a day, Stewart began his last "presentation." Posing as a contractor, he picked up two day laborers in downtown L.A., then drove to an airport hotel. Taking the men up to a room, he unexpectedly walked in on a chambermaid. In the confusion that followed he drew a gun, the two men escaped, and the maid locked herself in the bathroom. The police surrounded the joint, and Rollen demanded a three-hour press conference, hoping to make his last national splash. He didn't get it. After a nine-hour siege the cops threw in a concussion grenade, kicked down the door, and dragged him away.

About to be given three life sentences for kidnapping, Rollen threw a tantrum in the courtroom and now blames everything on a society that's "bigoted toward Jesus Christ." A cop who negotiated with him by phone during the hotel standoff had a better take on it: "With all due respect, maybe you look at a little bit too much TV." For info on the *Rainbow Man* documentary, write Sam Green, 2437 Peralta St., Suite C, Oakland, CA 94607.

From The Straight Dope Message Board

Subj: The four races of men
From: Jeuvohed
I know about Caucasoid, Mongoloid, and Negroid. What's the fourth?

From: Bermuda999
Hemorrhoid.

From: DMG550
Paranoid?

From: JonRandall
Herculoid.

From: FixedBack
Celluloid.

From: PUNditOK
Polaroid. While polaroids tend to be odd sized when compared with other races, there is no doubt that their rapid development gives them an evolutionary edge.

Financial Disclosure

Why does the U.S. dollar bill have the image of a pyramid with an eye in the capstone? Someone told me that it has something to do with a shadow society that secretly rules the country. If they're so secret, why would they be so obvious about their insignia? I want the straight dope—that is, unless they've gotten to you too.—Jason K., Scarborough, Ontario

They haven't. Ticks me off. Why should guys from the dailies get all the payola? As for the apparent paradox of a secret society advertising itself in one of the world's most conspicuous places, some say that's the beauty of it. The conspirators are geniuses, see? They know that the more they make themselves obvious, the more they'll be invisible. If

that sounds like a classic line of malarkey . . . bud, you're starting to catch on.

As you know if you've read the fine print, what you see on the back of a dollar bill is the great seal of the United States, established by Congress on June 20, 1782. The official interpretation is that the pyramid represents strength and durability. It's incomplete because so is the work of building the nation. The eye in the triangle is the all-seeing eye of Providence.

What makes the story interesting is that the eye and pyramid have links to Freemasonry. The eye, for example, is said to be a symbol of the Great Architect of the Universe—i.e., God. The symbolic significance of the pyramid and the eye were well known to educated folk of the eighteenth century, and one may argue that the Masons and the designers of the seal were merely drawing on a common fund of symbolic meaning. But what if . . . one pauses pregnantly . . . there's more to it?

Due to incomplete records, nobody knows exactly how many of the founding fathers were Masons. But there were quite a few, including George Washington, Ben Franklin, and possibly Thomas Jefferson. Franklin and Jefferson were on the committee assigned to design the great seal. This group produced a design calling for, among other things, an all-seeing eye. While the eye was cool, the design otherwise was pretty feeble, and the job wound up getting dumped on the secretary of the Congress, Charles Thomson. Thomson enlisted the aid of Philadelphian William Barton. The two cooked up the scheme we have today, incorporating the all-seeing eye plus a pyramid, because everybody liked the idea of Egyptian symbolism.

It's not known if Barton and Thomson were Masons, and judging from surviving correspondence there's no indication a Masonic connection crossed anybody's mind at the time. But it's crossed lots of minds since. Theories range from Nuts to Really Nuts to Grounds for Immediate Commitment. Joseph Campbell, in *The Power of Myth,* proposed a wacky but basically genial interpretation that works in Solomon's Seal and the Pythagorean *tetrakys* and Egyptian folklore. Upshot: the seal is a symbolic representation of democracy. Fine as far as it goes, but lacking the essential element of paranoia. For this we turn to the religious right, which sees the eye and pyramid as evidence of a Masonic plot (by George Washington!) to destroy Christianity.

And then, of course—you knew I was getting to this—there's the Illuminati connection. As you know from our previous discussions of this subject, the Illuminati are the grand cabal behind everything, including, some think, weird stuff on money. The question is, Who's behind the Illuminati? Wise individuals, I venture to say. Indeed, we may characterize them as wise guys. I'm thinking of Robert Anton Wilson and Robert Shea, who in the mid-'70s wrote the conspiracy satire *Illuminatus!*, which has become a cult classic. Wilson et al. have been shoveling baloney about the Illuminati/eye on the pyramid/world-domination conspiracy for more than 20 years, and some credit them with single-handedly keeping the thing alive. At the risk of belaboring the obvious, it's a joke intended to separate hip folk (who get it) from right-wing losers (who don't). So, Jason, let me ask you. You think it's real?

What has happened to 50-cent pieces? I suppose the collectors are hoarding all the silver ones, but what has happened to the cheap imitations? Nobody talks about this. Another cover-up conspiracy? —Bill Mitchell, Berkeley, California

Time to appoint another special prosecutor. I mean, who cares about presidential sex scandals? This is *big*.

The immediate reason you don't see halvies is that the U.S. mint doesn't make many—30 million in 1993, compared to 1.3 billion quarters. The mint says it doesn't make many because of lack of consumer demand; in fact, they've thought about eliminating the denomination altogether. Some coin experts say consumers don't demand half-

dollars because vending machines, pay phones, etc., won't accept them. A vending industry spokesman says nonsense, the machines don't accept them because people don't use them. A spokesman for the Coin Coalition, a trade group, says it's not the public that won't use halvies, it's retailers, who dispense most change. We could go on like this all day.

Time for Cecil to cut through the crap. In my opinion the main reason you don't see half-dollars is that virtually all of those minted from 1964 onward were snatched from circulation by hoarders, and people simply learned to do without.

It all started with the introduction of the Kennedy half-dollar in 1964. Though the earlier Franklin half-dollar had never been wildly popular, production had risen from 20 million in 1959 to 90 million in 1963, presumably due to rising demand. But demand for Franklin halves was nothing compared to that for Kennedy halves. That proved to be the half-dollar's undoing.

Virtually every Kennedy half minted between 1964 and 1970— nearly 1.3 billion coins—disappeared from circulation as soon as it was issued. Kennedy admirers took many, of course, but silver speculators got most of the rest. The price of silver was rising at the time, and though quarters and dimes were promptly switched to cupronickel-clad copper, the silver content of halves was kept relatively high, apparently because of lobbying by the silver industry. Whatever the reason, the half-dollar ceased to play any part in daily commerce.

The mint surrendered to reality in 1971 and began making half-dollars out of cupronickel-clad copper. But though production continued to be high—280 million halves were minted in 1974—it was still rare to see a half-dollar in everyday circulation, perhaps because by then it seemed such a novelty that anyone who received one immediately stashed it away as a souvenir.

In 1975 the first of nearly 530 million bicentennial half-dollars were issued. These vanished like the billions of other halves before them, no doubt because the finite (if large) number of coins produced led them to be regarded as collector's items. Issuance of standard Kennedy halves resumed in 1977 in more modest quantities, and today they can usually be obtained at banks, although it may take some asking around. But there is little demand for them, the economy having adapted to their nonavailability.

Too bad. What with inflation, a widely available (and accepted) high-value coin would eliminate the need to drag along a fistful of quarters when going to the Laundromat or buying a Sunday newspaper from a coin box. The vending companies also would love a popular high-value coin, since bill-accepting technology is much more expensive and failure-prone than coin mechanisms. The main job of the Coin Coalition, in fact, is lobbying for a dollar coin to replace the failed Susan B. Anthony coin—doomed, depending on whom you talk to, either by its similarity in size to a quarter or by the failure of the government to withdraw dollar bills upon introducing it. (Withdrawal of Canadian dollar bills was the main thing that put the Canadian dollar coin over.) There's talk now about taking another stab at it; let's hope the people at the Treasury have learned from their mistakes.

My mail is deluged with worthless credit-card solicitations and pleas for donations, all bearing telltale stamps of odd denomination: "Tractor 7.1 cents nonprofit," "Oilwagon 10.1 cents bulk rate," "Railroad Mail Car 21 cents presorted," etc. These stamps are almost never canceled. Can I reuse them for my own (nobler) epistles, provided they add up to 29 cents?—Gary Schwartz, Chapel Hill, North Carolina

Um, 32 cents. Guess your letter was delayed in the mail. But I know what you're talking about. As you probably guessed, you can't reuse these oddball stamps legally. The whole point of such stamps is that they don't require cancellation. Eliminating a step in handling saves the postal service money, which it passes along to mailers in the form of rate discounts. Thus the odd denominations. Skipping the stamp altogether and using a bulk-rate-postage-paid mark printed on the envelope (an "indicia") would save the senders even more money (no labor to stick stamps), but some bulk mailers prefer stamped letters on the theory that they're less likely to get thrown away unread.

What's to prevent you from reusing the stamps? Couple things. One, bulk-rate stamps are used on bulk mail—that is, a big presorted heap o' letters delivered directly to the P.O. accompanied by the necessary form. If your solitary letter shows up in a collection box, that's a pretty good clue it's not legit. Two, stamps intended for first-class mail have a phosphorescent ink on them to help orient the letter properly for cancellation. If the canceling machine doesn't detect any phosphorescent ink (most of the stamps you mention don't have it), the letter is kicked out for special handling, at which point your little dodge may be discovered.

Granted, it probably won't be. Given a volume of 550 million pieces of mail per day, it's likely most of your illicit missives will get through. Reused metered mail—e.g., clasp envelopes that don't show obvious signs of having been opened and readdressed—is even less likely to be detected; postage meters use phosphorescent ink, and it's perfectly OK to drop a single metered item in the mailbox.

Most mail without proper postage is simply returned. If you cheated in quantity and conspicuously encouraged your friends to do the same, the feds might decide to charge you with conspiracy and fraud. But the real deterrent is that most people have what's known as a life. You'd have to be pretty desperate for entertainment to take any deep satisfaction in cheating the government out of 32 cents.

By some accounts, the Social Security trust funds now have over half a trillion dollars, while others say the money in these funds is so phony it may as well have Art Linkletter's picture on it. Are the assets in these funds actually worth half a trillion dollars, or is it all a sham?—Daniel Moore, Chicago

Is it a sham? This is such a negative way of looking at things, Daniel. Better we should ask ourselves: What is reality?

Social Security, in theory, is a break-even proposition. Payments to retirees are supposed to be balanced by taxes collected from the poor stiffs who are still working (and their employers). Long ago some genius realized that once baby boomers got to retirement age, there was

going to be a lot more cash going out than coming in. So Social Security taxes were hiked to build a surplus that we could draw down later. This surplus, in theory (again), goes into a trust fund.

So far, so good. The problem is that the trust fund is not some gigantic sack of cash somewhere, or even a bank account. It's just a bunch of entries in the government's account books. All Social Security assets are automatically invested in special U.S. bonds, the proceeds from which pay off current government debts. In short, skeptics say, the trust funds are a scam: we're using the money we're supposed to be saving for tomorrow to help us scrape through today.

At this point the debate gets pretty woolly. Some in the don't-worry-be-happy school excuse the government's semi-fishy invest-in-ourselves approach by saying governments can't save the way people can. Nonsense. There is nothing to prevent the government from taking all the Social Security taxes it collects, burying the dough in a big can in the backyard, and disbursing the worm-eaten remains thirty years hence. Or, more plausibly, investing in Japanese savings bonds or GM notes or any other investment vehicle.

Would those investments be more "real" than investing in U.S. bonds? Depends how you mean. All unsecured financial obligations are built on air. If you walk into the Japanese savings bond agency or the GM treasurer's office and ask to see the assets underlying their financial instruments, what will they have to show you? Nothing; the money went to pay off current debts. Presumably, however, the venture as a whole prospers, and it is in the belief that it will continue to do so that one reposes one's hope for future repayment.

The question then becomes: Who's the best bet to pay off 30 years from now on an obligation issued today? The U.S. government, of course. Naturally, there is the possibility that we will run up such staggering deficits that interest payments will consume the entire federal budget or cause the government to default, in which case not only do pensioners get stiffed, so does everyone else. But that problem is independent of concerns about Social Security per se.

Not so fast, say the skeptics. When you strip away the fancy bookkeeping, the fact remains that the government is using the Social Security surplus not to build productive assets but to buy paper clips, million-dollar outhouses, and all manner of other foolishness. When the time comes to fund the baby boomers' pensions, Uncle Sam will have to raise the money as it always does, through taxes or borrowing, regardless of whether there's a paper surplus in some trust fund. Senator Daniel Moynihan thinks we should quit kidding and operate Social Security on a "pay as you go" basis—just collect enough this year in taxes to pay this year's pensions.

But Moynihan doesn't get it either. The Social Security surplus has the practical effect of reducing the real federal deficit—no small achievement. And while a pay-as-you-go policy would mean lower payroll taxes now, taxes would rise steeply when the baby boomers began shoving off for Sun City. If I were a Generation Xer faced with the prospect of paying crushing taxes to finance the golden years of my obnoxious elders, I think I'd just as soon leave things as they were.

How come the portraits on coins are always in profile, while the ones on paper money are always full face?—Jim Bohannon, Arlington, Virginia

You think this is a stupid question, eh? Pull out some cash and have a look. The coin portraits are in profile, every one. The old white guys on currency, on the other hand, are all in full face. (Well, up to twenties, anyway. I like to keep my liquidity low.) Is it coincidence . . . or plot?

Fact is, while full-face portraits on coins aren't completely unknown, they're definitely rare, mostly showing up on commemoratives. The reason is that it's tough getting a realistic likeness in full face, given the constraints of the medium. The relief on modern mass-circulation coins is low—typically just sixteen-thousandths of an

inch—to permit them to be cranked out by the boatload on high-speed equipment. That doesn't give the coin designer much room for the detailing that, on paper money or a stamp, makes a full-face portrait easily recognizable. In a profile view, on the other hand, you can often tell who's being depicted from the silhouette alone.

Currency designers prefer full-face or three-quarter views for the same reason any portraitist does—so the subject can face the viewer. The only time coin designers can depict someone in full face is on commemoratives, which are more carefully struck and can be in higher relief. Even so, the eye sockets are often set so deep that the subject looks like the victim of a famine.

Full-face portraits on coins were more common once upon a time. They enjoyed something of a vogue in the Middle Ages, mainly because, even though they were totally unrealistic, they were simple to execute with the primitive tools of the time. But as Renaissance princes acquired more power, they began to look askance at the amateurish full-face depictions of their august selves on the realm's coinage. Forsooth, they said, my two-year-old couldst do better than that. Guess I better have the royal coiner disemboweled. Mintmasters switched to the profile pronto.

Coin historian Richard Doty has dug up two examples of English coins illustrating the change during the reign of Henry VII, 1485–1509. The portrait on the first coin, apparently minted early on, is a nondescript full-face view that could have been most anybody. Henry, who had reached the throne by overthrowing his predecessor, probably concluded that it would be smart to let people know who was in charge, and so the later coin shows him quite realistically in profile. Or at least it realistically shows somebody. Paranoia being no less a factor then than today, maybe it was the royal gardener, so as to throw off assassins. Be that as it may, profiles on coins have been pretty much standard ever since.

I notice magnetic strips have been placed in bills denominated $10 and up, 1990 series and later. I have been told this is part of an anti-counterfeiting scheme, but I wonder. Can airports or other places with metal detectors pick up the dollar amounts when you pass through the gates? Is this another attempt by Big Brother to keep tabs on us?
—*P.R., Madison, Wisconsin*

Oh, right, like the government has nothing better to do than count your bankroll by remote control. Conceivably it would be useful to know if some international drug smuggler were trying to sneak a suitcase full of twenties on the next flight to Little Rock, but the "magnetic strips"—actually they're nonmagnetic polyester filaments—won't help Big Brother do that either. The filament, which is embedded in the bill to the left of the Federal Reserve seal and says USA TWENTY, is strictly an anticounterfeiting move. High-quality color photocopiers have made counterfeiting easy, and the number of fakes out there has been rising fast. Since it's embedded in the bill, the polyester filament won't be picked up by the copier and the lettering won't be visible when you hold the fake bill up to the light.

A more subtle anticounterfeiting measure, also introduced in 1990, is "microprinting," which consists of the words THE UNITED STATES OF AMERICA printed repeatedly in tiny type around the portrait of the bill. The type is virtually unreadable by the naked eye and can't be picked up by copiers, but high-speed counting equipment at the Federal Reserve will yank out any microprintingless bills it detects.

There's also magnetic printing on U.S. currency—always has been, in fact. But it can't be detected from afar, and even detecting it close up requires a more expensive bill-validating device than the average vending-machine manufacturer wants to invest in. Most bill-accepting machines strictly check optical characteristics and so can be fooled by a good copy. For added realism, put your fakes in a nylon stocking with some pebbles and give them a 10-minute rinse in a washing machine. That'll dull the finish and give them a worn appearance, meaning you'll be able to con not only electronic eyes but human ones too.

I learn all this from Frank Abagnale, a convicted check forger turned D.C.-based consultant who makes his money telling banks how to avoid getting scammed by the likes of his former self. He reports that if you use rice paper in a Canon 500 color copier you can make fake money that's virtually impossible to distinguish from the genuine article on casual examination. The copies are so good that the government prevailed upon Canon to replace the 500 with a new model, the 550, which has a computer chip that detects when you're trying to copy money and prints a black block instead.

Even better fakes are being cranked out now in countries like Iran. Apparently the bad guys (the Iranian government?) got hold of a multimillion-dollar intaglio printing press like the ones the feds use. They've cranked out anywhere from one to 20 billion dollars of fake cash, most of which is circulating in the Middle East. But it's started to show up here too, and some officials are so alarmed they're urging that $100 bills be abolished. The Drug Enforcement Administration is all for it, because big bills are used so often in drug deals.

Many countries use high-tech anticounterfeiting stratagems, such as holograms and multiple-color printing, in their currency. By comparison, faking a U.S. bill, whose basic two-color design hasn't changed since 1913, is child's play. The new bill designs now being introduced supposedly will make it tougher, but it won't help if the public doesn't get a clue. To demonstrate how easy it was to pass fake money for a TV news story, Frank Abagnale—with the blessing of federal agents—made some crude counterfeits on ordinary bond paper in an unsophisticated Canon 200 copier and successfully passed them at 10 stores in Philadelphia. Only one merchant noticed anything funny about the money, and he merely commented that, gosh, he hadn't realized the government was changing the paper it used to print currency. Excuse me, can anyone lend me carfare to Philadelphia? I want to see if I can sell 'em a bridge.

How does a person get listed in the Social Register? Obviously genetics must be a factor, along with piles of money. But many people with both appear to be excluded, while others lacking one or the other

are listed. Who decides, anyway? And why does such a silly institution continue in the first place?—Fania, Washington, D.C.

They leave you out again, kid? I told you they wouldn't be impressed by that bowling trophy. Although the Social Register folks declined to be specific, I gather you have to be invited. There's an anonymous admissions committee, and if you can get five people who are already in the book to nominate you, or, even better, if you can get married to a listee, you've got a chance. If that doesn't work, your best bet is to get yourself elected president of the United States—he always gets in, whether he deserves it or not.

The concept behind the Social Register takes a while to grasp. Here we have the 30,000 snootiest families in the country, and they consent to put their addresses and phone numbers in a book available in the public library. Think of the junk mail these guys must get. On the other hand, in a society full of climbers and frauds, I suppose there's a need for a quick-and-dirty way of distinguishing the quality from the shlubs. Screening ensures that the people who make it in aren't merely rich, they're Our Sort—no guarantee that a listee isn't a heel, but at least he's discreet.

The Social Register takes pride in not explaining itself. We know that it was first published in 1887 in New York and that there were separate editions in major cities until 1977, when everything was consolidated into one national book. Two editions are published annually—the main one in November, and a summer version in May.

The rest you've got to piece together for yourself, which isn't easy. Much of the book is written in some sort of Venusian Morse code. In the 1991 edition, for example, after the entry for Charles Norton Adams (no relation), we find the following: "Unn.Nrr.Srb.BtP.Evg.Myf.Ht.Cw." Goodness, you think, next time they ask the man for information they should untie the gag. But actually the letters are abbreviations for Charles's clubs. If we refer to the front of the book we learn that "Nrr" is the Newport Reading Room, "Srb" is the Spouting Rock Beach club, and "Unn" is either a typo or some place so exclusive that to have to ask about it is proof that you don't belong there. Mr. Norton isn't listed in the 1994 book, and one can only surmise that he is Dd.As.A.Stn.

In addition to the main listing, there are various special sections, such as Births, Deaths, and Marriages. (One longs in publications of this type for a section called Indictments, but no such luck.) Some sections are completely mysterious. In the front of the summer edition, for example, there is something called "Dilatory Domiciles." Dilatory in my book means "tending toward procrastination," which does not shed much light. One supposes that some editorial type was taking aim at "temporary residences" and missed. Equally puzzling, at least initially, is a section called "Married Maidens." What are we trying to say here—former virgins? On inspection, it turns out to be a cross-reference of women's married and maiden names.

There is much in the Social Register to remind you that this is not a book meant for thee and me. In the summer edition, for instance, we find the following note: "A listing of Yachts and Their Owners is included for the convenience of subscribers." Sure, like the subscribers are going around slapping their foreheads and saying, "Damn, what *is* the length, tonnage, and builder of Chumley's boat?" That said, there is something charming in knowing that Mr. Lawrence H. Mott's "Ellen" (home port Charlotte, Vermont) is 15 feet long with a beam of 4½ feet. Would that the same honesty had been applied to summer residences, all of which seem to have names like "The Pines." Come on, doesn't anybody live at "The Dump"?

On Getting Socially Registered

Regarding my column on the *Social Register,* Gregory Nigosian refers me to geographer Stephen Richard Higley's recent book *Privilege, Power, and Place: The Geography of the American Upper Class,* which maps out where rich folks live based on their listings in the 1988 edition. Great book, not least because it explains what "dilatory domiciles" means: listings that the listees turned in too late to make it into the main book (DDs appear in the summer supplement), along with changes of address.

Higley confirms what everybody suspected: the SR is heavily skewed toward old money and the East Coast. The seaboard states from Maine to Virginia account for two-thirds of the listings, with nearly one-third located in just two states, New York (5,838) and Pennsylvania (4,200). New money is grossly underrepresented. California has 2,517 SR households, fewer than Massachusetts (3,231), although it has five times the population. Texas has just 424 SR families (it *is* hard to imagine Ross Perot at the polo club, although the '94 book lists several other Perots). At the bottom of the list is North Dakota, with 1 SR family—no doubt the toast of Fargo.

Higley does not have much useful advice on how you can get into the SR. (Evidently you can just apply, like you can probably just apply to be pope.) But he does point out that it's pretty easy to get kicked out. There were 38,000 families in the 1984 book, but a great purge the following year reduced that number by 3,500, and more have hit the road since. Sad evidence of this comes from H.M., an SR listee from Chicago. H. (who according to his listing is actually H. the Third) got in because his mother's side married into a Mayflower family. But his four sisters were delisted because they married members of the steerage crowd, thereby diluting the gene pool. H.'s mom thinks he'll get the boot, too, once he marries his sweetie, whom H. cheerfully describes as NOKD—"not our kind, dear." He didn't sound real concerned. Kiss up to the gentry and you might increase your social stature, but I bet hanging with us mutts is more fun.

Excerpts From The Straight Dope Message Board

Subject: bathroom
From: NTTtgif
Why is going to the bathroom a group activity for women in general? Are they telepathically summoned, or what?

From: Ezotti
They all have to help. You don't want to know more.

From: Sonne Flwr
It's all about strategy.

From: Unimprssd
Personally, I choose to go alone, but I understand why other women flock to the lavatory like a herd of sheep. We like to talk and need a place to do it. It's an estrogen thing, I guess.

From: WildBabe96
I usually choose to go alone, too—except in the case of a blind date/double date combo, in which case I drag the bitch who set me up with the loser off to the bathroom with me to scream at her.

From: Editeers
Have you noticed the length of the lines into the women's bathrooms? Why stand there staring like a cow when you can finally chat with your buddy during the hour or so you have to wait in line?

From: CkJ246
Company.
And who are these women who pee all over the seat? Getting VD from the toilet seat is a MYTH. Sit down already!

From: Anne J2
I've always preferred to go alone, but I do have a theory. You need at least two people: one to use the stall, and one to hold the door in

case the latch thingie doesn't work. Ever try to use a toilet while leaning (or, worse, *pulling*) on the door to keep it shut?

From: ITURI

What's really bad is when the hinges swing freely in both directions and you have to ride that fine line between push and pull to keep it from (a) swinging outward and letting the whole world see you in all your glory or (b) having it swing inward under the pressure of your foot and smacking you in the head.

3

Nature's Way

The other day one of my professors asked why moths were attracted to light. Someone thought it might be because they thought it was the moon. But even granting that moths might not be bright enough to tell a porch light and a celestial body apart, why should they be interested in the moon? Please, Cecil, this may be worth extra credit to me.
—Shannon, Montreal

Always glad to help Straight Dopesters with their homework, *ma petite*. You going to let me have the gold star?

For many years it was thought the moon did have something to do with the attraction of moths to light. The so-called light-compass theory held that moths used the moon as a navigational beacon. By keeping it at a constant angle to their direction of travel, they were supposedly able to fly in a straight line.

The trouble came when the moths made their sightings on a close-up light source like a candle flame. Instead of heading in a straight line, they flew around the flame in an ever-narrowing spiral until finally, phhhht, moth flambé.

But this theory had more holes in it than a moth-eaten sweater. The main problem was that moths simply don't fly around lights in spirals.

This was shown by the ingenious bug researcher Henry Hsiao. He tethered moths to little Styrofoam boats in a tiny artificial pond—I love guys like this—and tracked their flight as they headed toward a light source.

He found that the moths flew more or less straight at the light until they got up close, at which point they veered off and circled around it at a more or less constant distance. They seldom actually touched the light.

A number of other theories also have been discredited. Some claim that, to the moth, bright lights mean open space and open space means safety. But moths are nocturnal, and the night sky has no light sources anywhere near as bright as a porch light. Besides, why should the moth feel compelled to fly around the light in circles?

Others argue that moths associate light with warmth. Yet ultraviolet lamps, which are much cooler than incandescent bulbs, attract more moths.

Henry Hsiao to the rescue. He said moths exhibit two kinds of behavior. When they're distant from a light source (they're drawn to light from as far as 200 feet away), they make a beeline straight toward it.

Why, nobody knows. Maybe they've tumbled to the fact that lights mean people, and people mean: wool sweaters! On an even more basic level, a light means: other moths! Par-*ty*!

However. When the moths get close to the light, a different kind of behavior takes over. Instead of being attracted to the light, the moth is actually trying to avoid the light.

When you think about it, this is only natural. To a creature of the night like a moth, daylight and by extension any bright light means danger.

Owing to a peculiarity of vision called a Mach band, the moth doesn't fly directly away from the light. A Mach band, which apparently is common to all sighted creatures, is the region surrounding a bright light that seems darker than any other part of the sky.

Hsiao conjectured that the moth's atom-size brain figures the darkest part of the sky is safest. So it circles the light in the Mach band region, usually at a radius of about one foot, depending on the species. Eventually either its momentum carries it away or it finds a dark corner to hole up in.

In short, moths like some light, but not too much. Hey, at some point in our lives we're all attracted to those bright porch lights. But that doesn't necessarily mean you'd want to live above a singles bar.

Is it true honey is really . . . bee vomit?—Lisa, Chicago

Well . . . yeah. This isn't something the Honey Marketing Association is going to make the centerpiece of its next ad campaign, but the fact is that honey is made from nectar the worker bees regurgitate, which is a polite way of saying vomit.

The bees collect the nectar from flowers and store it in their "honey stomachs," separate from their true stomachs. On their way back to the hive they secrete enzymes into it that begin converting the stuff into honey. Once in the hive they yuke up the nectar and either turn it over to other workers for further processing or else dump it directly into the honeycomb. The bees then beat their tiny wings to fan air through the hive to evaporate excess water from the honey. Last, they

cover the honeycomb cell with wax, figuring, Hey, we worked like dogs, but at least now we'll be able to get a snack whenever we want. Suckers. The humans steal the honey, pack it in bottles, and there you go—direct from the bees' guts to yours.

I know what you're thinking. You're thinking, Gosh, Unca Cecil, what *other* fun facts do you know about bees? Well, in my opinion, you can never know too much about an insect's sex life. Did you know that proportionally to its body size, the genitalia of a drone bee are among the largest of any animal on earth? Mention this to the girls over a game of bridge and you'll definitely get the conversation off Tupperware.

The size of its equipment is thought to be directly related to the drone's postcoital fate—namely, death. My bee book notes, "[The genitals] are contained in the abdomen, and presumably getting them out of the abdomen for the purpose of mating places such a strain on [the bee] that it dies in the process." As I understand it, the proximate cause of the drone's demise is that its privates are (urk) ripped off during the act. One more reason for caution, boys, when we are fumbling in the dark.

One last thing. Despite its status as bee stud, the drone is not itself produced as a result of sex. On the contrary, it develops from an unfertilized egg. (Fertilized eggs become either workers or queens.) My bee book drolly comments, "Thus the queen bee is capable of parthenogenesis and drone bees have no father, only a grandfather." You think your family is dysfunctional, be glad you're not a bee.

What Goes Down Must Come Up

You erred in describing honey as "bee vomit." Strictly speaking, it is bee regurgitation. Regurgitation is the voluntary bringing up of nutrients. Vomiting is involuntary.—Marty, Chicago

If it looks like vomit, walks like vomit, and quacks like vomit, I say it's vomit. My trusty *American Heritage Dictionary*, I'm happy to say, backs me up.

My boyfriend says plants and trees have natural life spans like ani-
mals. I say if a plant doesn't die of disease, drought, famine, fire, etc., it
will not die. Look at those age-old trees out in California. Please help
us settle this argument.—S.U., Chicago

Death, disease, drought, famine—at last a question that *speaks* to
me. To simplify matters, let's just talk about trees. One may speak of
trees having life spans, in the sense of having an average life expectancy. The *Encyclopaedia Britannica* notes that the "lifespans of
trees, like those of all organisms, are limited." But while this is certainly true—no tree is immortal—it's also deceptive. Trees may have
life spans, but they don't have *fixed* life spans, as animals do. It is reasonably certain that no human, no matter how coddled, would survive
past some definite point—say, 130 years. But this cannot confidently
be said of trees.

The most striking illustration of this is the bristlecone pine, *Pinus*
aristata. A 1948 field guide noted that bristlecones reached maturity
in 200–250 years, with "extreme ages of 300–375 years." Yet only 10
years later a researcher discovered a stand of bristlecones whose average age exceeded 4,000 years, and in one case 4,600 years.

Other examples are less dramatic but still instructive. Red maples
live 80–250 years; American chestnuts 100–300; white oaks 300–600;
bald cypresses 600–1,200. These extremely broad ranges suggest that
assigning a "life span" to trees is merely a statistical convenience
rather than a reflection of an inherent limit. It would not be surpris-
ing (to me, anyway) if much older examples of these species were
found.

Trees endure as long as they do basically because they're nonhierarchical organisms. In animals, all vital functions are controlled by the central nervous system, the guiding element of which is the brain. When the brain dies, so does the animal. By contrast, vital functions in trees are decentralized. A large part of the tree can die, and indeed routinely does die, without killing off the tree as a whole. Most of a mature tree is dead except for a few layers under the bark.

Trees have an astonishing capacity for survival. The oldest bristlecone pine is described as "a gnarled jagged piece of deadwood . . . overlaid on one side by a narrow strip of living bark barely sufficient to connect the few remaining living roots with its few remaining living branches. Yet every year the sap rises" (Feininger, 1968).

All trees die eventually, of course. Four thousand years is old compared to the life spans of gossamer creatures like ourselves, but in the context of geologic time it's the blink of an eye. As they get older trees become more susceptible to disease, pests, and other perils, and inevitably these take their toll. But think how different our conception of mortality would be if *we* were like trees: You probably won't last past 375 years, Jack, but play your cards right and you *might* squeak out 4,600. I don't know about you, but I'd definitely watch my weight.

This has been bothering me for years. How close to the ceiling does the housefly get before turning around to stand on it? Also, am I crazy to sit and ponder this?—Georgia R., Elizabethtown, Kentucky

Maybe, but I'm not complaining. At least you're not shooting up a post office. Besides, you're in good company. Many great minds of science have ruminated on this vital issue. They were less concerned with how close, though, than with how period, since landing upside down is no mean feat.

The leading theory for years was that the flies did a half barrel roll sideways à la the Blue Angels just before landing. This idea was shot down in 1958 when *Natural History* magazine published photos showing that in fact flies do a sort of backward somersault.

On approaching the ceiling, and while still flying right side up, flies extend their forelegs over their heads till they can grab a landing spot with the suction cups in their feet. Their momentum then enables them to swing their hind legs up, like a gymnast on a trapeze. Result:

inverted fly, home and dry. So the answer to your query is, they get real close. Hope that'll do.

'Scuse me, but . . . how do they grow more seedless fruit?—Just askin', Salt Lake City, Utah

Guess you can't just plant more seeds, huh? But the fact is, you wouldn't want to plant seeds even if you could. Sexual reproduction, which is mostly what you're talking about when you grow things from seeds, is too chancy. Tell me about it, you mutter. But if you think *you've* got problems, talk to a commercial fruit grower. An important function of sex, after all, is to shake up the gene pool. While that lends a certain charming variety to the offspring of us humans, it's not something you want to encourage in, say, a Thompson seedless grape.

Luckily, sex is only one method of propagating a species. There's also asexual reproduction. You're thinking: So that's how my parents did it! No, smarty-pants. Asexual reproduction means making copies of the parent plant by means of cuttings, grafting, and so on. The off-spring plants have the advantage—from a horticultural standpoint—of being perfect genetic duplicates or clones of the parent plant. So once you've bred the ultimate rutabaga or what have you, you can crank out exact copies unto the hundredth generation. And people do just that. Some grape "cultivars," as human-bred (and often human-dependent) varieties are called, date from Roman times—that is, the plants we have today are exact genetic copies of ones first grown 2,000 years ago.

What I'm telling you is that seedlessness is no big obstacle, plant re-production-wise. Most grape varieties, seedless or not, are reproduced by grafting. Ditto for citrus and fruit trees in general. (Actually, I believe they "bud" fruit trees, but let's not trouble ourselves with details.)

So you think you understand? Time to obfuscate the situation. It's possible to buy seeds that, when planted, produce seedless watermelons. Whence cometh this seed? It's the product of an unnatural union between different varieties of watermelon, resulting in a hybrid that, like many hybrids, is sterile. You plant the hybrid seeds, and you get a plant whose fruit matures but whose seeds are underdeveloped. To make more seed you have to keep mating the mommy and daddy plants. There is vastly more to it than that, but that's about all I can explain without charging you quarterly tuition. Pass me a grape.

When I was in college, not so many eons ago, it was pretty much an article of faith among us intellectual iconoclasts that, though we could put a man on the moon, we still had no idea how a bumblebee could fly. Do we?—Keith Hanson, Silver Spring, Maryland

Of course. You think this is on a par with quantum mechanics? The basic principles of bumblebee flight, and insect flight generally, have been pretty well understood for maybe 50 years. Somehow, though, the idea that bees "violate aerodynamic theory" got embedded in folklore.

The whole thing probably sprang from a faulty analogy between bees and conventional fixed-wing aircraft. Bees' wings are small relative to their bodies. If an airplane were built the same way, it'd never

get off the ground. But bees aren't like airplanes, they're like helicopters. Their wings work on the same principle as helicopter blades—to be precise, "reverse-pitch semirotary helicopter blades," to quote one authority. A moving airfoil, whether it's a helicopter blade or a bee wing, generates a lot more lift than a stationary one.

The real challenge with bees wasn't figuring out the aerodynamics but the mechanics: specifically, how bees can move their wings so fast—roughly 200 beats per second, which is 10 or 20 times the firing rate of the nervous system. The trick, apparently, is that the bee's wing muscles (thorax muscles, actually) don't expand and contract so much as vibrate, like a rubber band. A nerve impulse comes along and twangs the muscle, much as you might pluck a guitar string, and it vibrates the wing up and down a few times until the next impulse comes along. Cecil is sliding over a few subtleties here, but nobody ever said science for the masses was pretty.

Would one ocean pour into the other if the locks on the Panama Canal were blown? If not, let's say a mile-deep trench were dug from coast to coast. Would there be flooding then, huh?—Eliot R., Los Angeles

No, you mollusk. They don't have locks on the Panama Canal because one ocean is higher than the other, they have them because the land is higher in the middle—85 feet higher, to be exact. As I have explained in the past, the level of the sea is more or less uniform throughout the world, making the concept of "sea level" possible.

But that's not to say you wouldn't get any flow from one ocean to the other if somebody dug your "mile-deep trench" from coast to coast. Scientists studying the feasibility of a sea-level canal (not a mile deep, but deep enough) have found that the Pacific at Panama is about eight inches higher than the Atlantic on average, because of currents and such. In addition, tidal variation on the Pacific side of Panama is much greater than that on the Atlantic side—20 feet versus 1 foot.

That means the Pacific would flow into the Atlantic through the sea-level canal, producing currents that could reach nearly 6 mph. While that wouldn't cause flooding, it would definitely complicate navigation.

But that's the least of the problems a sea-level canal would present. It would also allow Pacific and Atlantic marine species to mingle, with

unpredictable but probably bad consequences for the environment. Worse, constructing it would require either 1) tens of billions of dollars or 2) nuclear explosives. So don't expect it anytime soon.

I recall reading that if you attach a polygraph machine to a tree and then project harmful thoughts at it, the machine will register "lies" or "stress." Did I imagine this? Do trees have not only emotions but ESP?—Javier Ramirez, Los Angeles

Feh. You undoubtedly read something about a crackpot classic from the '70s called *The Secret Life of Plants,* by Peter Tompkins and Christopher Bird. The centerpiece of the book was the work of one Cleve Backster, an expert in lie-detector machines. On a whim in 1966, Backster hooked up a plant to a polygraph and found that it reacted sharply when he merely thought about burning one of its leaves. To test the plant's reaction to the extinction of other forms of life, Backster dumped some brine shrimp into a pot of boiling water. The plant, obviously outraged, showed a violent response (or so Backster claimed). Ergo, plants have ESP.

Tompkins and Bird cited other research supporting Backster's findings. One researcher claimed that plants sulked when insulted. Electronics whiz Paul Sauvin said he'd wired up a philodendron to a sensing device tuned in to a radio gizmo in a nearby car. When Sauvin beamed a telepathic message to the plant from his home two miles away, it triggered a signal that caused the car to start.

Another researcher found that an ordinary green pea registered a half-volt discharge at the moment of its death. If enough peas were wired together in series, he speculated, you could generate 500 volts, enough to cause a human to explode. Luckily, he explained, most recipes for peas don't involve wiring them in series, so the actual danger was slight.

Other scientists, however, were unable to replicate these findings. They concluded that plant telepathy was a fantasy. Proponents responded that the plants were just refusing to cooperate with hostile researchers. Matters came to a head at a conference in 1975, when Backster admitted he'd never bothered to repeat his original experiments. He did report, however, that he had begun a promising new line of research. He'd poured milk into a container of yogurt and immediately detected a sympathetic response in another container of yogurt nearby. This greatly amused the assembled reporters, who phoned in stories about the "world's first inter-yogurt communications system." The conference ended in disarray, and little has been heard from the psychic-plant crowd since.

Botany Update

Longtime readers will recall the heated debate in this space some years ago over the identity of a tree, originally spotted in Los Angeles, that at certain times of the year smelled like, uh, sperm. (To be precise, like semen. But you know what we mean.)

It wasn't our idea to get into this repulsive topic. It did, however, capture the imagination of the Teeming Millions. Not that the Teeming Millions were much help getting to the bottom of it. Despite repeated pleas, no one ever sent us an identifiable sample, and we never settled the matter.

The controversy flared anew on our America Online message board. But this time our call for samples got results. In fact, we got two samples—one from Robert Williams, the other from Brian Maffitt.

Just one little problem. They weren't the same tree. What's more, neither of them was among the trees suggested in our previous go-round on this subject.

According to a plant expert at Morton Arboretum near Chicago, one specimen was an ailanthus, a.k.a. tree of heaven, and the other was a species of chestnut. The chestnut was pretty dry by the time I got it, but the ailanthus—no question, definitely spermlike.

Previously the consensus was that the sperm tree was the carob tree, with one radical holding out for the California privet. Now we've got three or four possible sperm trees out there.

So there you have it. The truth ain't pretty. But I feel you need to know.

From The Straight Dope Science Advisory Board

Decades ago, when I was a lad, I remember a late '50s or early '60s cartoon called the Eighth Man or 8-Man, something like that. It was your typical cartoon superhero fare except that this little critter got his superhuman strength from smoking cigarettes (I think they were cigarettes). Whenever he found himself in a weakened state, he'd simply light another doobie and off he'd fly. I've yet to find anyone else who remembers this 'toon, so it may simply be the result of my own early drug dependence. Oh, and I also recall that whatever text showed up on-screen, such as a traffic sign or store names, was in Chinese, Japanese, or some other 'ese. Ring any bells?

Ah, America's confused love/hate relationship with the cartoon. In the early '90s, Bart Simpson's proclamation that he was an "underachiever and proud of it!" prompted some schools to ban students from wearing T-shirts featuring the yellow-skinned character. Next MTV's Beavis and Butthead are blamed for the death of a child due to Beavis's obsession with fire. Yet in 1965, a superhero was arguably teaching kids to smoke—a good 20 years before villainous Joe Camel hit the scene—and nobody objected.

Having said that, whatever drugs the watching of "8-Man" inspired you to abuse didn't affect your memory of the show; you've pretty much got it down. "8-Man" originated as a weekly comic strip in Japan (those in the know, and who obsess over such things, refer to these Japanese comics as *manga*), and eventually was produced as a half-hour cartoon show (56 episodes were produced). The animated

"8-Man" was a hit in Japan, and, as was the case with other Japanese series ("Astro-Boy," "Gigantor," "Speed Racer," etc.), it was soon imported into America, redubbed, re-edited, retitled (from "8-Man" in Japan to "The Eighth Man" here), and put out on the airwaves. Both manga and *anime* (Japanese animation, also beloved by these same social misfits) versions followed the same general plot: police detective Peter Brady is murdered by a notorious gangster, then brought back to life—as a humanized robot with superhero strength named Tobor (read the name backwards and groan)—by a brilliant scientist, and goes on to fight crime.

After having read that, I know what you're thinking: This 8-Man sounds like it might have inspired a popular '70s live-action show. And while it is possible, it's still highly doubtful that producer Sherwood Schwartz was watching "8-Man" when naming the middle boy on "The Brady Bunch." Other, more fanciful minds have found similarities between "8-Man" and a little show called "The $6 Million Man" (and, years later, the film *RoboCop*).

Now about those cigarettes. While most doctors will tell you to *quit* smoking if you want to be able to continue participating in any sort of strenuous activity such as beating up criminals, 8-Man/Brady/Tobor was advised the opposite. Feeling run-down? Light up! When in need of a burst of energy, 8-Man recharged his atomic energy supply with tiny strength pills, which were in the form of cigarettes. After a few drags on his special smokes, 8-Man was as alive with pleasure as any of the playful subjects in a typical Newport ad, and once again ready to battle his nefarious foes.

It seems that back in the '60s, when this series first aired, parents were either blissfully unaware of what was happening on the shows their kids watched, or they were smart enough to realize, unlike today's fretful folks, that they were just harmless cartoons. 8-Man may have been unique in that he got his strength from smoking a substance manufactured in a lab and wrapped in rolling papers, but characters on other shows from this same era got their strength in equally suspicious ways—at least by today's standards. Henry Cabot Henhouse III was transformed immediately into Super Chicken after gulping down his "Souper Sauce," and both Roger Ramjet and Underdog were popping pills to get their anabolic highs.

Just try getting *that* on TV today. Better, apparently, that kids be watching the slightly masked profanity and the supposedly hilarious running gag of a child being violently killed each week on the abysmally written, acted, and animated *South Park*.

—*SDSTAFF Scott,*
Straight Dope Science Advisory Board

Chapter **4**

Time And Weather

One thing I have never understood is daylight saving time. Why can't we just put the clock forward a half hour next spring and then never touch it again?—Chris Tittle, earth

The newspapers have been trying to explain this for years, and still nobody gets it. Time to bring out the big battalions. People have the idea that the purpose of daylight saving time is to give them more time to frolic on summer evenings. Hah. The real purpose is to conserve energy. You want to line up the hours of daylight with the hours most people are up and about: that way, they'll use the lights less and we'll waste less oil, coal, etc.

On December 21 sunrise is around 7:20 A.M. and sunset around 4:40 P.M.—business hours. Fine. Problem is, as the day lengthens you get more daylight in both A.M. and P.M. but you need it mostly P.M. Rather than try and nudge the clock ahead every day, you bide your time till April. Then bam, you switch to DST, thereby shifting an hour of wasted daylight from morning till evening. When the days start to get shorter again, you shift the hour back. It's a hassle, but it's more effective than this half-hour-split-the-difference nonsense.

Now for questions from the class.

- *Why do we need to change the clock at all? Why don't we just get up earlier?*

Yeah, right. Besides, this is the twentieth century. You do what the clock tells you to do. When the masterminds behind it all want people to dance to a different tune, they don't retrain the populace, they change the clocks.

• *Why are farmers against daylight saving time?*

Because they're idiots. They claim DST makes them get up when it's pitch dark. Like hell. Farmers can get up when they want (subject to the OK of the cows, of course). Except on market days, they don't have to be in sync with the rest of us. They just don't feel like resetting the alarm. TDB.

Idiocy Of Farmers Explained

As a farmer, I resent being called an idiot. The reason we are against daylight saving time is that our crops can't stand the extra hour of sun in the dry part of the year. They burn up and wilt.—J. Bass, Dallas, Texas

This is a joke, right?

You didn't know how close to the truth you were when you attributed the farmer's schedule to the cows in your column about daylight saving time. It's true clock time doesn't mean much to a farmer or his cows. The problem arises when the milk cans, filled from the bulging udders of cows ready to give milk at the same point in "God's time" each day, end up sitting on the station platform while the trains (running on Man's time, which has been set back an hour) obstinately refuse to show up to carry the precious fluid to you waiting city dwellers with your dry Cheerios. Get with the program, Uncle Cecil.—Terry Stibal, Mount Vernon, Illinois

You think the farmers have ever heard of, say, a refrigerator?

I left the farm 35 years ago, but I still remember the farmers' quarrel with DST, at least in Wisconsin. It had nothing to do with cows and clocks, but rather with farmers and clocks. As soon as farmers began

*working according to the clock instead of according to the sun, along
came DST and robbed farmers of two hours each day. This is how.
Field crops become damp with dew every evening, and are dried
by the sun every morning. Crops ready by 8 o'clock "sun time" now
were not ready until 9 o'clock DST. Thus one hour was lost in the
morning. Then, at the end of the day, farmers working by DST
knocked off at 7 o'clock, which was only 6 o'clock "sun time." Thus
they lost another hour in the evening. The unanswerable question, of
course, is why farmers ever work according to clocks.—Frederick A.
Kreuziger, Dallas*

I'll say. I was kidding when I said farmers were idiots, but now I'm
starting to wonder.

*Why, on Groundhog Day, if the groundhog sees its shadow, does it
mean that there will be six more weeks of winter? Presumably if the
weather was nice enough to see a shadow, winter would be over.—Nep
Smith, Los Angeles*

First thing we have to do is cleanse the problem of extraneous detail. This has nothing to do with groundhogs. In Europe the same legend has attached to bears, badgers, and hedgehogs. German immigrants brought it to North America in the nineteenth century and, not finding any hedgehogs, settled on the somewhat similar (it's small, it hibernates) woodchuck, a.k.a. groundhog. Not that you need animals of any sort. Medieval English proverbs strip the proposition to its paradoxical core: "If Candlemas Day [also February 2] be bright

and warm, ye may mend yer auld mittens and look for a storm." Some writers (e.g., Gail Cleere in *Natural History*) trace the belief back even further "to an ancient pagan celebration [by Scottish Celts] called Imbolog, which marked a 'cross-quarter' day, one of the days that fall midway between the four mileposts of the solar year"— namely, the solstices and equinoxes.

Incredibly interesting, but why did people figure good weather to-day meant crappy weather later? Beats me, and from what I can tell, pretty much beats everybody else, too. Best, or perhaps I should say only, theory: sunny days in winter are the product of cold, dry arctic air masses, while cloudy days result from mild, moist tropical air. Unfortunately, while this may be true as a general proposition, the predictive value of cloudy weather on February 2 pretty much sucks. According to *Canadian Geographic* weather columnist David Phillips, a multidecade, multicity study in Canada found that groundhog-driven predictions were right only 37 percent of the time. Which means, I guess, that you'd be right 63 percent of the time if you said good weather on 2/2 meant good weather ahead. But what kind of weather proverb would that make? If the choice is between right and catchy, go with catchy. It always works for me.

A quick question from a bunch of us born in '67: When did the "Age of Aquarius" officially dawn, and is it still going on now?—Saul Kaiserman, Brooklyn

This may come as a surprise, baby busters, but there's going to be a short wait. The Age of Aquarius, introduced with such hype back in the '60s, isn't actually due on the scene until A.D. 2150. Obviously, when they talked about it being "a long, long time before the dawn" they weren't kidding. But you have to realize that astrological ages last quite a spell—2,150 years, to be precise. (The previous age—the Age of Pisces—began with the birth of Christ.) I'm told you have to sort of sidle into these things gradually. Get a good book and some crossword puzzles and I'm sure the time will fly.

Then again, everybody has different ideas about these things. A gent named Marc Edward Jones, who wrote a book called *Fundamentals of Number Significance* in 1978, claims the Age of Aquarius commenced with the discovery of Pluto in 1930. The Age of Aquarius, in

Jones's view, was thus ushered in by the Depression and World War II. Not an auspicious start for an era of peace and love, but like I say, these things start off slow. (Jones also thinks each age lasts 2,500 years, and I've got another book of the occult here that says they last 2,000 years. Trying to get a straight story on this stuff isn't easy.)

Jones sees the Aquarian Age as "the equalitarian new age of mankind," characterized by "a universality of cooperation freely accepted and tendered by all people everywhere." But don't dust off those love beads yet. This cooperation stuff cuts both ways. Some interpret it to mean we're going to have a highly regimented society in which you cooperate or die, the prototype being modern Japan. So it could be jumping jacks and the company song in the morning and 12 hours on the job per day. But don't worry. You'll still be able to whistle while you work.

More Bad News On The Aquarius Watch

Your recent column seemed a little vague on what the Age of Aquarius is and when it will begin. The idea of an astrological "age" arises from the precession of the vernal equinox through the twelve astrological signs (or the thirteen modern astronomical constellations) of the zodiac. The modern astronomical constellations have precisely mapped boundaries. If we use these to measure our "ages," we can say definitively that the vernal equinox will enter Aquarius in 2660 and leave in 4360. The Age of Aquarius will begin and end in those years.

Astrologers, however, have little use for modern astronomy (or anything else that requires rational thought). They have traditionally divided the zodiac into 12 "signs" of equal width. Since the vernal equinox makes a complete circuit of the zodiac in 25,785 years, the corresponding "age" of each zodiac sign lasts 2,148 years. But nobody has ever delineated exactly where each "sign" (and thus each "age") begins and ends. Your definition of the Age of Pisces as lasting from A.D. 1 to 2150 is good enough, but you could shift it a century or two either way and nobody could argue.—Jim Klann, Glendale Heights, Illinois

Often I hear of people complaining about their bones or joints hurting when they think the weather is going to change. Is there any truth to this? Can people really tell when the weather is going to change, or is this just some psychological phenomenon that has people feeling ghost pains when they hear a cold front is coming in?—Ann R., McAllen, Texas

Medical opinion is divided on this question. The most commonly expressed views may be summarized as follows:

1. Yes, people can tell when the weather is changing, because their joints ache.
2. No, they can't.
3. Some say yes, some say no. More research is needed.
4. You talkin' to me?

But don't be too critical. We've had only about 2,000 years to work on this (2,400 actually, Hippocrates having discussed the effect of weather on chronic diseases in 400 B.C.). One more big grant, and we'll have it for sure.

Many, perhaps most, people with arthritis and other chronic joint ailments say their symptoms are affected by the weather. Their doctors tend to believe them, going so far as to advise the most intractable cases to move to a warm, dry climate.

At the same time, you get various fonts of negativity saying this is all bunk. For example, Donald Redelmeier and Amos Tversky note in a 1996 paper that:

1. "No study using objective measures of inflammation has found positive results."
2. In studies using subjective measures of pain (i.e., as reported by the sufferers), "some find that an increase in barometric pressure tends to increase pain, others find it tends to decrease pain, and others find no association."
3. "Some investigators argue that only a simultaneous change in pressure and humidity influences arthritis pain, but others find no such pattern."

You see what I'm saying. We're not making much progress. And I'll tell you why we're not making much progress. Because guys like Redelmeier and Tversky come along and make sweeping pronouncements on the basis of minimal evidence. Having kissed off the previous 30 years' worth of research, R & T proceed to do their own investigation, which is larded with sentences such as "The mean of these correlations was 0.016 and none was significant at $P < 0.05$." Conclusion: the weather/joint pain connection is BS. Surprise factor in this result: zero. Total number of patients tested: 18.

Eighteen! Dadgummit, boys, we're not going to settle 2,000 years' worth of argument by testing 18 lousy patients!

To which one might reply, nice talk coming from somebody who's notorious for generalizing on the basis of one experiment in the backyard. Well, sure. But I'm writing for the newspapers, where most research consists of interviewing people in taverns. R & T are writing in the *Proceedings of the National Academy of Sciences*.

Another problem is that everybody who looks into this seems to be testing something different. Are we talking about indoor climate or outdoor climate? Forecasting the weather or reacting to it? High or low pressure/temperature/humidity or changing conditions?

You probably figure I'm building up to my usual lament about the sorry state of medical research. Well, no. The situation is perhaps less confused than some people make out. You'll recall R & T's comment that we can't tell whether an increase in barometric pressure increases pain, reduces pain, or doesn't do anything. To illustrate, they cited four studies. On examination, we find that two studies say an increase

in barometric pressure is strongly linked to an increase in pain in arthritis sufferers, while the other two say it's strongly linked to a *decrease* in pain. At first glance, that seems to support R & T's view that research results have been all over the map. But the strong statistical correlation claimed in all the studies suggests that it may be a *change* in pressure, not necessarily the *direction* of the change, that is linked to increased arthritis pain. In any case, I'm not ready to concede that generations of arthritics have been making the whole thing up.

I have never heard of a tornado occurring outside North America. Is this weather phenomenon unique to North America? Is this because only North America has mobile home parks, which attract tornadoes? The straight dope, please.—Dean, Dallas

Silly boy. Tornadoes occur throughout the world. I have reports here of tornadoes from Moscow, Peshawar (Pakistan), and even Vienna. But they do occur most frequently in North America, and in particular in the central plains of the United States. Something like 700 tornadoes a year occur in the States; Australia, with 200, is a distant second.

Roughly 90 percent of U.S. twisters occur in a 300-mile-wide corridor extending from West Texas to Canada. That's because conditions there are ideal for tornado formation. First you get warm, moist surface winds blowing up from the Gulf of Mexico, while cool high-altitude winds blow over the tops of the Rockies. This situation is inherently unstable, because cool air wants to sink while warm air wants to rise.

However, for reasons we need not delve into here, the mountain air causes a temperature inversion, which prevents the warm surface air from rising. It's like clamping the lid on a pressure cooker. The surface weather systems build up a big head of steam until they break through the inversion, whereupon they shoot up to towering heights. This sets in motion the violent up- and downdrafts that lead, through circumstances still imperfectly understood, to the formation of more tornadoes than anywhere else in the world.

What does a cloud feel like to the touch?—B.P. Jones, Chicago

Like a funeral director's handshake, B.P.—cold and clammy. But why are you asking me? Chances are you've already felt a cloud. It's called fog, which is nothing more than a cloud at ground level.

Who in the world dreamed up the idea that there's a pot of gold at the end of the rainbow?—Anonymous, Los Angeles

Who knows? The expression has been proverbial at least since 1836, and the idea of chasing rainbows period goes back a lot earlier than that. The catch, of course, is that you *can't* get to the end of the rainbow, owing to the fact that it's an optical effect dependent on the relative orientation of the sun, you, and a suitable collection of airborne water droplets. If you're not directly between the droplets and the sun, no rainbow. If you spot a bow and try to chase it, it simply recedes before you until the angles don't line up anymore, at which point it disappears.

Rainbows are strictly in the eye of the beholder. You may see a small local bow created by the mist from a squirting garden hose, but somebody on the other side of the hose will see nothing. Not only can't you get to the end of the rainbow, you can't even sidle around it; no matter what you do, the rainbow always appears to face straight toward you. As a result, chasing rainbows has come to symbolize—depending on your degree of cynicism—either pursuing a fool's errand or dreaming the impossible dream.

Do you have any info on the so-called "green flash"? It's not a super-hero, but rather an optical phenomenon involving a burst of pure green light that occurs just as the sun rises or sets over the ocean. I've seen it several times, but my friends won't believe me, saying it's just delayed mescaline aftereffects. Set these unbelievers straight.—E.N., Hollywood, California

Adds a sort of postmodern element to the process of scientific discovery, doesn't it? "I believe I've discovered a new perturbation in the space-time continuum! However, it could just be the drugs." Don't worry, though—there really is such a thing as green flash. Usually it's a thin green band or splotch visible for a split second at or near the top edge of the sun as it sinks beyond the horizon. You can see it at sunrise, too. Sometimes it lasts longer; sometimes it's blue or violet or turns from green to blue. To see it you need a clearly delineated horizon and a haze-free sky. The ocean (or any large body of water) will do fine, as will a desert or mountain.

Most people have never seen green flash and think it's a myth, ascribing it to retinal fatigue on the part of the observer or other causes. One reason they're so adamant is that green flash is impossible to photograph with an ordinary camera; the image is too small to register. But researchers managed it in the 1950s using telescopes. (For some of their handiwork, see the January 1960 *Scientific American*.)

Green flash is caused by atmospheric refraction—that is, the bending of sunlight as it passes through the air so that it splits into a rainbow of colors. Refraction causes the solar disk to be surrounded by

ghost images like those on a cheap TV, with a violet-blue-green "shadow" above and a red-orange-yellow one below. None of this is visible except at sunrise and sunset, when refraction hits the max and the sun's light is so reduced that the ghosts don't wash out. The red ghost disappears below the horizon, the orange and yellow ones are absorbed by the atmosphere, the blue and violet ones scatter (usually), and what's left is green. Count yourself lucky if you've seen it; you're one of a privileged few.

What is the deal with the millennium? I understand that people think years ending in zeroes are significant, so it follows that a year ending in three zeroes is really significant. But for years I have heard people talking about the "arrival of the millennium," meaning either

*that we're going to have heaven on earth or that civilization will col-
lapse. Either people are envisioning the muthah New Year's Eve party
of all time or there's something else going on. What? And what happened the last time the millennium came around?—N. E. Buddy, via
the Internet*

My feeling is it's mostly media hype. Although maybe we should be
more concerned than we are. There is, after all, the chance of a nuclear confrontation between India and Pakistan, and some think half
the world's computers will shut down due to the Year 2000 Bug. But
frankly, I'm seeing way less millennial anxiety now than I did 30 years
ago, at the height of the Cold War. As for commemorating the millennium, as opposed to merely fearing it, what are we supposed to do?
Celebrate a thousand years of progress? "Yeah, the electric light, that
was a heck of an invention. And that Ottoman Empire—boy, weren't
those the days?"

Although many now assume "the millennium" is the calendrical
period beginning on January 1, 2001 (or, in the unenlightened view,
January 1, 2000), that's not the traditional interpretation. In Christianity, the millennium is the thousand-year period referred to in
Revelation 20 in the Bible: "And I saw an angel coming down out of
heaven. . . . He seized . . . Satan, and bound him for a thousand years
[during which time those found to be righteous will reign with
Christ]. When the thousand years are over, Satan will be released
from his prison and will go out to deceive the nations in the four corners of the earth—Gog and Magog—to gather them for battle." Satan's eventual defeat will be followed by the end of the world and the
last judgment.

Since the early days of Christianity, "millenarians" have argued that
the angel was going to come down out of heaven sooner rather than
later. But when? Countless dates have been proposed, but one school
of thought reasons as follows:

1. A couple passages in the Bible, notably 2 Peter 3:8, state that "one
   day is with the Lord as a thousand years, and a thousand years as
   one day."
2. God created the world in six days, and rested on the seventh day.
3. Therefore, the ordinary world will last 6,000 years, and the

Christian millennium will occupy the subsequent (and last) thousand years. I realize there's a leap of logic here, but if we're going to insist on strict rationality, we wouldn't be having this discussion at all.

4. A momentous event such as the birth of Christ would surely have occurred an exact number of millennia following the creation of the world, e.g., at the four- or five-thousand-year mark, and an exact number of millennia before the end of the world.

5. The world as we know it obviously didn't end in A.D. 1000 (or 1001).

6. So it's bound to happen now.

As I say, it's not ironclad logic. Stephen Jay Gould, in his book *Questioning the Millennium,* says if we accept the famous calculation by Archbishop James Ussher that the world began on October 23, 4004 B.C., then, allowing for the fact that there was no year zero, the everyday world ended October 23, 1997, and we're in the millennium now. I can accept the idea that you and I made it through. But Dennis Rodman?

What happened on the last calendrical millennium? For centuries it was assumed that there was worldwide (well, Christendom-wide) panic, but many historians now believe this was grossly exaggerated by subsequent chroniclers. So far this millennium is shaping up to be a bust too. Still, while most of us personally don't expect the arrival of the millennial angel, one can't help but think: there are some that do. Will they celebrate with a picnic . . . or apocalyptic slaughter? Added to which is the possibility that, owing to the aforementioned Y2K problem, the cop cars won't work. I don't know what you were planning to do this New Year's Eve, but I'm staying in bed.

From The Straight Dope Message Board

Subj: What do you want on your tombstone?
From: JA1166
What do we want our tombstones to read after we are gone?

From: OttoPlndrm
"Windows has experienced a fatal exception error in module PHIL.EXE."

From: JA1166
Here lies Joan Arndt.
She be dead cause
She Arndt alive.
Hope to see you
On the other side.

From: TUBADIVA
For myself, no funeral, no burial, no headstone . . . but I want one of those big circular wreaths like you see sometimes, and a banner on it: "Good Luck In Your New Location."

Chapter 5

Myths And Legends

As a volunteer worker with PWAs (people with AIDS), I've been solemnly assured that AIDS was created in a lab by the CIA/KKK/ KGB, etc., to kill off all the commies/blacks/capitalists, etc. Obviously this is just a modern take on that ancient and dishonorable tradition of blaming disaster and disease on your least favorite minority, as the

Jews were blamed in the Middle Ages for the Black Death. It did bring to mind, though, the stories that some Native Americans tell about the deliberate introduction of smallpox as a form of genocide. One version I've read has Custer's cavalry handing out infected blankets on the reservations, and on the Pacific Northwest coast, where I live, some of the First Nations believe this sort of thing was going on as recently as the 1930s. I'm skeptical, not because I attribute any high morality to the Europeans—some of whom would have cheerfully infected natives if they thought they could get away with it—but precisely because of the boomerang effect. Even today it seems to me the only thing keeping a lid on biological warfare is the fact that it will potentially kill as many of your people as of the enemy. Bearing in mind that absence of evidence is not evidence of absence, is there any "smoking gun" in the form of documents, eyewitness testimony recorded at the time, or guilt-racked confessions, to indicate that whites ever really did attempt such a germical holocaust?—Philip Torrens, Vancouver

A common reaction to this story is that it has to be folklore. Giving infected blankets to the Indians—why, that's awful! That's disgusting! That's . . . ethnic cleansing. Hmm. Maybe this story bears a closer look.

And in fact it does. On at least one occasion a high-ranking European considered infecting the Indians with smallpox as a tactic of war. I'm talking about Lord Jeffrey Amherst, commander of British forces in North America during the French and Indian War (1756–63). Amherst and a subordinate discussed, apparently seriously, sending infected blankets to hostile tribes. What's more, we've got the documents to prove it, thanks to the enterprising research of Peter d'Errico, legal studies professor at the University of Massachusetts at (fittingly) Amherst. D'Errico slogged through hundreds of reels of microfilmed correspondence looking for the smoking gun, and he found it.

The exchange took place during Pontiac's Rebellion, which broke out after the war, in 1763. Forces led by Pontiac, a chief of the Ottawa who had been allied with the French, laid siege to the English at Fort Pitt.

According to historian Francis Parkman, Amherst first raised the possibility of giving the Indians infected blankets in a letter to Colonel

Henry Bouquet, who would lead reinforcements to Fort Pitt. No copy of this letter has come to light, but we do know that Bouquet discussed the matter in a postscript to a letter to Amherst on July 13, 1763:

> P.S. I will try to inocculate the Indians by means of Blankets that may fall in their hands, taking care however not to get the disease myself. As it is pity to oppose good men against them, I wish we could make use of the Spaniard's Method, and hunt them with English Dogs. Supported by Rangers, and some Light Horse, who would I think effectively extirpate or remove that Vermine.

On July 16 Amherst replied, also in a postscript:

> P.S. You will Do well to try to Innoculate the Indians by means of Blanketts, as well as to try Every other method that can serve to Extirpate this Execrable Race. I should be very glad your Scheme for Hunting them Down by Dogs could take Effect, but England is at too great a Distance to think of that at present.

On July 26 Bouquet wrote back:

> I received yesterday your Excellency's letters of 16th with their Inclosures. The signal for Indian Messengers, and all your directions will be observed.

We don't know if Bouquet actually put the plan into effect, or if so with what result. We do know that a supply of smallpox-infected blankets was available, since the disease had broken out at Fort Pitt some weeks previously. We also know that the following spring smallpox was reported to be raging among the Indians in the vicinity.

To modern ears, this talk about infecting the natives with smallpox, hunting them down with dogs, etc., sounds over the top. But it's easy to believe Amherst and company were serious. D'Errico provides other quotes from Amherst's correspondence that suggest he considered Native Americans subhumans who ought to be exterminated. Check out his research for yourself at web.maxwell.syr.edu/nativeweb/subject/amherst/lord_jeff.html. He not only includes transcriptions but also reproduces the relevant parts of the incriminating letters.

My father is convinced that the so-called lost city of Atlantis is at the bottom of Neptune Lake in North Dakota! Should I call a sanitarium or go to this lake and help him find this lost land?—C.W. Rozet, Wyoming

The bottom of Neptune Lake, eh? Sounds to me like Pops has spent too much time looking at the bottom of a beer glass.

Then again, why not North Dakota? Just about every other spot on the globe has been spoken for by the zillions of would-be Atlantis discoverers. It's said that more than 20,000 books have been written about the lost island (it was more than a city), Atlantis having been pretty much the crackpots' default area of obsession before they had the Kennedy assassination.

Haven't seen much so far on Neptune Lake, though admittedly I've still got about 19,990 books to go. In the meantime, here's a rundown of the leading theories about Atlantis's location:

- *Plato made the whole thing up,* the weasel. Plato, of course, is the guy who related the Atlantis legend circa 348 B.C. in two of his dialogues, *Timaeus* and *Critias.* The entire account covers maybe 20 pages of printed text. A character in the dialogues says the legend had been told 200 years previously to the Athenian statesman Solon by an Egyptian sage.

  But no independent account of Atlantis exists in Greek or Egyptian literature or anywhere else. Modern efforts to equate Atlantis with well-established myths about Elysium, the land of fallen heroes, etc., are speculative BS. The common view among scholars is that Plato manufactured the story to support his theories about the ideal state, appeal to Greek patriotism (in his story the Greeks defeated the Atlanteans), etc.

Much of the story does seem fictional. For example, the destruction of Atlantis is said to have occurred 9,000 years before Plato's day. This requires us to believe that the story had been accurately transmitted since prehistoric times by word of mouth—this by a species most of whose members can barely remember what they had for lunch.

However, Plato has his characters insist at a couple of points that the story's true. And if you can't trust Plato, whom can you trust? (I mean, besides me.) Let's not forget that everybody thought Troy was fictional until Schliemann dug it up in Turkey.

• *Atlantis was in the Atlantic.* Duh, you say. Obviously you haven't read the 20,000 books. Plato clearly states that Atlantis was just outside the Pillars of Hercules at Gibraltar. However, no traces of a giant lost island have been found, and oceanographers are pretty confident none will be. "Plate tectonics," the believers reply. What about plate tectonics? The major shifting of the continents occurred millions of years before man's arrival, and you sure didn't have any big chunks disappearing overnight, as in Plato's account.

German inventor Otto Muck proposed that Atlantis was an island in the Azores that was destroyed as a result of an asteroid crashing into the earth on June 5, 8498 B.C., at 8 P.M. That Otto, what a wild man.

• *Atlantis was Minoan Crete.* The most popular current theory outside the it's-BS school. It's been reasonably well established that the center of the Minoan empire on the island of Crete was substantially destroyed by a volcanic eruption on the nearby island of Thera (Santorin) circa 1490 B.C. If we assume Plato based the Atlantis story on a legend in which some clueless translator mistakenly multiplied the numbers by ten, the 9,000 years of Plato's story become 900 years. Behold, 590 B.C. (Solon's time) minus 900 equals 1490 B.C. What's more, when reduced by a factor of ten, certain geographic dimensions given by Plato for Atlantis, plus a lot of the descriptive detail, accord reasonably well with what's known about Minoan Crete. (Now that I look more closely, some accounts give the number of books about Atlantis as 2,000, not 20,000. For Atlantis buffs, a shaky grasp of the tens table may be a problem of long standing.)

Drawbacks of this version: Crete is in the Mediterranean, not the Atlantic. Also, this version is essentially unprovable short of somebody unearthing a sign in Crete saying Now Entering Atlantis. See *Lost Atlantis* by J. V. Luce for a—dare I say it?—lucid account.

- *Atlantis was located just about anywhere else you'd care to name in our sector of the galaxy.* Proposed sites include Morocco, Nigeria, Asia Minor, Tunisia, the North Sea, the Bahamas, the southeastern United States, the Martian polar ice cap, and for all I know, Neptune Lake. Pops may have flipped, but he's got a lot of company.

Recently I read the useless fact that the quack of a duck will not echo. 1) Is this true? (I currently do not have access to either a duck or a canyon, or I would find out myself.) 2) Why not? (Assuming it is true.) 3) Are there other noises that will not echo? 4) Again, why not?—G. J. Thelin, Fresno, California

This is another example of faxlore—myths and factoids kept in circulation by people who evidently will believe anything. Next time I organize a poker game, I know whom I want to invite.

Personally, I recognized this claim immediately for what it was: quackery. Preliminary inquiries confirmed this. Sure, there's such a thing as destructive interference, in which colliding waveforms cancel each other out. But how this would cause 100 percent attenuation of an echo 100 percent of the time in uncontrolled conditions was beyond even me.

But never mind my opinion. What we need here is science. Knowing the only way to settle the question for good was an experiment, I assigned Jane to assemble the apparatus and conduct a test. Here is her report:

"I spoke with several friends about the duck's quack question, and even called the Michigan State University animal science department. No one could confirm or deny the claim, and no one at MSU seemed eager to stage a formal experiment, the wimps. I mentioned my dilemma to a visiting friend, and he said his wife, Shareen, had an in with the director of Mott Hashbarger Children's Farm and School in Flint. She had, on occasion, borrowed farm animals for events, and she was willing to get a duck and bring it down. After a quick phone call to the farm director, who gave his blessing, she obtained a duck and put it in a pet carrier.

"But where to find a good echo? I live in mid-Michigan, after all. I called Glenn Brown, a sound engineer who has done work across the country. As luck would have it, Glenn remembered one place where, as a kid, he would go to produce great echoes. It's at the back of East Lansing High School—a sort of courtyard between two classroom wings, about 30 feet wide and 170 feet long. The hard surface of the buildings and perhaps a low hill opposite are highly conducive to reflecting sound.

"So, with friends, duck, and camera in tow, we drove to ELHS. In the courtyard without the duck we easily produced some impressive echoes. Next we got the bird and sat down in the middle of the courtyard. We thought he would produce a big quack and the experiment would be over. No such luck. He just wouldn't quack. Probably he was nervous. Who wouldn't be? He was a sitting duck.

"The three of us certainly quacked, though, such that we thought we might want to change the name of the experiment from 'does a duck's quack echo' to 'how to make three humans quack like a duck.' We tried to be inconspicuous, since school was in session and students could see us. However, a duck and three quacking humans is not the sort of scene that fades readily into the woodwork. The duck quacked in the cage, which was useless for our purposes, but when we took him out he was mute.

"Finally Shareen had an inspiration. She held the duck by his body so that he could flap his wings, and ran up and down the length of the courtyard hoping to replicate the experience of flying. So much for being discreet. Incredibly enough, this wacky stratagem worked. The duck loved it and quacked like crazy for a minute. Yes, the quacks echoed. This was heard by the three of us and by an unidentified East Lansing High School teacher who came out to make sure we weren't engaging in duck torture. I was able to record the event but didn't get a good sound recording of the echo itself. But I do have a dandy clip of Shareen running up and down with the duck. I call it my 'duck tape.'

"I wanted to reward my friends somehow, and offered to buy them lunch. They asked for roast duck. They're such comedians. They settled for soup and quackers."

That Jane. What can I tell you? She quacks me up.

Is it true the black doctor who invented blood plasma bled to death in front of a hospital because the white doctors refused to admit him?—Anonymous, Kansas City, Missouri

For the real story on this classic legend Cecil is indebted to Scot Morris of *Omni* magazine, who wrote about it in his book *Omni Games*. Here's the dope:

Charles R. Drew was a black surgeon who pioneered techniques for

preserving blood plasma that saved countless lives during World War II. Later he became medical director of Freedmen's Hospital in Washington, D.C. In 1950, while driving three other black doctors to a conference in Alabama, Drew fell asleep at the wheel. The car swerved and rolled over, breaking his neck and crushing his chest. According to legend, he desperately needed a blood transfusion, but doctors at a hospital in Burlington, North Carolina, refused to admit him, and he died.

This story is told in several black history books and has been repeated by Dick Gregory, among others. But it isn't true. Morris spoke with Dr. John Ford, one of the passengers in Drew's car. "We all received the very best of care," Ford said. "The doctors started treating us immediately."

Drew didn't receive a transfusion because his injuries wouldn't permit it. "He had a superior vena caval syndrome—blood was blocked getting back to his heart from his brain and upper extremities," Ford said. "To give him a transfusion would have killed him sooner. Even the most heroic efforts couldn't have saved him. I can truthfully say that no efforts were spared in the treatment of Dr. Drew, and, contrary to popular myth, the fact that he was a Negro did not in any way limit the care that was given to him."

The Drew story is similar to one told about blues singer Bessie Smith. She, too, supposedly bled to death after an auto accident when a white hospital refused to admit her. The alleged incident, which occurred in Mississippi in 1937, was even the subject of a play by Edward Albee. But as Morris notes, "Though the whole truth will probably never be known, it is certain she did not die this way." Morris's efforts notwithstanding, I'll bet these macabre legends won't die for a long time.

What's the meaning of the number of feet the horse has off the ground in statues of war heroes? I recall hearing one foot off meant the person was injured and recovered, while two feet meant he was fatally wounded.—Laury Hutt, Baltimore

Your columnist confesses he went into this figuring it was a crock. Your columnist goes into pretty much everything figuring it's a crock, for the obvious reason that when you consider most popular beliefs, the percentages are on your side. However, it's not like I wasn't willing to be convinced.

First we reviewed the literature. This consisted of looking at tourist guidebooks, which, as far as I can tell, are the main perpetuators of this yarn. Here's a typical version from one such guidebook, *Hands On Chicago* (1987), by Mark Frazel and Kenan Heise: "At Sheridan Road and Belmont Avenue, the statue of [General Philip H.] Sheridan beckons troops to battle. The horse General Sheridan rides is named Winchester. . . . Winchester's raised leg symbolizes his rider was wounded in battle (the legs of [General Ulysses S.] Grant's horse [as seen in another Chicago statue] are on the ground, meaning he was not wounded)." The book makes no mention of what two legs in the air means, but many people seem to think it indicates the rider died in battle.

Next I scoured texts on sculpture for any indication that sculptors actually used such a code. In vain. Not that I was exactly shocked, but one must be thorough. A historian for the U.S. Army Center of Military History also dismissed the story as a myth.

We then got down to the guts of the investigation. I got photos of 18 equestrian statues featuring historical figures (Napoleon, George Washington, etc.) in cities ranging from Chicago to Leningrad (well, that's what it was when I looked this up—now it's St. Petersburg). I then checked to see whether the individuals depicted had been wounded or killed.

This involved some guesswork. Does getting grazed by a bullet count as a wound? If the guy was assassinated, does that mean he was killed in action? Does it count the same if the horse has both front feet off the ground versus having one front foot and one back foot? I wrestled with these questions late into the night. Giving the code the benefit of the doubt, I determined as follows:

Code corresponds with subject's fate: 8
Doesn't correspond: 8
Not enough information to tell: 2

Significantly, in the two equestrian statues I turned up by Augustus Saint-Gaudens, one of the most famous sculptors of his day and someone who surely would have respected a code had there been one, I found that one piece did correspond with the code and one didn't.

Granted, in this world of doubt and pain, one can be certain of nothing. But I say the code is BS.

The Teeming Millions Say Neigh

Recently you scoffed at the idea that in equestrian statues of war heroes, the number of feet the horse has raised indicates whether the rider was killed or wounded in battle. You are WRONG, WRONG, WRONG! There is at least one place in this great nation of ours where the horse code holds true—namely, that most hallowed of Civil War battle sites, Gettysburg, Pennsylvania.

At Gettysburg, a statue that has all four of the horse's hooves on the ground means that the rider survived the battle without a scratch. One foot raised means the person was wounded but survived, and both forelegs raised indicates that the man was killed at Gettysburg. Obviously you are an imposter—the real Cecil (a true American) would of course have known this. I advise you to turn yourself in at once.—Theodore S. Shouse, Washington, D.C.

Just goes to show you, Theodore, there's good in all of us, even a zit like yourself. You've undoubtedly pinpointed the origin of the horse-statue myth. Others have told me they also heard it first at Gettysburg. Turning to *Gettysburg: The Complete Pictorial of Battlefield Monuments* by D. Scott Hartwig and Ann Marie Hartwig (1988), we find photos of six freestanding horse statues (478 monuments and memorials are pictured all told). Sure enough, all six conform to the code you describe, except that the horse of General John F. Reynolds, who was killed at Gettysburg, has one foreleg and one hind leg raised, not both forelegs.

Does this mean there really is a code? Nah, it's just coincidence. You'd hardly invent a code to cover a lousy six statues—a code, moreover, that seems calculated to rile the family and friends of many of the depicted heroes. The horse in the statue of General John Sedgwick, for example, has all four feet on the ground. Sedgwick was killed in action, but at Spotsylvania, not Gettysburg. We're supposed to believe Sedgwick was denied his sculptural Purple Heart because he died in the wrong battle? Tell me another one. Further inquiries have turned up nothing to corroborate the existence of a code. Expunge it from your mind.

Many years ago my grandmother told me that her grandfather's ethnicity was "black Irish." Recently I've heard three different explanations concerning the origin of the term:

1. *It refers to a mixture of Irish and Spanish blood dating from the time of the Spanish Armada, when many shipwrecked Spanish sailors were washed up on the Irish coastline and wound up staying.*
2. *It refers to a mixture of Irish and eastern European blood.*
3. *It refers to a mixture of Irish and Italian blood from the time of the Roman Empire.*

No books have been written on the subject, and no entry is to be found in either the Encyclopaedia Britannica *or the* Oxford English Dictionary. *So naturally one turns to you.—Christian Ard, San Francisco*

Naturally. One saves the big guns for last.

It seemed to me a reasonable first step would be to see if they'd heard of the black Irish in Ireland. Having inquired of several Irish natives, either in person or via the Internet, I'd say the answer is no—the black Irish are strictly an American hang-up.

People talk about the black Irish as though it were a mythical race on a par with the lost tribes of Israel. But in fact all they mean

(usually) is that somebody named McNulty has dark, and in the classic case black, hair. Even if we make the dubious assumption that dark-hair genes were completely absent in the original Gaels, it seems likely that the incidence of dark-haired folk in a nation whose population only slightly exceeds that of the city of Los Angeles can be accounted for strictly by routine mixing due to immigration, trade contact, and so on. But you can see how exciting an explanation that makes. So people have come up with all kinds of fanciful tales instead.

The wildest notion is that black hair is evidence of Spaniards marooned in Ireland following the wreck of the Armada. But as we discussed in this column long ago, the number of shipwrecked Spanish sailors who remained in Ireland for any length of time was trivial.

I have also heard it said the black Irish are descended from the first settlers of Ireland—maybe the Phoenicians. The red Irish, meanwhile, are descendants of the Normans, and the blond Irish are descended from the Vikings. One of many drawbacks to this theory is that it seems to leave the Gaels completely out of the picture.

A more plausible but still essentially unprovable version of this idea is that black hair is a vestige of an indigenous population of short, dark-haired types overrun by the fair-haired Gaels. Supposedly there are more black Irish in the western part of the country, which fewer Gaelic invaders reached. There is archaeological and, I'm told, linguistic evidence of pre-Gaelic settlement, but how it was concluded that they were short and black-haired I do not know.

We could go on like this for another couple pages, but why? While the Irish in me finds it entertaining, the Yankee thinks it's a damfool waste of time.

In my search for a new coffeemaker, a concerned friend advocated a boycott of both Braun and Krups brands because they were made by German companies that manufactured concentration-camp crematoria in the 1930s and '40s. Can this be true? I'm drinking tea pending your reply. Also, did Adolf Hitler really name the Volkswagen?—Yvonne Pelletier, Chicago

Is it true Mercedes-Benz manufactured the ovens used in the Nazi death camps?—Ross, North Hollywood, California

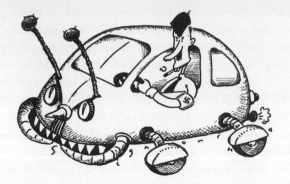

Not one of your more lighthearted questions, but what the heck—you ask, we answer. None of the companies mentioned built crematoria, but Daimler-Benz, maker of Mercedes-Benz cars, committed other crimes. Testimony at the Nuremburg war crimes trials suggests the ovens were mostly built by heating-equipment manufacturers and such. The crematoria at Auschwitz were built by I. A. Topf and Sons of Erfurt, and those at Dachau and Lublin by C. H. Kori GmbH. A horrified spokesperson for Braun, a maker of small appliances bought by Gillette in 1967, assures me the firm's main business during the 1940s was electric shavers. Krups mostly made small household products like scales.

How Braun got dragged into this God knows. (Eva Braun?) Krups is probably being confused with the Krupp works, for many years the leading German munitions maker. (You've heard of Big Bertha, the giant cannon used by the Germans during World War I? It was named after Bertha Krupp, the wife of the family-owned firm's patriarch.) Krupp didn't make crematoria either, but it did use 100,000 slave laborers to make weapons at Auschwitz and other death camps. Boss Alfried Krupp was sentenced to 12 years for war crimes but was freed in 1951—cynics say because the Korean War had just broken out and the United States needed Krupp's industrial might as a bulwark against the Reds. Its assets restored, Krupp again became a corporate giant and remains so today.

Krupp doesn't make consumer products, but other former slave employers do. Daimler-Benz, for example. The firm avidly supported

Nazism and in return received arms contracts and tax breaks that enabled it to become one of the world's leading industrial concerns. (Between 1932 and 1940 production grew by 830 percent.) During the war the company used thousands of slaves and forced laborers, including Jews, foreigners, and POWs. According to historian Bernard Bellon (*Mercedes in Peace and War*, 1990), at least eight Jews were murdered by DB managers or SS men at a plant in occupied Poland. There was a report that Daimler-Benz built mobile poison-gas vans, but this has never been corroborated and is doubtful.

Many big German companies used slaves during World War II. The most important was I. G. Farben, the German chemical monopoly. IGF had a substantial interest in one of the companies making Zyklon B, the poison used to gas the Jews. (The director of that company got five years; the heads of the other ones were hanged.) The Allies ordered IGF broken up after the war, but the pieces are still around, including such well-known companies as Bayer and BASF.

I guess you could boycott the products of these firms, but you have to ask yourself how far you want to take this. Tom Fuchs, author of *The Hitler Fact Book*, notes that a major participant in the Holocaust was the German state railway system, whose management boasted of its efficiency in delivering the Jews to their murderers. Does that mean next time you tour Germany you walk?

As for the VW, Hitler didn't name it but there's no question he helped create it. Ferdinand Porsche had been working on a popularly priced "people's car" (whence "Volkswagen"). At a 1934 meeting Hitler told him to make the car an air-cooled four-seater with a streamlined shape "like a beetle." Your vish is mein command, said Ferd. Hitler announced the new car at the Berlin Auto Show. The Nazis sold VW "subscriptions" and a factory was built, but only a few cars were made before hostilities began. During the war the plant churned out V-1 buzz bombs and a jeep-like vehicle of a design later sold in the United States as "The Thing." Only after the Nazi surrender did civilian VW production begin in earnest.

Ferdinand Porsche was long viewed as an unwilling participant in Hitler's war machine, but a recent investigation suggests he and his company may have been in deeper than was previously thought. A five-year study by a team of German historians found that as much as

80 percent of VW's wartime workforce of 16,000 may have been slave laborers.

In 1991 the head of the investigative team, Bochum University history professor Hans Mommsen, declared at a symposium, "It's quite clear that Porsche was responsible for hiring concentration-camp inmates for the factory's labor camp." Porsche contacted SS leader Heinrich Himmler directly to request slaves from Auschwitz, Mommsen said.

It should be noted that the investigation was commissioned by Volkswagen itself. The company has dedicated a stone memorial to the slave laborers at its headquarters in Wolfsburg, and I suppose we shouldn't hold current management responsible for crimes committed 50 years ago. But the whole business does put the funky Beetle of one's youth in a new light.

On a recent NBC Today Show *segment, some Martha Stewart wanna-be said you shouldn't throw rice at weddings because it kills birds. Supposedly birds eat the rice, it swells in their stomachs, and they explode over playgrounds. Having cooked a lot of rice, I know it takes boiling heat and a good 20 minutes to get it to swell (aside from*

so-called Minute rice). It seems to me if any bird has an intestinal tem-
perature near boiling, eating a few grains of rice is the least of its wor-
ries. Also, despite zillions of weddings, I don't recall seeing piles of
blown-up pigeons near churches, nor do I remember seeing inordinate
numbers of bird carcasses near rice paddies in southeast Asia. Is there
any basis in fact to the rice = bird killer story, or is this yet another ur-
ban myth?—David Thomas, via the Internet

Cecil humbly concedes that the final word cannot yet be written on this subject. Instead, as is his custom, he merely recites the facts as ascertained to date:

1. Personally I think the whole thing is nonsense, but if I just said that I'd be 500 words shy of a column.
2. Having momentarily tired of the Internet, I had little Ed go on the Mara Tapp show on WBEZ radio in Chicago to see if any of the Teeming Millions had seen birds exploding over playgrounds. Number of calls from kibitzers who wanted to hear what their voices sounded like on the radio: zillions. Number of sightings of detonated birds: zero. Told ya.
3. One guy's idea of a major scientific contribution was to tell us he'd been in a cooking class in Minnesota ten years before, and they'd experimentally determined that dried rice doubles in volume when soaked. Like I didn't know this, you goof.
4. Though maybe the guy's point was that you didn't need to have boiling or even hot water to do this. Little Ed isn't sure. You look at his notes, you think, Wow, nice shorthand. Unfortunately, he was writing in longhand.
5. My brother-in-law told me that dried barley expands to three and a half times its original volume when soaked, so if you're looking for things to throw at weddings instead of rice, I guess barley shouldn't be high on the list. Then again, my brother-in-law also told me he read in a World War II memoir about how they would parachute in bags of rice to the troops in Burma or someplace, and occasionally when a bag went astray people on the ground would later find an empty bag and an exploded cow nearby. But when I spent three hours in the library reading the memoir in question I found zip to support this tale,

and it wouldn't surprise me if my brother-in-law hallucinated the bit about barley too.

6. Getting back to WBEZ, another guy claimed he had a friend who was a physical anthropologist, and she told him that when she wants to separate the bones in a skull, she fills it with rice and lets it sit in water overnight, whereupon the rice expands and forces the bones apart. The guy said that in his opinion this didn't qualify as exploding. Maybe not, but it's not as if having some bird swell up until its skull cracks open is a big improvement visualization-wise.

7. Some people think that, from the point of view of bird endangerment, a distinction should be drawn between regular rice and Minute rice. These people are losers.

8. When we queried the experts at Cornell University—you may remember what a big help they were in exposing the grim truth about green potato chips—the director of education and information services wrote back as follows: "I do not have a prepared response [and why not?], but the simplest answer is, 'ricebirds' (bobolinks) have been eating rice throughout recorded history! It's really no different than the birds eating any grain, including millet or wheat, which they do all the time." Testify, sister.

9. My assistant Jane—I tell you, nobody's going to say I didn't throw enough resources into this—says that, judging from her review of pertinent Web sites, the cool thing to do instead of throwing rice is to release clouds of butterflies. I'm not quite picturing this, but I guess you go to the bridal supply house and buy a box full of butterflies and hope most of them survive till the wedding. This is an improvement?

10. A Presbyterian minister called WBEZ to say that the reason they didn't want you to throw rice at weddings was that it was like spreading little roller bearings all over the floor, and insurance companies didn't want the bride and groom to fall and break their necks. Now that I think about it, using birdseed instead of rice is basically replacing roller bearings with ball bearings. Maybe we should rethink butterflies.

11. I've said this before, I'll say it again: Ain't science great?

Things We Didn't Need To Know

Concerning your column about whether you shouldn't throw rice at weddings because birds eat it, it swells up in their guts, and they explode—well, maybe not rice. However, one day in D.C. I tried to figure out what I was seeing on the sidewalk, even though it was gruesome. It was [WARNING! Disgusting part follows!] a dead pigeon, its throat split vertically, and oozing out of it like stuffing out of a turkey, solidly packed split and whole kernels of dried corn. It really did look like that is what killed the bird. Maybe it had an obstruction of some sort.

I like your column a lot.—Eloise Needleman, Annapolis, Maryland

Uh, thanks, Eloise. Just the same, I'm glad we never went out on a date.

I also have a note from Tim Erskine, who reports that he saw a bird "torn asunder" by the rice in its stomach. Tim says he saw this 25 years ago. This is not what I would call high-quality scientific evidence. Then again, it's not like I want anybody sending me something fresh.

Other baby steps on the road to knowledge:

1. Numerous parties feel I should take up a related myth about feeding Alka-Seltzer to seagulls. "The birds have no means to pass gas orally or ventrally," Wayne writes, "so they just go in a burst of feathers!" Uh-huh. Wayne is hereby named High Commissioner of Experimental Alka-Seltzer Seagull Feeding. I expect a full report.

2. An anonymous benefactor sent me a long excerpt from the Web site run by the USA Rice Federation. One learns that rice farmers set aside 500,000 acres of rice fields for overwintering waterfowl habitat, with 300 pounds of "residual grains" left per acre! Think of it: thousands of circling birds, detonating like flak bursts in *Twelve O'Clock High*! But the rice federation says bull. They quote another expert from Cornell, who says birds have powerful muscles and grit in their stomachs to grind up the rice before it reaches critical mass.

3. The federation also says Ann Landers told the exploding-bird

story in a 1988 column, retracted it, then spread the same line of baloney in a 1996 column. You see why eradicating ignorance is so god-awful slow.

Further Reports

Mail about the effect of rice on our feathered friends continues to flood this department. The latest bulletins:

1. Tim Neil of Crowley, Louisiana, "Rice Capital of the World," reports that thousands of birds swarm to eat the rice falling out of trucks near his hometown. Number of sightings of exploding birds: none. No, I take that back. He did see one explode. However, this was because a wad of birdshot hit it.
2. The fact that birds eat rice in fields proves nothing, Paul Erickson claims. Rice in fields is not dehydrated, and doesn't expand when eaten. Rice in the box *is* dehydrated, and does. Nonetheless, Paul continues, birds who eat dehydrated rice don't explode. They just die.
3. But Tim Neil says the rice dropped by the trucks was both "processed and unprocessed." I'm assuming that "processed" includes "dehydrated." So take that, Paul.
4. A young person who obviously has way more time on his hands than I do reports that, in the interest of science, he captured four sparrows and fed them a daily diet of, respectively, Minute Rice, Uncle Ben's, normal rice, and bird feed. Mortality after seven days: zero, although the rice-fed birds did look "kinda droopy." However, they did fly away energetically when released. Conclusion: dried rice does not cause birds to explode or otherwise die. Good lad.
5. At U.S. Air Force survival school in Spokane, Washington, students are told to drop Alka-Seltzer into wading pools in order to secure an easy lunch of seagull, says Brian Bourke. Many pilots carry Alka-Seltzer with them on sorties for this reason.
6. Ex-serviceman Allen Greiner reports that while stationed on the Gulf Coast, he and his friends used to entertain themselves by tossing Alka-Seltzer to circling seagulls, who would catch the

tablets in midair. If the gull succeeded in swallowing the Alka-Seltzer, it would falter after a short time, foam at the beak, then projectile-vomit its stomach contents. Afterward the bird would be as healthy as ever. Bet this comes as a surprise to downed pilots tossing Alka-Seltzer into wading pools.

7. Garrett Datz says he was at a wedding where they wanted to release live butterflies instead of having the guests throw rice. The idea was to release them from the top of the tent the wedding was held under. Unfortunately, they had the butterflies in boxes for hours and then in release cages for another few hours. By the time the critters were let go, they had all died and plopped onto the assembled party, which to me sounds like something out of *Carrie*.

8. Steve Waldron reports having attended a wedding in which the bride and groom decided it would be neat to release two white doves at the end of the ceremony. However, the birds purchased at a pet store for this purpose had clipped wings and no survival skills. They made it as far as a tree, where they were attacked by squirrels as the children watched. I will spare you further details. The organist said he was not going to play for any more weddings where the ceremony called for an animal sacrifice after the recessional.

9. Arnold Wright Blan says when his cousin got married, instead of throwing rice or birdseed, the couple had little jingle bells attached to business cards that the wedding guests were supposed to jingle as the newlyweds left for the honeymoon. Arnold considers this the tackiest wedding stunt he has ever heard of. He concludes, "I think the bride came up with this, since she wouldn't have enough class for a one-room schoolhouse."

10. Obviously numerous social and ecological disasters await if you try to use anything besides rice at a wedding. My feeling is, if rice is out, elope.

The Last Word

While we're on the subject of exploding birds, rice, and Alka-Seltzer, perhaps you'll tackle another one, if it has not yet been resolved in the annals of science. I remember faintly from early childhood that if you give a frog a cigarette, it will continuously inhale until it explodes, a rather graphic example of the perils of smoking.—Peter Kreutlein

Peter, I'm counting to three. If you're not out of here by then, there's going to be an explosion. And it won't be the frog.

Once during our vacation last summer my daughter demanded a swim in the pool immediately after dinner. I told her to wait at least 30 minutes. Being of the age (12) that no longer accepts what I say as gospel, she insisted on an explanation. "Because my parents made me do it" was the best I could do on short notice. Was I right to insist she wait? Or was I conned by my parents?—Joe Nadeau, Oshkosh, Wisconsin

Sorry to undermine your daughter's faith in you, pops, but you might as well get used to it. Wait till she asks you to repartition the hard drive. As you no doubt suspect, the idea that swimming right after eating means instant death is a myth.

From the 1930s through the 1950s, water-safety experts believed swimming after eating would lead to stomach cramps that would double you over in agony, causing you to sink like a stone. This was thought to be a leading cause of drowning. As late as 1956 the Red Cross water-safety manual devoted several pages to the topic, complete with a staged photo of a gasping "victim."

That same year, however, University of Georgia swim coach B.W. Gabrielsen published a book called *Facts on Drowning Accidents* that revealed that swimming after eating was implicated in fewer than 1 percent of drownings. Thereafter, the wait-an-hour hysteria began to subside. It's now thought stomach cramps are rare. It still isn't a good idea to do strenuous swimming right after eating, lest you exhaust yourself. But a quick dip in the pool after dinner is harmless.

Diving In The Pool, However . . .

There is another possible side effect to swimming after eating, which I witnessed at the impressionable age of nine. My friend Peter and our moms were visiting other friends, who owned a pool. My mother refused to let me back in the water when I was done eating. Peter's mother made no such restriction, and I watched with envy as he headed for the diving board. After a dramatic belly flop, Peter threw up in the pool. No more diving for anybody that day. Since then I assumed the rule was "wait an hour before you do anything violent," but that quiet paddling was OK.—Juanita, Caspar, California

From The Straight Dope Message Board

Subj: Antibacterial Soap
From: MYOOZ1K
If you drop a bar of antibacterial soap in the shower, does it become riddled with bacteria, or is the "anti" completely effective?

From: DEVILFISH
Well, it would probably depend on the bacteria, but I would tend to think that it would pick up as many bacteria as a non-antibacterial bar would. So, initially at least, it would still be riddled with bacteria. As to its continued status as "riddled," that would depend on how well the antibacterial component works. With your typical antibacterial soap, I doubt this component is very effective.

From: AFiggis
Actually, antibacterial soap works exactly the same as antigravity. If you drop it in the shower, it repels against the bacteria and slides around faster. If you drop it in a really infested shower, like, say, a Wrestlemania locker room, the bar will actually levitate above the tiles.

Subj: Requested change for AOL message boards [SR]
From: TBEA925
Much hoohaa has been reported lately about the ratings system for television shows. The rating appears in the upper left corner when the show starts, so parents can have some clue what is going on without taking the time to be actively involved in their children's lives. Revisions to these ratings were recently begrudgingly approved by some of

the major networks to reveal more detail about the shows (violence, sex, language, etc.).

The Straight Dope message board needs a similar rating system. The rating should appear as part of the subject line in square brackets so the reader can avoid the post if he or she chooses to do so.

The proposed initial set of ratings would be:

[SR] – The post is some Stupid Rant about something that just happens to be bugging the writer at that particular moment.

[F] – The post is part of some ongoing and lengthy Flame war(s) between assorted posters on the board. Noninterested parties can skip the entire thread, delete it, and recover the space in their personal filing cabinet without missing anything.

[GP] – The post refers to the Gry word or anything to do with a Parkway, or some similar Gallagheresque Post, demonstrating the astonishing unoriginality of the poster. This includes questions about olive/baby oil, why is abbreviation such a long word, how does Teflon stick to the pan, etc.

[J] – The post is intended as a Joke. This is for readers who don't get it.

[DH] – The poster is currently in some Drug-induced Haze, and the post concerns Phil Collins's "In the Air Tonight" or the perennial favorite "Wow . . . have you ever, like, listened to *Dark Side of the Moon* while watching 'The Wizard of Oz'? Tooootally awsome, duuuude!"

[E] – The poster wants an E-mail response, they don't want to bother retrieving the answer to their question that someone has researched for them.

This system will, no doubt, be revised and improved in the oncoming years. It is hoped that this rating system will protect unsuspecting children from exposure to unpleasant situations, and help preserve the peace and harmony of the Teeming Millions during their visit to the message board.

6

Medical Bulletins

I'm sure you've never been asked this before, but is it okay to eat clay? I'm a student at the Art Institute and I've been eating clay for four years. You are probably not familar with the process of clay, so I will briefly explain. When the clay is completely dry but has not been fired it's called greenware. That's when I eat it. But I once ate a whole teacup after it had been fired (bisqueware). I don't have anyone to ask, because they'll think I'm crazy. Please give me an answer.—Marian, Chicago

No question, telling people you eat teacups does have a way of bringing conversation to a halt. But be bold. Say to yourself, It's not weird, it's performance art. What you've got is a form of pica, the craving to eat the inedible or to eat normal food in obsessive quantities. If

you think teacups are a little over the top, try toilet air-freshener blocks, which one lost soul used to consume at the rate of one or two a week.

Some cravings are so common they have names of their own, such as pagophagia, a hankering for ice (one sufferer admitted to a five-tray-a-day habit supplemented by bags of crushed ice obtained at convenience stores); xylophagia, a yen for wood toothpicks; coniophagia, a lust for dust from venetian blinds; and my personal favorite, gooberphagia, pathological consumption of peanuts. Other cravings include ten bunches of celery a day, a peppermint Life Saver every five minutes, salad croutons by the handful, coal, foam rubber, and worse. One woman, a nonsmoker, reportedly "would burn cigarettes to obtain the ashes" and, when her husband smoked, would follow him with cupped hand to catch the ashes as they fell.

The particular condition you've got is called geophagia, the desire to eat clay or dirt. It's common among poor rural black women, especially during pregnancy—in fact, during the nineteenth century dirt- and clay-eating was called cachexia africana. It's so common that one writer (R. Reid, *Medical Anthropology*, 1992) thinks we should reassess our whole attitude about it, the idea evidently being that if one person does it it's sick but if thousands do it it's an affirming cultural experience, possibly even conferring some medical benefit, although Lord knows what. Incidentally, many geophages are switching to laundry starch, something to think about if your taste for teacups begins to flag.

Geophagia and pica in general are often associated with iron-deficiency anemia. No one knows whether anemia is a cause or an effect, but it's worth looking into in your case, since one can't help thinking that art students as a class could stand a little more, you know, red meat. According to the medical literature, a lot of pica sufferers, including pregnant women with pickles-and-ice-cream-type cravings, have been cured with a regimen of iron supplements.

Then again, maybe you just like clay. Admittedly, the stuff isn't as weird as the match heads and such that some folks go in for. And given that kaolin, a type of clay, is the active ingredient of the well-known childhood remedy Kaopectate, I'll venture to say you don't suffer much from diarrhea. Still, a fair number of clay-eaters have shown up in emergency rooms with obstructed or even perforated intestines, the latter problem being one you put yourself at particular risk for if you start eating fired teacups in quantity. It's all very well to obsess, but let's not get carried away.

What is the connection between handedness and death? I have heard that statistically lefties are more accident-prone and die earlier. I'm a lefty, and I'm getting scared. Does it work like smoking—if I quit now will my stats improve? Thank goodness the insurance companies don't ask, but I'll bet my life-insurance agent watched carefully as I signed my policy.—Dan Kaplan, Evanston, Illinois

I feel your pain, brother—I'm left-handed too. So were all the major candidates in the last two presidential elections, assuming your idea of major is Bush, Clinton, Dole, and Perot (though I suppose Dole's war injury makes him a special case). Five of the last ten U.S. presidents have been left-handed, although lefties account for only 10 percent of the population.

Obviously we have a gift for leadership. The only problem is that a lot of us don't live long enough to use it. At any rate, that's the thesis of psychologist Stanley Coren, the man largely responsible for changing the image of lefties from lovable klutzes to doomed race. Coren's 1992 book *The Left-Hander Syndrome* argued that for a variety of reasons, ranging from less immunity to disease to a higher accident rate, lefties didn't live as long as righties. Based on a survey of the relatives of a thousand recently deceased people in California, Coren claimed that the average lefty died nine years sooner than the average righty (66 versus 75).

Many scoffed at this, the chief objection being that the life-expectancy gap was implausibly large—larger even than the gap between smokers and nonsmokers. Insurance-company actuarial departments would have to have been in a coma not to have noticed a difference this huge before now.

Other research has failed to substantiate Coren's claim, finding either a much smaller difference in life expectancy or no difference at all. Coren's own previous study of baseball players' life spans (drawn, charmingly enough, from the *Baseball Encyclopedia*) found only an eight-month gap, and even that has been vigorously disputed.

Coren now seems to have conceded that the nine-year gap may be a

little off. A study of British cricket players found a two-year gap, which he's described as reasonable.

Still, even a two-year gap is sizable. If it turns out to be legit, you wouldn't be surprised to find life-insurance applications with "left-handed" on the risk-factor checkoff list right after "smokes" and "does drugs."

So we're left to ponder the question: Can this be, pardon the expression, right?

A lot of people say no way. If Coren's research shows that relatively few old people are left-handed, they argue, that's because lefties in the old days were forced to convert, like medieval Jews.

Me? I'm not so sure. As a general proposition, no one doubts that lefties differ in fundamental ways from righties.

There's a fair amount of evidence that left-handedness is caused by minor brain damage at birth (though there seems to be a genetic component as well). Possibly as a result, lefties are clumsier if perhaps also more creative.

Looking through the medical literature, I find studies reporting that lefties have a higher accident rate, are more likely to have their fingers amputated in power-tool accidents, suffer more wrist fractures, etc. What's more, lefties suffer a higher incidence of allergies, epilepsy, schizophrenia, and certain learning disabilities.

Lefties, a 1992 article in the *Atlantic* notes, also show unusually high frequencies of depression, drug abuse, bed-wetting, attempted suicide, lower-than-normal birth weight, sleeping disorders, and autoimmune diseases.

Not to mention the fact that, as we've already seen, they have a significantly greater danger of becoming U.S. president. If that won't

take years off your life, I don't know what will. My advice to fellow southpaws: keep your head low, avoid power tools, and never, ever accept a convention draft.

Did you ever uncover the mystery behind the tiny ring that one sometimes gets in the ears? You know, that tiny pitch you may hear in one ear that temporarily blocks out sound and you think some CIA agent is trying to contact you through some unknown computer chip in your head? (Well, maybe not that scenario.) Or you think some alien planet is trying to reach you? Or you feel like you have a calling somewhere, but you have no idea where? Did you ever get that, or hear of it, or am I just completely mental?— Nina Keinberger, Chicago

You realize, Nina, that the last two choices aren't an either/or proposition. I've heard the tiny ring, although I'd call it more a tone, like the ones used in hearing tests. Other people hear low-pitched "ocean noise," roaring, buzzing, cricket sounds, sirens, or some combination of the above. However you experience it, the sensation of sound without an external stimulus is called tinnitus. Lots of people get it—including, I would venture to say, virtually everyone who's ever been to a rock concert. One U.K. study found that nearly 40 percent of respondents reported experiencing tinnitus at least occasionally, roughly a sixth had persistent symptoms (episodes lasting more than five minutes not associated with exposure to noise), and around 2 percent described their tinnitus as severe.

Doctors traditionally have distinguished between objective, or "real," tinnitus and subjective, or "false," tinnitus. In objective tinnitus an actual sound can be detected with a stethoscope or, in the odd case, simply by standing near the patient. The noise may arise from some deformation of the blood vessels, in which case it may signal a tumor or aneurysm; twitching of the muscles of the middle ear; a eustachian tube that remains open when it shouldn't; and so on.

Subjective tinnitus, which is far more common, is tougher to pin down. Clinicians caution that tinnitus should be considered a symptom of some larger problem, and in fact it's often associated with other symptoms, like hearing loss or dizziness. But in many cases no definite cause can be established. "Subjective tinnitus . . . is presumed to originate from some type of electrophysiologic derangement in the cochlea, cranial nerve VIII, or central nervous system," one Mayo Clinic review notes, but beyond that the subject remains mysterious. After running through a list of theories, all of them too numbingly complex to present here, one research team observed tartly, "None of these speculations has been (nor can many of them be) put to the experimental test." In short, the CIA and alien planets can't be ruled out.

There is no cure for subjective tinnitus, but some progress has been made in alleviating it. Around 1825 the French doctor Jean-Marc-Gaspard Itard (whom regular readers of this column will remember as the tutor of the wild boy of Aveyron) was the first to notice that tinnitus would diminish or subside if masked with a similar external sound. For example, if the patient complained of hearing a high-pitched noise Itard recommended listening to a fire of green wood, the hissing of which often brought some relief. Later generations of patients found it helpful to listen to a water fountain, FM radio static, or even an electric razor. (Although not just any electric razor. When one tinnitus sufferer sent his lucky razor in for repair, he was devastated when the company sent back a new one instead—unlike the old one, it had no effect on his tinnitus.) Since the 1970s sufferers have been able to avail themselves of electronic tinnitus maskers, which may be combined with (and worn like) a hearing aid. One researcher claims two-thirds of severe tinnitus cases can be helped by hearing instruments of one kind or another.

Failing that, there's the drug lidocaine, which also works about

two-thirds of the time, the main drawbacks being that you have to in-
ject it intravenously and the relief is short-lived. I don't know how
much this bugs you, Nina, but here's hoping the alien planets don't
come calling too often.

*We all know smoking cigarettes can kill you, but it seems to me that,
as with most vices, there's a difference between use and abuse. People
who drink too much destroy their livers, but people who have one
drink of red wine per day actually help their hearts. I'll gladly accept
the fact that smoking several packs a day is harmful, but what about
having only three cigarettes a day, one after every meal? Does it really
do any harm? Is there any chance it's actually good for you?—Michael
Dare, Hollywood, California*

Well . . . I hesitate to mention this. But after years of research saying that smoking was the worst threat to public health since the
plague, several recent studies suggest it may have at least one health
benefit: it prevents or at least slows the onset of Alzheimer's disease.
For obvious reasons, these reports have been accompanied by a certain amount of embarrassed hemming and hawing. From a big-picture
standpoint smoking is definitely bad for you, and nobody wants to give
people an excuse to do more of it.

Still, facts are facts. I quote: "A statistically significant inverse association between smoking and Alzheimer's disease was observed at all
levels of analysis, with a trend towards decreasing risk with increasing
consumption" (*International Journal of Epidemiology*, 1991). "The

risk of Alzheimer's disease decreased with increasing daily number of cigarettes smoked before onset of disease. . . . In six families in which the disease was apparently inherited . . . the mean age of onset was 4.17 years later in smoking patients than in non-smoking patients from the same family" (*British Medical Journal,* June 22, 1991). Nicotine injections significantly improved certain types of mental functioning in Alzheimer's patients (*Psychopharmacology,* 1992). One theory: nicotine improves the responsiveness of Alzheimer's patients to acetylcholine, an important brain chemical.

I know, I know. Now that chimney at work will claim he's keeping himself (and due to secondary smoke, you) from going senile. Tell him it's a little early to start gloating. Some of the research is contradictory. At least one scientist thinks smokers are less likely to develop Alzheimer's mainly because they die of smoking-related diseases first. Smoking isn't like low-to-moderate alcohol use, which is probably harmless and may even be beneficial. Although the data are unclear, many believe the relationship between smoking and disease is linear: the more you smoke, the greater your risk—but any smoking presents some risk. Right now the only known benefit of smoking is a societal one: if the heavy smokers die young, they won't deplete the retirement funds for everybody else.

Smoking Is Good For You

First off, as a loyal fan I acknowledge your omniscience, so this is not meant to be taken as a correction at all, since you are truly incorrigible. However, you may want to reassure the reader looking for advantages of smoking that a form of inflammatory bowel disease called ulcerative colitis is thought to be prevented by smoking. Relapses of this disease, marked by weeks of bloody diarrhea, are frequently provoked by suddenly giving up smoking. Not that this would make a good ad campaign for the folks at RJR, since ANOTHER form of inflammatory bowel disease called Crohn's disease, with only slightly different symptoms, occurs mostly in smokers.—Anonymous, Chicago

Bummer about the Crohn's disease. Think of the great cigarette ads you could write:

SMOKE SARCOMAS

Look sharp, feel sharp
. . . and avoid weeks of bloody diarrhea

Anonymous also sent me a reference to a medical-journal article titled "Beneficial Effects of Nicotine" (Jarvik, *British Journal of Addiction,* 1991) that summarizes the many positive aspects of this wonder
drug. "When chronically taken," it says here, "nicotine may result in:
(1) positive reinforcement [it makes you feel good], (2) negative reinforcement [it may keep you from feeling bad], (3) reduction of body
weight [by reducing appetite and increasing metabolic rate], (4) en-
hancement of performance, and protection against: (5) Parkinson's
disease, (6) Tourette's disease [tics], (7) Alzheimer's disease, (8) ulcerative colitis and (9) sleep apnea. The reliability of these effects varies
greatly but justifies the search for more therapeutic applications for
this interesting compound." Yeah, and what other medical miracle lets
you blow smoke rings?

*How do "ear candles" work? Recently my hearing became impaired,
and I was advised that my ears were impacted with wax. A friend recommended that the wax could be removed if I stuck a candle in my
ear and lighted the other end. To humor her, I accompanied her to a
homeopathic-remedy shop. Ear candles were prominently displayed.
An ear candle is a hollow paper cone impregnated with ordinary
candle wax. The large end is about one inch in diameter. The other end
is small enough to go into the ear. As I lay on my side with the candle
in place, my friend lighted the other end. The candle burned slowly
and smoothly, with (I was told) some wisps of smoke circulating down-*

ward to the small end. There was no discomfort or noticeable warmth. After about ten minutes she removed the candle and snuffed out the flame. Immediately my hearing in that ear was back to normal. The end of the cone had a considerable amount of earwax in it. The process was equally successful in the other ear.—Saxe Dobrin, Santa Monica, California

Uh-huh. Not that I'd ever doubt the Teeming Millions, but I prefer to conduct my own experiments. Ear candling is the latest New Age fad, being to the '90s what colonic irrigation was to the '80s. Colonic irrigation was never a procedure I was inclined to investigate close up. But with ear candles I figured, How bad can it be?

Having rounded up a couple of M.D.s and a volunteer candlee, I went to my neighborhood new-age apothecary shop to buy ear candles. I discovered to my surprise that 1) they were 11 inches long—I'd assumed they were the size of a birthday candle—and 2) they cost $3.50 each. This gets you a hollow cone made of wax-impregnated cloth with a raw-materials cost of maybe 10 cents, a profit margin that makes even ballpark hot dogs look like a deal.

Figuring that the M.D.s' medical education had probably been a little light in the ear-candling department, I also bought an ear-candling manual. In the "theory and research" section I read that candle flame creates a "slow vacuum" that softens the old wax and draws it into the base of the candle. I had no idea what a slow vacuum was, but I was prepared to believe a candle might cause earwax to wick up.

I read on. "Our theory is that [various benefits] are possible because all the passages in the head are interconnected, allowing the candles to drain the entire system osmotically through the membrane of the ear." I also learned that the nerves have a "thin coating of spinal fluid" that can become polluted; that said fluid circulates 14 times a day to cleanse itself; that the cranial bones can become misaligned; and that candling cleans the "lymphs" as well as the "cochlear hairs." Whew, too deep for me. But the manual did have pictures, so even dopes could do it right.

The medical team consisted of Keith Block, a family practitioner with an interest in alternative medicine, and Cecil's good friend Clark Federer. Clark was a surgeon rather than an ear-nose-throat guy, but I meant to be prepared for any eventuality. Our subject was Pat, a

30-year-old male who'd had earwax removed via conventional medical treatment some years earlier.

First we peered into Pat's ears with an otoscope, the familiar flashlight-type examining device. The poor guy had enough wax in there to make his own candles. We put him on the table, lit the candle, and stuck it in his ear in the prescribed manner. Then we watched, struggling to suppress the thought that we should also be chanting and maybe sacrificing small animals.

When the candle had burned down to two inches, we snuffed it and examined the treated ear with the otoscope. No change, except that possibly the wax was dented where the candle had been stuck in. Upon slicing open the candle stub, however, we found a considerable quantity of brown wax and whitish powder. The manual had the audacity to intimate that the powder was candida yeast extracted from the ear, conceding that possibly "1% to 10%" was from the used candle. The disappointed M.D.s were more inclined to say it was 100 percent, but just to be sure we burned another candle in the open air. When we sliced it open we found wax and powder identical to that in the first. Conclusion: it's a hoax. Ain't it always the way? Maybe we're not doing enemas anymore, but we're winding up with the same old end result.

Your Worst Fears Confirmed

As an otolaryngologist with 15 years' experience, I have had more than one occasion on which a victim of ear candling has been presented to my office with excruciating symptoms caused by melted wax adhering to the eardrum. This often necessitates minor surgery and puts the patient's hearing at risk. In addition to debunking the efficacy of ear candling, you should mention the inherent danger to hearing.—C. Christopher Smith, M.D., F.A.C.S., Dover, New Hampshire

Why is it when a doctor gives you a physical examination, he taps your knee with a rubber hammer? My knee always jerks when he does this, and the same goes for everyone I have ever spoken to. Which makes me wonder if anyone has ever failed it, and what became of them. Does the medical community just go on looking, looking, hoping

to find a person who fails the test? Or is there actually some hideous disease which has as one of its early symptoms that your knees do not jerk when struck?—Bill Kinnersley, via the Internet

I consulted the Straight Dope Science Advisory Board about this, and one member informed me that if no knee-jerk reflex can be elicited, "this is one of the diagnostic signs that the patient is dead." Ho ho! But of course there's more to it than that. The actual purpose of knee tapping is to test for pathological conditions that, while not common, are far from nonexistent. These conditions fall into two categories:

1. *Hyperactive deep tendon reflex* (knee jerks too much): amyotrophic lateral sclerosis, brain tumor, cerebrovascular accident (stroke), hepatic encephalopathy (associated with liver disease), hypocalcemia (low calcium), hypomagnesemia (low magnesium), hypothermia, multiple sclerosis, preeclampsia, spinal cord lesion (e.g., tumor), and tetanus.

2. *Hypoactive deep tendon reflex* (knee doesn't jerk enough): botulism, Eaton-Lambert syndrome, Guillain-Barré syndrome (nerve inflammation), peripheral neuropathy, polymyositis, syringomyelia, tabes dorsalis, and other ailments too scary to pronounce, much less have.

When the doctor tests your reflexes she's tapping the tendon that connects the muscle to the bone, which causes the muscle to stretch slightly. This sends a nerve impulse to your spinal cord, where it triggers a motor impulse that returns via a parallel nerve and causes the muscle to twitch.

A faulty reflex in itself is not conclusive evidence that you have one of the problems listed above. For example, in the case of preeclampsia, a form of hypertension, you also have to be pregnant. But a bad reflex does tell the doctor to investigate further. One way to do this is by testing other reflexes. The doctor usually starts with your knee-jerk response, also known as the patellar reflex, because it's quick and easy. But she can also whale away on your elbow (triceps reflex), crook of your arm (biceps reflex), wrist (brachioradialis reflex), or back of your ankle (Achilles tendon reflex).

If you've got feeble reflexes all over plus muscle weakness and blurred and double vision, maybe you've got botulism. If you've got hyperactive reflexes on one side of the body only, that's a sign of brain tumor or stroke. If your patellar reflexes bite but your triceps reflexes are OK, that may mean you've got a lesion (injury) below your second lumbar vertebra. If you jump even though the doctor didn't use her little hammer at all, don't worry, babe, that's normal. It means you saw the bill.

A friend of mine, who is paranoid about everything, recently told me that fluorescent lights cause cataracts. Everything I've read about these lights before talks about them glowingly—that they're so energy efficient I should replace every lamp in my home with fluorescent bulbs. And of course I and millions of other people toil under them for most of our waking hours every day. Are we all going to go blind? Why have I not heard about these harmful effects before? Is my paranoid friend nuts too, or is there some conspiracy to keep this information out of the press and away from the general public?—Mary M.Q.C., Chicago

If there is, my payoff from the Bulb Trust must have gotten lost in the mail. The reason you haven't heard much about the dangers of fluorescent lighting is that there isn't much to hear. No study has ever established a link between fluorescent lights and cataracts, and there haven't been many studies period. While fears about the bulbs aren't entirely groundless, right now the danger is strictly theoretical.

Concerns about fluorescent lights are a by-product of research into the harmful effects of ultraviolet radiation from the sun. Laboratory experiments have shown that UV light can damage the proteins and

enzymes found in the lens of the eye, and several studies have suggested that outdoorsy types and others who get more sun than average are at greater risk for cataracts.

Fluorescent bulbs generate UV light too—that's how they work. When you turn on the juice, a mercury arc in the bulb emits UV light that strikes a phosphor coating on the inside of the tube. The phosphor, in turn, emits visible light.

The amount of UV light emitted by bulbs is a lot less than what the sun puts out, but the fact that many people work under fluorescent fixtures day after day has stirred fears about the long-term effects. Not to worry, the experts say. The amount of UV light that escapes from the tube is minimal, since the phosphor absorbs much of it and the glass tube is opaque to most of the rest. Supposedly you receive as much UV rays from one hour's exposure to sunlight in November in New York City as you do from an entire year's exposure to a fluorescent tube. What's more, the ultraviolet light emitted by the tubes is mostly in the UVA range rather than the more dangerous UVB range.

Concerns about the sun are more urgent. The danger of ultraviolet light remains controversial and, given the difficulty of epidemiologic studies, may never be definitely settled. But enough is known to warrant such basic precautions as wearing sunglasses outdoors. The wraparound kind are especially recommended, one of the few times when being hip is actually good for you.

Just one thing: make sure your sunglasses block UV light. A cheesy pair that blocks only visible light could make things worse. The reduced visible light will cause your pupils to dilate, allowing the UV light to pour in. To avoid frying your lenses like an egg, make sure any sunglasses you buy have a tag or label that says they block UV light.

As I was slogging through yet another interesting assignment for medical school, I happened upon this interesting tidbit:

"BEZOARS. Bezoars are foreign bodies in the stomach of animals and humans that are composed of food or hair that has been altered by the digestive process. Historically, bezoars were esteemed for their alleged therapeutic properties and aesthetic value, and one was included in the crown jewels of Queen Elizabeth I." (From Pathology, *second edition, 1994, by E. Rubin and J. L. Farber, page 649.)*

What "therapeutic and aesthetic" uses were people able to come up with for hair balls? Is Queen Elizabeth's Royal Hair Ball on display somewhere?—Mark Phillips, Baltimore

If they can promote the work of Michael Bolton as aesthetically desirable, I don't see what's so tough about hair balls. Actually, if you can suppress the thought of where they came from, bezoars are said to be kind of pretty. While I can't say I've laid eyes on one, I'm told they're hard and glassy, somewhat like pearls, which are produced in a similar way. The original bezoars (also called bezoar stones) came from the wild goats of Persia as well as certain antelopes and other cud-chewing animals. They were believed to offer protection against poison and for that reason were highly prized during the Renaissance by the Medicis, presumably for when they had the Borgias over. Bezoars were later obtained in the New World from Peruvian llamas, but these were held to be of inferior quality—although it's gotta take a sharp eye to tell a good hair ball from a bad one. Reportedly, a gold-framed bezoar was listed in the 1622 inventory of Elizabeth I's crown jewels; make sure you look for it on the palace tour.

Little was heard about bezoars in modern times until 1987, when a

seven-centimeter specimen was removed from the stomach of a
35-year-old man in Kansas City. Tan and egg-shaped, this bezoar is
thought to have been the result of the man's habit of eating pieces of
plastic foam cups. It was not embraced by the world of fashion, however. Too bad. Given an aggressive PR strategy, it could have been the
hottest thing since the chia pet.

Things I Didn't Need To Hear

*Re your recent discussion of bezoars, one month ago I operated on
an 18-year-old woman who was having intestinal problems. She would
become full after eating only small amounts. I surgically removed the
large bezoar in the enclosed photo. It measured 8–9 inches. The young
woman chewed her hair. I thought you would find this interesting.
—Lieutenant Colonel Victor L. Modesto, M.D., Womack Army Medical Center, Fort Bragg, North Carolina*

Saints preserve us. The thing is roughly the size and shape of a
turkey leg. And how nicely the Polaroid brings out those vivid postop-
erative colors! Now, if you'll excuse me, I have to go to the bathroom
and barf.

*When I was a little kid my mother always warned me not to sit too
close to the TV because it would "ruin your eyes." Now I am saying the
same thing to my two sons. Is this really true? Exactly what eye damage can occur? Is there an optimal distance from which to view a television screen? I am aware of the mental damage that children can
incur from watching television but have never been clear about the ad-
verse physical effects of this pastime.—David Horowitz, Los Angeles,
California*

First the good news: according to most eye specialists, claims that
you'll ruin your eyes by sitting too close to the TV, reading in bed, using inadequate light, etc., are old wives' tales. The bad news is that the
old wives may have been right.

First let's dispose of the TV threat. Virtually no one believes that
under ordinary circumstances television watching poses any special

danger. (Well, physically, anyway.) Prior to 1968 or so some sets emitted excessive X-rays, but that problem has now been eliminated. More recently concern has arisen about computer video display terminals (VDTs), which typically are viewed at much closer range than televisions; research is inconclusive so far but continuing. To be on the safe side some eye doctors say you shouldn't let your kids get closer than five feet to the TV screen, the room shouldn't be pitch black, etc. But the intention is to prevent eye fatigue, not eye damage.

The more general (and more interesting) question you raise is this: is it possible to ruin your eyesight through overuse, close work, inadequate light, and so on? The usual answer from the MDs is no. But don't be too sure. A fair number of people believe that some eye problems, notably myopia (nearsightedness), are a "product of civilization," as one researcher put it.

The most striking demonstration of this was a study in the late '60s of eyesight among Eskimoes in Barrow, Alaska. These people had been introduced to the joys of civilization around World War II. The incidence of myopia in those age 56 and up was zero percent; in parents age 30 and up, 8 percent; in their children, 59 percent.

The same phenomenon has turned up in studies of other newly civilized peoples, suggesting that modern life somehow causes nearsightedness. But how? Nobody knows. The shift among the Eskimoes appeared to be too sudden to be explained by genetics alone (although there is little question that a predisposition to nearsightedness is inherited). On the theory that too much close focusing while young permanently distorts the eyeball, some experts gave kids regular doses of atropine, which relaxes the eye muscles. (Eye doctors use it to dilate your pupils prior to an exam.) A few claimed this halted myopia but failed to convince many of their peers, and there was the obvious practical problem that with your eyes dilated you couldn't see for beans.

Other researchers blame dietary deficiencies, e.g., not enough copper or chromium; excessive exposure to pesticides; and so on. But nothing has been proven.

Animal studies tend to support the idea that myopia is caused by eyestrain. Normal monkeys are not myopic; neither are monkeys whose eyes are kept completely sealed off from light. But monkeys whose eyes were sutured so they could see only dimly (I realize this is the kind of thing that outrages animal rights activists) did become myopic, presumably because they could see something and strained their eyes trying to see more.

The idea that the civilization means bad eyes is by no means universally accepted. The Alaska Eskimo study, for example, was criticized for not testing a random sample—presumably the main reasons kids were brought to the Barrow clinic in the first place was that their parents thought they had vision problems, which of course skewed the results. Other studies have failed to find a correlation between environment and vision.

So what's a father to do? Search me, pard. If you buy the environmental argument you could feed the kids whale blubber and chuck the books, TV, and needlepoint lessons, but the tradeoff might not be worth it. Having to wear eyeglasses is hardly a major handicap these days whereas being an uneducated mope is. Till such time as the myopia-inducing component of civilization (if any) is isolated, you're probably best off chalking up a little nearsightedness as a small price to pay for indoor plumbing.

About 15 years ago I read an obscure government publication on the use of uranium in dental porcelain. It said uranium is added to dental porcelain for cosmetic reasons: to make the porcelain more luminous, like natural teeth. It was estimated that this use of uranium causes about 2,000 cases of cancer per year. I've since mentioned this to many dentists, but none of them had ever heard of this.

Cecil, I'm counting on you to find out what's going on here. Preferably before I need more dental work. And while you're at it, what is the safest dental material?—Pearl E. White, Chicago

You read right, friend—no mean achievement these days. In one of those classic wacky moves, manufacturers once upon a time put uranium in dental porcelain to give crowns and false teeth that certain glow.

Real teeth have natural fluorescence. If you shine a black light on

your teeth, they gleam a brilliant white. To give dental work the same glow, the use of uranium in dental porcelain was patented in 1942.

The timing of this was suspicious. You have to wonder if those Manhattan Project scientists, toiling over crucibles of hot uranium, got to thinking, Hey, if this atom-bomb thing flops, we can always go into teeth.

The glow imparted to false teeth by uranium was not a consequence of radioactivity. Uranium merely happens to fluoresce in the presence of UV light. Fluorescence is harmless; lots of compounds do it. Uranium's advantage was that it would survive the high heat of porcelain manufacture.

Still, you did have the problem that uranium was radioactive. In the wake of Hiroshima and Nagasaki, it occurred to the dental-ceramics industry that a substance that had destroyed cities might not be such a good thing to use in somebody's mouth. Manufacturers discussed the situation with the Atomic Energy Commission in the 1950s. The debate proceeded along the following lines: On the one hand, putting uranium in people's mouths might possibly give them cancer and kill them. On the other hand, their teeth looked great. It was an easy call. The industry was given a federal exemption to continue using uranium.

In the 1970s, some people began to wonder if this had been the world's smartest decision. The amount of uranium used in dental porcelain was small—0.05 percent by weight in the United States, 0.1 percent in Germany. Nevertheless, the fake teeth bombarded the oral mucosa with radiation that was maybe eight times higher than normal background radiation. None of the research I came across mentioned a specific number of cancer deaths, but clearly this was not something you'd do for the health benefits.

There was also the unavoidable fact that the aesthetic gains achieved using uranium were slight. To see the teeth fluoresce you needed UV light, and, as one study sniffily noted, "UV lamps are used mainly in some discotheques and restaurants" frequented by "only a very small fraction of the population with these types of restorations."

But come on, you're thinking. If even one guy with fake teeth looked good in a disco, wasn't that worth a little risk?

Even that advantage turned out to be illusory, however. Though it was claimed that the best uranium compounds replicated the white fluorescence of natural teeth, research showed that some porcelain teeth fluoresced red, violet, or bright yellow. In other words, not only were you nuking your gums, when you opened your mouth you looked like a neon sign.

That put the matter over the top. Numerous authorities urged that the use of uranium in dental porcelain be discontinued, and in the mid-1980s the federal exemption was revoked. Most dental porcelain sold today is uranium-free.

What's the safest dental material? One guess: real teeth. Guaranteed against silent horrors unless someone sneaks up and bites you. Brush 'em after every meal, because who knows what the dental industry will think up next?

I recently acquired a satellite dish and have become a shameless junkie of old Westerns. In half of these B movies of plains life, it seems there is always a woman giving birth. After they give her the obligatory wooden spoon to bite on, someone always yells to boil some water. What's with the water?—Ryan Bailey, via the Internet

Really. Your first thought is that the boiling water was dreamed up by male scriptwriters who had never witnessed the miracle of childbirth. Anyone who's actually assisted at one thinks: I don't need boiling water, I need a bucket and a mop. A midwife we talked to jokingly suggested it was an excuse to get the husband out of the room.

But there was probably more to it than that. Midwives and such have been heating water since time immemorial to wash mother and

baby following delivery. Water could also be used for warm compresses to soften the perineum, easing the pain and reducing the chances of tearing.

You didn't necessarily boil the water, though. Boiling water kills germs, but this was not widely understood until the late nineteenth century. Prior to that time few saw the need for cleanliness. Doctors in the 1780s, for example, complained about midwives with dirty hands poking around in the mother's innards during labor.

Truth is, as long as it was just midwives doing the poking, sterility wasn't that important. Only when doctors got involved did it become a matter of life and death. During the nineteenth century, as doctors began to supplant midwives at the bedsides of women giving birth, there was an alarming rise in complications such as puerperal fever. This often fatal illness resulted from the infection of vaginal or other tissue torn during childbirth. Midwives weren't major carriers of this disease, because they saw only a handful of patients a week. A doctor, on the other hand, might handle diseased tissue during an autopsy and then proceed to the delivery room, where he'd unwittingly infect the mother.

Some doctors tried to warn of the danger, notably the Hungarian physician Ignaz Semmelweis. But few paid much heed until 1880, when Louis Pasteur showed that puerperal fever was caused by a particular type of bacteria. Meanwhile, the English physician Joseph Lister was persuading his colleagues of the importance of antiseptics in surgery. By 1885 hospitals had begun to adopt antiseptic methods such as boiling water to sterilize instruments, including those used during childbirth. (Previously many cases of tetanus had resulted from cutting the umbilical cord with a dirty knife or scissors, and of course there were the infamous forceps.) Presumably word about antiseptic practices eventually reached the prairies, and boiling water both to sterilize things and, after it cooled, to wash the hands of the attending midwife/doctor/cowpoke became a standard part of the prenatal drill.

That's not to say no one ever boiled water before the 1880s. Here's a recipe for a concoction intended to hasten the delivery of a stillborn, from *The Midwives Book* (1671) by Jane Sharp: "Take Oyl of worms, of Foxes, and of the Lillies of the Vallies, each alike, boyl a young blind Puppey in them, so long that his flesh part from the bones; then press forth all strongly, and add to the straining, Styrax, Calamint, Benzoin, Opopanax, Frankincense, Mastik, of each one dram, a little Aqua Vitae, a little wax; mix them and make of them an Ointment; then let her drink often of this Potion following."

I mean, lest you get too rosy an impression of midwives.

When I was about 12, my health teacher told our class that roaches sometimes crawl into sleeping people's ear canals and get stuck. This causes pain and hearing problems. Within a week of being told this, I suffered pain and hearing problems in one ear. I freaked out, went to the doctor, and fully expected him to pull a roach out of my ear. Instead, he took out a lot of earwax. This marked the beginning of my ongoing battle against earwax. I've been wondering ever since: What is earwax for? Why do I produce way too much of it? And was my health teacher right about roaches?—Bob Vesterman, via the Internet

Afraid so, Bob. But let's not jump into that right away. Earwax—called cerumen by doctors because they don't want people to realize they're talking about earwax—is a normal secretion of special glands in the outer ear. The wax coats the outer part of the ear canal, trapping germs and debris and preventing them from reaching the eardrum. If you didn't have any your ears would, at a minimum, itch like hell. In other words, earwax is good! You should be organizing Earwax Appreciation Week!

Still, all things in moderation. In most people earwax is produced in modest amounts and migrates out of the ear naturally. But a few people such as yourself are, let's face it, freaks. You may be tempted to remove excess earwax with a Q-tip or the like. Don't; you'll pack it in tighter. Better you should try an over-the-counter preparation such as Debrox or ordinary mineral oil. You put in a dropperful and pack your ear with cotton; the earwax softens and comes out.

If that doesn't work you need to see a doctor. We found this description of a doctor's Cerumen Management Kit:

1. a suction pump with a one-eighth-horsepower motor and 1,500-cubic-centimeter collection bottle;
2. an otoscope, a lighted ear-examining device;
3. stainless-steel ear forceps with "alligator type three-inch serrated jaws," so the earwax knows who's boss;
4. a stethoscope—who knows why; maybe they just figure if you're a doctor you need a stethoscope;
5. an "emesis basin," I guess to catch the drippings; and
6. a headlight with rechargeable nicad battery pack. I mean, you gotta be ready for anything. Some doctors say, forget all the apparatus, just squirt in some warm water. But we'll leave those decisions to the pros.

Now, about roaches crawling into ears. You may think this is some kind of deranged myth. Uh-uh. Happens all the time. In fact, a controversy has raged since 1980 over the best way to get the little bastards out. The conventional remedy: drown the critter with mineral oil. "One cannot use the commercially available roach sprays," one M.D. sagely notes, "because of technical difficulty and for possible medicolegal reasons"—i.e., the patient might sue. But mineral oil isn't ideal either, because the insect takes a while to go through its death throes in the patient's ear.

One proposed alternative is 2-percent lidocaine anesthetic. The value of this was seemingly demonstrated when a patient showed up at a hospital with cockroaches in both ears. (Unanswered question: what was this guy *doing?*) Recognizing a golden opportunity for a controlled clinical trial, the attending physicians put mineral oil in one ear. "The cockroach succumbed after a valiant but futile struggle, but its removal required much dexterity on the part of the house officer," they wrote. In the other ear the doctors put lidocaine. "The roach exited the canal at a convulsive rate of speed" and was promptly stomped by an intern.

But lidocaine has drawbacks too. Another doctor who tried it reported that 1) the roach died *in situ* and was hell to get out, and 2) the roach had punctured the eardrum, so the lidocaine penetrated the inner ear and the patient had the whirlies for the next five hours. Also, subsequent tests have shown that lidocaine works much more slowly than your top-quality mineral oil.

A promising alternative: suction. Of course, one must take care not to inadvertently seal the ear canal with the suction tip, thereby risking "tympanic membrane barotrauma" and possibly sucking out the patient's brains.

What else? How about fly larvae in the ear? Happens. Also earwigs, with those scary pincers. You know the story. Earwig gets into a guy's ear, chews through his brain, causes horrible agony. Finally it stops. The doctors say, good news: the earwig came out the other side! Bad news: it was female and laid eggs. You've also heard that this is BS, that earwigs don't really crawl into ears. Not so; two known cases. The part about eating out your brains may still be a myth, but who knows?

What is déjà vu and why does it occur?—Eric Palmer, Wilkes-Barre, Pennsylvania

I could have sworn I'd answered this question before. However, having scoured the files, I guess it just seems like I did. Is this a déjà vu experience? No, this is an out-to-lunch experience. I feel it's important to make these fine distinctions lest the meaning of this too casually flung about term become even more muddled in the popular mind.

The definition of déjà vu commonly cited in the medical literature these days is "subjectively inappropriate impressions of familiarity of

the present with an undefined past." This definition unfortunately eats, since it requires you to understand the thing being defined before you can understand the definition.

A better take on it is that déjà vu is the uncanny sensation that you are reliving some unknown past experience. I throw the word *uncanny* in there because it exudes the musty air of cheap paperbacks we like to cultivate in this column and also because an essential feature of déjà vu is that it seems intensely strange at the time.

The other essential feature is that the relived past experience is unknown—you cannot recall having previously had the experience, and indeed you may realize that it's impossible for you to have had it. You just somehow feel that you have.

The déjà vu phenomenon is a favorite of creative types. Proust mentions it, fittingly, in *Remembrance of Things Past*. In *David Copperfield* Dickens has his title character say, "He seemed to swell and grow before my eyes; the room seemed full of the echoes of his voice; and the strange feeling (to which no one is quite a stranger) that all this had occurred before, at some indefinite time, and that I knew what he was going to say next, took possession of me."

Depending on the survey, anywhere from 30 to 96 percent of respondents report having experienced déjà vu. But one suspects the high-end figures are a function of having worded the question too vaguely. Déjà vu doesn't mean merely going through the same situation twice, as many journalists seem to think. Nor should it be confused with other mental hiccups such as flashbacks, precognition (the sense that the present situation has been foretold), and so on.

Déjà vu is said to occur more frequently in those under 30. The experience is usually brief, lasting from a few seconds to a few minutes, but in pathological cases may be prolonged. Although the term déjà vu (French for "already seen") suggests it's primarily a visual phenomenon, it can involve all the senses, which is why some prefer the term *deja vecu,* "already experienced." The opposite of déjà vu is *jamais vu,* ("never seen"), the sensation that a familiar situation is completely strange.

What causes déjà vu? Almost all who've studied the subject have come up with their own explanations, and hey, why not? Our knowledge of the brain is so fragmentary that no explanation can be definitely discounted. Still, the chances that déjà vu is a sign of telepathy, reincarnation, or visitations by one's astral body, as some have suggested, seem pretty slim.

Among the quasiscientific explanations, what might be called the split-image school holds that two parts of the brain participate simultaneously in the process of perception. If for some reason the impression from part A arrives in one's consciousness out of sync with the impression from part B, one has the sensation of experiencing the thing thing twice.

Others explain déjà vu by analogy to a tape recorder. They propose that memory storage is accomplished by means of a "recording head" and memory recall by a "playback head." During déjà vu the two heads are erroneously situated above the same bit of mental blank tape. An experience is thus recorded and remembered simultaneously, with the result that the present is experienced as the past.

There are lots more theories, but you get the idea.

Déjà vu was a hot topic in the 1890s among French psychiatrists, who came up with the name. But later researchers dismissed it as a curiosity. The Dutch psychiatrist Herman Sno sparked a revival of interest in the 1990s, arguing that déjà vu provided insight into the functioning of both the normal and abnormal brain.

It's long been known that prolonged or frequent episodes of déjà vu are associated with various psychiatric or neurological disorders. Some

now consider déjà vu, in conjunction with other symptoms, to be diagnostic of a type of epilepsy. Researchers have found that electrical stimulation of the brains of epileptic patients in some cases can trigger the déjà vu phenomenon.

Nothing you need to worry about. On the contrary, it seems pretty clear that what some consider a glimpse of the supernatural is more than likely just a cognitive burp.

Can eating foods with poppy seeds (i.e., bagels, muffins, etc.) really cause someone to fail a routine corporate drug test? I've heard the answer is yes, but I am a skeptic. Aren't drug tests specialized? Are they really testing for opium, which I understand to be the only drug made from the poppy? And even if the test did search for opium, wouldn't the number of poppy seeds needed to make even a minute amount of opium be far greater than that in the foods we eat poppy seeds in? Help!—Peter Schilling, Minneapolis

Let's not beat around the bush. The answer to your question is yes—eating a couple of poppy seed rolls, bagels, etc., can cause you to fail a routine drug test. This news will produce one of two reactions, depending on whether you're a law-abiding citizen or a drug fiend:

1. Panic (if you are a law-abiding citizen): "I could lose my job by eating breakfast!"
2. Elation (if you are a drug fiend): "I could keep my job by claiming I ate breakfast!"

So the real corporate drug test is to tell your employees about poppy seeds and watch their reactions. The happy ones get the ax.

At this point you figure I'm going to say: Whoa, relax! A drug-testing lab is savvy enough to be able to distinguish between muffin eaters and opium addicts.

Uh-uh. While many drug testers and researchers claim they can separate "false positives" from the real thing, other researchers dispute this. Sure, some guy with pinhole pupils and a tendency to walk into walls is going to have a hard time claiming he got that way due to excessive bagel consumption. The fact remains that if you got fired due to a borderline positive and had no follow-up tests or corroborating signs of drug use, a good lawyer would be able to cram that drug test—and your pink slip—down your bosses' throats. Currently, 87 percent of positives are reversed on follow-up.

This murky situation may not last long, though. Largely because of the poppy seed problem, the federal test threshold for morphine and codeine was scheduled to be raised in late 1998 from 300 nanograms per milliliter to 2,000. The feds figure they might miss a few drug abusers but they'll eliminate most of the false positives. No doubt many corporate drug testers will follow suit.

Now let's take some questions from the floor.

Q: *You're telling me the poppy seeds in baked goods come from the same type of poppy used to make opium?*

A: Maybe not all, but a lot of them do. Of the 90 or so species of poppy, one, *Papaver somniferum,* is commonly used for two things: drugs and food. In the United States, possession of opium poppies with intent to grow more is a crime. But possession of opium poppy seed is perfectly legal—in fact, you can (or could) buy opium poppy seeds from gardening catalogs. (But God help you if you try to grow anything with them—see Michael Pollan's scary article on this subject in the April 1997 *Harper's*). So-called bread-seed poppies (*P. paeoniflorum*) are also legal, though botanically they're the same as *P. somniferum*.

Q: You mean I could get high eating poppy seed rolls?

A: No, goofball, I said they might make you flunk a drug test. The amount of morphine and codeine in poppy seeds varies enormously. One study found that Dutch, Czech, and Turkish poppy seed contained minimal opiates, Australian seed was up there, and Spanish seed sounded like it should be sold by creepy-looking guys on street corners. But, while test volunteers who ate poppy seed products sometimes flunked urine tests, nobody really got what you could call stoned. (Possible exception: one volunteer who ate 23 grams of seeds was accused of "giggling and acting silly.") You're limited by the fact that the poppy seeds are usually contained in food—you get full long before you get high.

Still, if you're desperate enough there are ways to get a buzz from poppies. In parts of England prior to World War II, tea made from boiled poppy heads was recommended as a way to cure what ails you, or at least not get overly concerned about it. Poppy tea has come back into favor among U.K. drug users in recent years, and some people have reportedly become addicted to the stuff. One guy boiled 14 poppy heads daily, which he obtained from florists. Another addict was a baker who each day drank two liters of tea made from four kilograms of poppy seed. His secret was discovered when he went into convulsions. Serves him right. Even the Bible warns about bad seed.

One day, in response to a case of the munchies, I started scarfing forkfuls of cold macaroni and cheese from a dish in the fridge. I soon gave myself a case of hiccups, which I proceeded to douse with a drink of milk. This got me to thinking: What are hiccups? Do they have a role in how our bodies function? Why does rich food (even macaroni and cheese) cause hiccups? Why does drinking cure hiccups? And, paradoxically, why does drinking (of alcohol) also cause hiccups?
—Daniel J. Drazen, via the Internet

You're lucky to be writing me now, Dan. For years very little was known about hiccups and even less was written about them. Today that's changed. We still don't know jack, but scientists have told us so at great length.

Here's what we know. When you hiccup, your diaphragm and nearby muscles convulse, causing you to briefly gulp air. Within 35

milliseconds the glottis (the opening at the top of the air passage) slams shut, producing the characteristic "hic."

If you're able to stifle the hiccup right away, great. But if you hiccup more than seven times you'd better settle in for the long haul. Once in hiccup mode you typically will hiccup 63 times or more. Maybe a lot more. The hiccup record, last time I checked, was 57 years.

Hiccups are commonly caused by distension of the stomach, which you get if you eat too much, drink carbonated beverages, or swallow too much air. This suggests that a hiccup as a sequela to boozing may be more the result of fizzy mixers than alcohol itself. Or else you just slurp.

Lots of other things can cause hiccups too, some of them pretty scary. Skimming through a long list, I see skull fracture, epilepsy, diabetes mellitus, myocardial infarction, tuberculosis, meningitis, bowel obstruction, and ulcerative colitis.

But it's not always, or even usually, so bad. A 27-year-old man complained that he'd been hiccuping for four days. The doctor looked into the guy's ear and saw a hair tickling the eardrum. The hair having been washed out, the hiccups stopped.

Why do we hiccup? I don't know, and as far as I can tell, neither does anyone else. Unlike gagging, sneezing, etc., hiccups serve no known useful function. Some speculate that hiccups "may represent a vestigial remnant of a primitive reflex whose functional or behavioral significance is now lost," as one researcher put it.

Or maybe they're just, you know, hiccups—an accidental reflex triggered by a stimulus to (usually) the vagus or phrenic nerves. This travels up the line to a nerve-control center that for some reason sends out a "commence hiccup" impulse via the phrenic nerve.

The vagus and phrenic nerves go all over, which explains why so many things cause hiccups. For example, a 16-year-old girl began hiccupping after receiving a blow to the jaw. A brain scan found that a blood vessel was pressing against the vagus nerve in her neck. Surgeons inserted a Teflon spacer between the nerve and the blood vessel, and the hiccupping stopped. When the spacer later fell out, the hiccupping resumed.

That brings us to the question of hiccup cures, of which a great many have been proposed. Unfortunately, to paraphrase the distinguished physician Charles Mayo, the number of remedies is in inverse proportion to the likelihood that any one of them will actually work.

Home remedies are mostly based on the idea that you have to disrupt the hiccup cycle. These include holding your breath, induced sneezing, breathing into a bag, drinking water while covering your ears, pulling your tongue, pressing on the eyeballs, sudden fright, or—this is interesting—eating dry granulated sugar. Merely drinking water, if done soon enough, may work by washing down a glob of food in your throat that's pressing against a nerve.

If the preceding are unavailing, a doctor may try a drug such as chlorpromazine, tickling the pharynx with a catheter stuck through the nose, hypnosis, or acupuncture. Still no go? Time for stern measures. In 1833 it was recommended that you blister or burn the skin above the phrenic nerve on the neck and back. This has now been supplanted by a marginally more civilized procedure in which the nerve is sliced or crushed.

Sometimes unorthodox procedures are efficacious. Doctors tried everything they could think of on a 60-year-old man who'd been hiccuping for two days. No luck, so "digital rectal massage was performed, resulting in abrupt cessation of the hiccups." I'll bet.

If that's not your cup of tea, the case of a 32-year-old man with persistent hiccups offers hope. His hiccups stopped when he had sex. But it was only temporary, and additional therapy was soon required. The obvious question to have put to this guy: you sure you want this cured?

From The Straight Dope Message Board

(Collected by OpalCat, keeper of the Straight Dope "Page o' Flames")

Is it really true that after a guy goes swimming his penis shrinks, or does it expand? My boyfriend and I were wondering if you can have sex underwater if your penis is not the normal size.

Never did have a problem with that, as such. My main problems were:

1. Drowning.
2. Getting fish to hold still.

From The Straight Dope Science Advisory Board

How does a person go about getting the title of "esquire"?—apongras

Become either a lawyer or the son of a British nobleman. *Black's Law Dictionary* says: "In Eng. law, a title of dignity above gentleman and below knight. Also a title of office given to sheriffs, serjeants, and barristers at law, justices of the peace, and others. In the U.S., title commonly after the name of an attorney; e.g., John J. Jones, Esquire."

Now, you might ask: What allows one to use this title? Is there a ceremony? Is it conferred by a university? Is it just some affectation that snobbish folk use? Can I be Joe Blow, Esq., just because I like the ring to it? Or do I need to get authorization, and if so from what and where?

The answer is that any snob in the world (or at least in the United States) can use the title. In England there's this whole business about hereditary nobility and getting knighted and all that, so it might be a little risky to start calling yourself "esquire" there. (Although what's going to happen? The Snob Cops arrest you?) But we're not in England, we're in America! The land of the free, the home of the brave! You can call yourself anything you want ... although you do take the risk that you will be thought a snooty jerk. Since this has never bothered lawyers, they have gotten into the habit of calling each other "esquire." This is a little like elected officials addressing each other as "honorable," another classic instance of whistling past the graveyard. But I digress.

Among lawyers, it's thought pretentious if you sign yourself "Esq." in written communications, but you're supposed to dignify other lawyers with the appellation. So a lawyer's letters go out "Yours very truly, Snidely Whiplash" but the envelope comes back addressed to "Snidely Whiplash, Esq." Also, you never put "Ms." or "Mr." in front of the name when you use "Esq." Still, this is strictly custom, and even if you never saw the inside of a law school there's nothing to prevent you from calling yourself esquire . . . except the fact that you might be thought a lawyer.

—SDSTAFF Dianne (Esq.)
Straight Dope Science Advisory Board

Chapter 7

Issues

A while ago I saw a tagline on alt.fan.cecil-adams from someone who was darn proud to be a member of the National Rifle Association. I asked if the Second Amendment to the U.S. Constitution still holds water today since the intent was to provide guns and protection against the other side of the puddle. This sparked a huge debate on the Net about the right to bear arms with, as usual, both sides claiming they are right. I figured it's time to take it to the top and ask you to settle it all for us. Is it time to reevaluate the Second Amendment, if only so that those who argue can at least now argue an up-to-date amendment?—Colin Joyce, Scranton, Pennsylvania

Maybe so. But you have to realize that the NRA crowd doesn't want an "up-to-date" amendment. On the contrary, they'd happily settle for a proper interpretation (in their view) of the Second Amendment

we've got. So let's put the question this way. What did the framers of the Bill of Rights intend the Second Amendment to mean, and does their intention have any continuing legal relevance in view of the (supposedly) dramatically altered social landscape upon which we gaze today? The answer to the second question is easy: yes, else why have a constitution? But the answer to the first is knottier.

Historically there have been two interpretations of the Second Amendment: the states-rights argument and the individual-rights argument. The states-rights view is that the Second Amendment merely guarantees the states the right to organize militias and citizens the right to join. (Militia here means any armed force raised for the common defense, not just the National Guard.) The individual-rights view is that the Second Amendment means what it says: citizens have the right to keep and bear arms. The states-rights view currently prevails in federal case law, but the individual-rights view is probably closer to the framers' intent. A reasonable restatement of the amendment might go something like this: "Since we as a nation have found it necessary to organize citizen militias to defend against tyranny and may be compelled to do so again, and since these militias are necessarily composed of volunteers supplying their own weapons, the right of individuals to keep and bear arms shall not be infringed."

OK, some gun-control advocates will concede, but that merely means infringed by the federal government. As an article in *Mother Jones* put it, "The legal precedents are clear: Almost any state or local gun-control action is fine; the Second Amendment does not apply. On the federal level, only laws interfering with state militias are prohibited."

This is a crock. The legal precedents are far from clear. They are also pathetically sparse, suggesting a reluctance on the part of the courts and the legal community generally to deal with the issue. (An enlightening article in the *Yale Law Journal* a few years ago was titled "The Embarrassing Second Amendment.") In almost every other aspect of law the Bill of Rights has been broadly construed to restrain the states as well as the federal government. Few today would argue that states can abrogate the right to free speech guaranteed by the First Amendment. Yet many are prepared to let them gut the Second, on the grounds that the framers did not foresee urban violence on the scale we face now. Maybe they didn't, but so what? Civil-liberties advocates don't accept urban violence as an excuse to curtail other constitutional rights, such as the protection against unlawful search and seizure.

Accepting the Second Amendment at face value doesn't mean you can't regulate gun ownership. No one can argue plausibly that the authors of the Bill of Rights meant to make the authorities powerless to disarm criminals. The framers likely would have objected to a blanket proscription of handguns, which they would have seen as legitimate weapons of self-defense, and arguably they would have opposed a ban on assault rifles, the AK-47 being to today's oppressed what the long rifle was to those of 1776. But local gun registration presents no obvious constitutional problems. Criminals don't register guns, of course; that's the point. Arrest a carful of mopes with guns and no permits and you have a good ipso facto case for throwing the book at them. How much better to approach gun control on a reasonable basis rather than make a religious war out of it.

Taking Another Shot

Why is it that Cecil Adams, as well as the NRA, have different copies of the United States Constitution from my own? The Second Amendment in my own library clearly starts out with the words "A well-regulated militia . . ." What is well-regulated about a private citizen with a stash of guns in his basement? The opening words of this amendment seem to clearly indicate that the possession of guns was not meant to be beyond control.—Ed Cohen, Chicago

Let's put it this way: it was not meant to be beyond regulation. The question is whether the power to regulate encompasses the power to ban. So far as guns are concerned, the courts have held that it does. You may say outlawing guns altogether was not what you had in mind. But it's certainly what some people have in mind, at least with respect to broad categories of firearms such as handguns, and a few would happily prohibit guns, period. Federal case law currently offers virtually no protection against such draconian measures.

Put yourself in a gun owner's shoes. While the first half of the Second Amendment is no miracle of clarity, the second half is about as plain as it can be. "The right of the people to keep and bear arms shall

not be infringed." But gun-control advocates deny that this sentence means what it seems perfectly evident it says, and the courts have backed them up. Gun owners' recognition that one of their most cherished rights has been interpreted out of existence accounts for the apocalyptic tone in which their arguments are often framed.

But let's get back to "well-regulated." A number of serious scholars have disputed the idea that this phrase necessarily means "subject to a lot of regulations." The historian Robert Shalhope, for example, makes a good case that for the framers it meant "duly constituted"—that is, subject to civilian authority. The framers, in other words, did not propose to have armed gangs of self-appointed militiamen roaming the streets. Some take Shalhope's argument a step further and say that "well-regulated" applies only to the militia and does not constrain an individual's right to keep and bear arms in any way.

A more reasonable interpretation, however, is that if the government can regulate the militia it can regulate the individuals in it, provided it does so in a way that does not make a shambles of their basic Second Amendment rights. For that reason I think even if the amendment had been interpreted more in line with the framers' intent, the regulatory landscape would not necessarily look a lot different from the way it does now. But it's silly to think the framers would guarantee a right in one half of the Second Amendment only to allow the government to unguarantee it in the other half.

However odd it strikes us today, the framers regarded private gun ownership as one of the pillars of their liberty. They had recently defeated one of the most powerful nations in the world with an army that in the early going had consisted of amateur soldiers using their own weapons. They considered these citizen militias vastly preferable to standing armies, which in their experience had been instruments of oppression. They also had no professional police force upon which to depend for defense of their lives and property. It seemed natural to them that ordinary folk should have the right to own guns.

That was then, you may say, and this is now. In the 1990s it may well be foolish, as a matter of public policy, to allow law-abiding private citizens to own guns (although I'm not persuaded this is so). But it seems pretty clear that's what the founders intended, and it eats at the heart of the constitutional process to simply wave that right away. No one doubts today that slavery is bad, but the constitution as written permitted it, and a duly ratified amendment was required to put the matter right. Likewise we should concede that the Second Amendment means what it seems to mean and that if we want to control guns to the point of prohibition, amending the amendment is the honest thing to do.

Do Americans really have to pay income tax? I have been told the 16th Amendment, which authorized the income tax, is invalid because Ohio was not legally a state at the time of ratification. So far I haven't had the nerve to actually try this argument out on the IRS, but with Christmas coming I could use the extra cash. What do you think, Cecil, is it worth a shot?—Tex R. Zister, Chicago

This is my absolute favorite anti-income-tax argument. Most claims that Americans aren't required to pay income tax rely on legal

interpretations so tortured only a tax resister could possibly believe them. But the Ohio thing has just enough plausibility to give even sane people pause.

It all started when Ohio was preparing to celebrate the 150th anniversary of its admission to the Union in 1953. Researchers looking for the original statehood documents discovered there'd been a little oversight. While Congress had approved Ohio's boundaries and constitution, it had never passed a resolution formally admitting the future land of the Buckeyes. Technically, therefore, Ohio was not a state.

Predictably, when this came to light it was the subject of much merriment. One senator joshingly suggested that his colleagues from Ohio were drawing federal paychecks under false pretenses.

But Ohio congressman George Bender thought it was no laughing matter. He introduced a bill in Congress to admit Ohio to the Union retroactive to March 1, 1803. At a special session at the old state capitol in Chillicothe the Ohio state legislature approved a new petition for statehood that was delivered to Washington on horseback. Congress subsequently passed a joint resolution, and President Eisenhower, after a few more jokes, signed it on August 7, 1953.

But then the tax resisters got to work. They argued that since Ohio wasn't officially a state until 1953, its ratification of the Sixteenth Amendment in 1911 was invalid, and thus Congress had no authority to enact an income tax.

Baloney, argued rational folk. A sufficient number of states voted for ratification even if you don't count Ohio.

OK, said the resisters, but the proposed amendment had been introduced to Congress by the administration of William H. Taft. Taft had been born in Cincinnati, Ohio, in 1857. The Constitution requires that presidents be natural-born citizens of the United States. Since Ohio was not a state in 1857, Taft was not a natural-born citizen, could not legally be president, and could not legally introduce the Sixteenth Amendment. (Presumably one would also have problems with anything done by presidents Grant, Hayes, Garfield, B. Harrison, McKinley, and Harding, who were also born in Ohio.)

Get off it, the rationalists replied. The 1953 resolution retroactively admitted Ohio as of 1803, thereby rendering all subsequent events copacetic.

Uh-uh, said the resisters. The Constitution says the Congress shall make no ex post facto law. That means no retroactive admissions to statehood.

Uh, we'll get back to you on that, said the rationalists.

A call to the IRS elicited the following official statement: "The courts have . . . rejected claims that the Sixteenth Amendment . . . was not properly ratified. . . . In *Porth* v. *Brodrick*, 214 F2d 925 (10th Circuit 1954), the court dismissed an attack on the Sixteenth Amendment as being "clearly unsubstantial and without merit," as well as "far fetched and frivolous."

Just one problem. The Porth decision didn't specifically address the Ohio argument. It just sort of spluttered that attacks on the Sixteenth Amendment were stupid.

OK, they're stupid. But great matters have turned on seemingly sillier points of law. It's not like the Ohio argument couldn't have been defeated on the merits. One suspects that from a legal standpoint "ex post facto" doesn't mean exactly the same thing as "retroactive." And of course the weight of 150 years of history, during which time everyone *thought* Ohio had been properly admitted, ought to count for something.

I'm not defending the crackpots. But if you're a parent you recognize that "because I said so" isn't much of an argument. Guess it's different if you're a judge.

Better Late Than Never

You recently dealt with the argument that the 16th Amendment (income tax) was never properly ratified because Ohio was not a state of the union. You mentioned that the IRS referred you to the Porth case and that it "didn't specifically address the Ohio argument." Well, there have been court decisions that specifically addressed the Ohio argument. I enclose a copy of Knoblauch v. Commissioner of Internal Revenue *(Fifth Circuit 1984), 749 F2d 200 [etc.].—Bernard Sussman, Bethesda, Maryland*

I got a lot of mail about this, much of it actually pretty intelligent, which I hope is a trend. However, the case law isn't much help. Bernard cites two decisions: *Knoblauch* and *Bowman* v. *Government*

of the United States. *Knoblauch* does briefly address the Ohio argument, but merely cites earlier cases in which said argument was rejected by the courts. Turning to the earlier cases, one finds the following declarations:

1. In previous cases having nothing to do with the Ohio argument we upheld the constitutionality of the Sixteenth Amendment, so too bad for you, Bobo.
2. Since 1803 everybody had assumed that Ohio was a state, and we don't feel like upsetting the apple cart now.

Bowman deals with the issue in greater depth, but its finding boils down to: We ain't messin' with this one, Jack. Take it up with Congress.

Cecil understands that the courts don't want to open the door to substantive review of the Ohio argument, lest they be inundated by clowns seeking to have the government dissolved due to clerical error. Still, one can't help thinking the preceding arguments, while they may be legally solid, aren't exactly satisfying.

The Teeming Millions (well, dozens) to the rescue. As Cecil suspected, and as he certainly would've demonstrated had he the space and that law clerk he's been asking for, the Ohio argument can be refuted point by point, to wit:

1. The ban on ex post facto laws refers only to criminal matters. Case law, 1798. Ohio's retroactive admission to the union was OK.
2. Persons born in U.S. territories—not just in states—are U.S. citizens. (For example, Puerto Rico.) So Taft was a natural-born citizen and could legally serve as president.
3. Even if he wasn't, so what? Presidents don't introduce constitutional amendments; members of Congress do.
4. Ohio was a state even without the 1953 resolution. The statehood admission process was somewhat casual in 1803; it required no formal resolution of admission.

Whew, you say. The republic saved again. Not that this'll stop the tax resisters. While the Ohio argument has some entertainment value, most tax-resister arguments are just stupid—e.g., the claim that the IRS is unlawful because it's an "establishment of religion." Taft not a citizen of the United States? These people aren't citizens of earth.

What's the scoop on hemp? Is it true that in earlier days of our country over 90 percent of paper was made of hemp? Is it true hemp is one of the strongest fibers known to man? Why is it illegal to grow it, since it is only about 1 percent THC? In fact, it is only a relative of the plant that is cultivated for smoking, is it not? It just seems that cultivation of hemp would be such an easy solution to the deforestation problems we are having.—Tyler Hartley, Lincoln, Nebraska

Our deforestation problems! Yes, absolutely, hemp is a perfect solution. I myself can recall thinking as a youth (puff) that we've got terrible deforestation problems these days (puff). What can we do about them? (Puff. Long pause.) What was I just talking about?

One of the nuttier developments of recent times is the sudden interest in nonpharmacologic hemp cultivation among people who've never grown so much as a radish. It's true that prior to criminalization hemp was grown commercially for paper, cloth, rope and twine, and other products. It grows pretty much anywhere, doesn't require much tending, and produces plenty of strong fiber.

During World War II the government relaxed the antihemp laws

and encouraged midwestern farmers to grow the stuff for the war effort. It's said that a parachute rigging made of hemp saved the life of George Bush when the young bomber pilot bailed out of his burning plane.

What with the renewed interest in natural fibers, there's a good case to be made that hemp farming should be promoted rather than suppressed. What the hell—we might as well legalize the stuff altogether, since we know perfectly well that cannabis smoking doesn't cause insanity or any of the other horrors that federal narcotics authorities feared when they clamped down in the late 1930s.

But let's not get goofy about this. Hemp cultivation isn't going to save the planet, as some claim. It won't halt deforestation, which is driven mainly by the demand for lumber and agricultural land.

Hemp wasn't a mighty industry in the United States prior to passage of the Marijuana Tax Act of 1937. Only about 1,300 acres of hemp—about two square miles—were under cultivation. It was cheaper to import the stuff than grow it.

Even so, total U.S. consumption was only about 2,000 tons, and most of that was used for rope and such. Textile manufacturers had long since abandoned hemp for cotton, which was easier to process. An improved hemp-processing technology had been invented, and the industry might have rebounded had it not been for the antihemp crusade. But nobody knows for certain.

The suppression of hemp wasn't, as some have alleged, the result of an unholy conspiracy between federal narcotics commissioner Harry Anslinger, the Du Pont corporation, and William Randolph Hearst. No question, Anslinger was a zealot who thought marijuana was a menace to society, and Hearst's newspapers had done their best to whip up antihemp hysteria. But so had everybody else in the press. Lurid antimarijuana stories appeared in the *New Yorker*, for God's sake.

The hemp industry didn't pose a significant threat to Du Pont and its new synthetic product, nylon. The most widely publicized early use of nylon was for women's stockings. Hemp wasn't used for this purpose.

Getting back to the present, let's not pretend that hemp and marijuana are two different things. They come from the same plant, *Cannabis sativa*. The "industrial hemp" variety, which is useless for recreational purposes, is tall and spindly, whereas the stuff prized for high-potency smoke is short and bushy. While it's reasonably easy to tell the two apart when you're up close, they can't be readily distinguished during aerial surveillance. Federal drug officials are probably right when they say legalization of hemp cultivation would greatly complicate enforcement.

Given the unlikelihood of total decriminalization of cannabis, Cecil can appreciate that proponents of the weed might want to sneak partial decriminalization in through the back door. On the one hand I think, Hey, whatever works. But on the other hand I think, This is just the kind of hypocrisy we '60s types used to try so hard to avoid.

Put This In Your Pipe And Smoke It

I enjoy your usually well-researched columns but am sorely disappointed at your lack of depth on hemp cultivation. You said it "won't halt deforestation, which is driven mainly by the demand for lumber." Uh, if hemp becomes a source for cellulose, won't the demand for lumber ease? I heard of a bumper sticker in a rural area last Sunday: "If

you don't like logging, wipe your ass with plastic." Hemp makes paper. Those hurting loggers could sorely use a new commodity to make a living from.

You dismissed the Hearst conspiracy claim with nothing but your assertion that "everybody else" did it. Just why and how was hemp suppressed? Why did the press do their best to whip up antihemp hysteria? I had my suspicions about the conspiracy theory and had hoped you would be the one to clarify it. A simple denial does not cut it.

"Hemp wasn't used for [nylon stockings.]" No it wasn't, but it certainly could be. Why isn't it just as good as the petroleum and wood pulp the companies use now? Maybe it is control of the oil wells and tree plantations? Hmm? If it was good enough during WWII, why is it goofy now?

If my current profession goes belly-up, there ain't much call for my *specialty. I might* need *a subsistence crop. You're not helping my survival. There is a growing number of people who think the government should* not *be enforcing their brand of oppression and indeed the laws should be scrapped as a monstrous waste and enemy of liberty. Denying Americans the potential of this plant (whether it will save the planet or not) while the rest of the world passes us by and continues to enjoy its bounty is folly. In Russia they grow huge fields of . . . [impassioned plea truncated, no room.]—William Hathaway, via the Internet*

William. Kick back. Have a toke of this. Feel better? Look, I'm the first to concede that the gentle weed is harmless and ought to be legalized. But the day I start believing this dope-will-save-the-planet stuff is the day I switch to Kool-Aid. To address your claims and some of the dozens of others that flooded my mailbox:

- *Hemp is ideal for paper, cloth, and a thousand other products.* Don't be ridiculous. Even hemp advocates concede the stuff has a lot of drawbacks. It makes a fairly coarse cloth (OK for jeans, though) and, given current technology, doesn't lend itself to high-volume, low-cost paper production. (Granted, research in this area is continuing.) Many proposed uses are speculative or far-fetched. Check out back issues of *HempWorld* magazine, available on-line at hempworld.com. Amid the rah-rah stuff you'll find some clear-eyed assessments of hemp's pros and cons.

    By the way, William, "lumber" is usually understood to mean "construction lumber." There's been talk of using hemp in particleboard and such. But take it from someone who's been there, there's still no substitute for a wood two-by-four.

- *Cecil has been duped by the antimarijuana conspirators.* If somebody tells me he was abducted by aliens, it's not my job to prove he *wasn't*. It's his job to prove he *was*. I've yet to see any credible evidence for the alleged Anslinger/Hearst/Mellon/Du Pont antidope cabal. Most historians of U.S. drug laws say the outlawing of cannabis was the work of narcotics commissioner Harry Anslinger, a formidable figure who persuaded Congress that this little-known weed was undermining the republic.

What exactly motivated Anslinger is a matter of debate, but it seems silly to blame a fat-cat conspiracy. As I said earlier, hemp was a minor crop in the 1930s and posed no competitive threat.

• *The legalize-hemp-cultivation movement is not simply a backdoor attempt to legalize marijuana.* I'm sure many of the agribusiness types in the hemp coalition have never smoked a joint. But for a much larger crowd, your eco-green-save-the-whales types, hemp has become a kind of alternative vegetable. (Literally—I've even seen hemp recipes.) No doubt many of these people have persuaded themselves that hemp is mankind's last hope, but don't tell me it hasn't occurred to a lot of them that legal hemp might be a step toward legal marijuana. One hemp shoemaker has a product out called H.I.G.H. Tops. Another, U.S. Hemp, stamps a marijuana leaf on its shoes, and owner Cathy Troutt was quoted in *HempWorld* as saying, "we aren't going to lie about our feelings on marijuana." Good for you, Cathy. Wish everybody else were as upfront.

Do individuals have any rights to the airspace above the land they own? Can I, for example, declare the space above my house a no-flight zone (I know that it would be virtually impossible to enforce this), or can this only be done on a national level?—Dawood Salam, Toronto, Ontario

I understand your feelings. You paid good money for that house. Why shouldn't you be allowed to shoot down bothersome aircraft flying overhead? Well, under the enlightened policy prevailing in the Middle Ages, you would have. For centuries the common-law doctrine was *Cujus est solum, ejus est usque ad coelum et ad inferos*—literally, "To whomsoever the soil belongs, he owns also to the sky and to the depths." In other words, you had complete control over everything above and below your property. You want to declare a no-flight zone over your manse? Go right ahead. True, during the Middle Ages there were pretty much no flights, period. But it's the principle that counts.

This happy state of affairs began to crumble as soon as practical aircraft appeared on the scene. Lobbyists for the infant air-transport industry argued that air travel would be impossible if air carriers had to get permission from the owner of every private property their planes

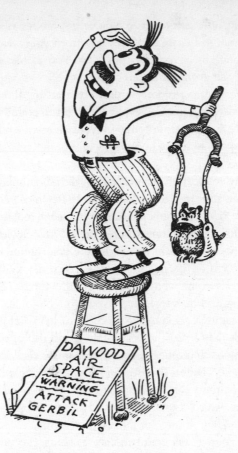

flew over. Possibly also there were whispered promises of frequent-flyer miles in exchange for friendly votes. All I know is that the politicians immediately caved. In 1926 the U.S. Congress passed the Air Commerce Act, which declared that the "navigable air space" of the United States was a public highway, open to all citizens. Navigable airspace was defined as the sky above "the minimum safe altitudes of flight" as determined by federal regulators—typically 500 to 1,000 feet above the ground. You see the practical effect of this. One minute you're lord of all you survey; the next you're living under the freaking interstate.

Usque ad coelum as a principle of private ownership was formally given the boot by the U.S. Supreme Court in *U.S. v. Causby* (1946).

The court laid down a new rule: you've got air rights only insofar as they're essential to the use and enjoyment of your land. Military aircraft using a nearby airport during World War II had flown over the Causby family chicken farm at an altitude of 83 feet, scaring the chickens and rendering the property unfit for the raising thereof. The court generously ruled that the Causbys had a right to compensation. Big of them, wasn't it? Bah. Under the previous system Old Man Causby could have taken out a few bombers with his shotgun, and that would have been that.

If it's of any comfort, *usque ad coelum* didn't completely disappear; it was merely transferred to nations. The 1944 Chicago Convention on International Civil Aviation declared that each country had sovereignty over the airspace above its territory. Thus, Soviet leaders were within their rights when they ordered the destruction of commercial flight KAL 007 after it strayed over their territory in 1983. Sure, the loss of hundreds of innocent people was unfortunate. But you can be sure the next guys who flew near Russia brought a map.

Even on a national scale *usque ad coelum* isn't what it used to be. A 1967 treaty declared that the "exploration and use of outer space, including the moon and other celestial bodies . . . shall be the province of all mankind." Though the frontier of outer space was not defined, some experts argue that it begins about 90 kilometers above the earth's surface. This is the lowest level at which orbital flight is practical, and it's also out of range of most nations' guns.

But some courageous countries are pushing the envelope in this arena. One valuable portion of outer space is the so-called geostationary orbit, located approximately 22,300 miles above the earth's equator. Satellites in this orbit appear stationary relative to the ground, which is useful for communications, weather surveillance, and other purposes. Recognizing a revenue opportunity when they saw one, eight equatorial countries proclaimed in the Bogotá Declaration of 1976 that they owned the portion of the geostationary orbit above their territories. They demanded that any nation wishing to place satellites in said orbit first obtain permission from the country beneath. Since the equatorial nations' ability to enforce this claim at the time was approximately zilch, the United States and other developed countries said: In your dreams. But you wait. If Ecuador ever perfects that 23,000-mile-range surface-to-space missile, I'll bet negotiations get reopened real quick.

Per Aspera Ad Astra

Your column on usque ad coelum *would have cogently answered Dawood Salam's question about establishing a no-flight zone over his house except for one thing: Didn't you notice the letter came from* Toronto, Canada? *Since when does an act of Congress apply to Canada? Since when does a decision of the United States Supreme Court affect Canadian law? Your answer may be relevant to U.S. readers, but it is irrelevant to Mr. Salam's case. Please finish your answer and tell us what the relevant Canadian statutes say.—Jay Shorten, via the Internet; similarly from many others*

Complaints, complaints, that's all I hear. I do a first-class column, complete with charming story about intrusive Big Government ruining this guy's chicken farm by flying planes too low overhead, and all I get is nitpickers saying I wrote about the wrong country. See if I try to eradicate any more of *your* ignorance. For the record, Canadian case law says pretty much the same thing as U.S. law about an owner's rights to the airspace above his land. A commonly cited case in this regard is *Bernstein of Leigh* v. *Skyview & General* (1978). Skyview was in the business of taking aerial photos of real estate and offering them for sale to the owners. When they did this with the property of one Baron Bernstein, he sued Skyview (which obviously had flown over his property) for trespass, citing the *usque ad coelum* maxim; i.e., he owned everything above his land to the very heavens. The court wrote, "In a pig's eye, you bleeding sack of . . ."—sorry, wishful thinking. What the court actually wrote was that an owner has air rights only insofar as they're necessary to the use and enjoyment of his land. Thus, one can't prevent planes from flying overhead—pretty much the same deal as in the United States. Happy?

We ran across the enclosed item in Marilyn Vos Savant's column in Parade *magazine and were astounded by her reply. Our first thought*

was that we should ask Cecil the same question. However, we're equally interested in your response to her answer.—Claire and Harold, San Rafael, California

Here's the question from Marilyn's column:

"Q: Is it true that the rich pay very little tax?

"A: No, and this is the myth, more than any other, that has created the unwarranted and destructive dissension among the so-called economic classes in this country. The wealthy pay a truly stunning amount of tax, and there are virtually no exceptions. Anyone who thinks otherwise has been misguided."

Regarding Marilyn's answer, I'll just say that when you make sweeping claims like this you might want to back them up with a little detail. She's not wrong, though. As a general proposition, the wealthiest Americans do pay the bulk of the individual income taxes collected in the United States. That's a point worth making, since the belief that the rich pay zip while the little guy gets slugged is the impetus behind the "flat tax" proposal, the stupidest idea to come down the pike since pet rocks.

Here are the numbers for 1992 from the *Statistical Abstract of the United States*:

- The top 7 percent of those filing returns, those reporting adjusted gross income of $75,000 or more, paid 51 percent of total U.S. income taxes.

    People making $75,001, a group that includes many households in which both spouses work, may object that they don't feel particularly rich. They should talk to a single mom who's mopping floors. But let's work our way up the income scale:

- The top 3 percent of filers, those making $100,000-plus, paid 40 percent of the taxes.
- The top four-fifths of 1 percent of filers, who make $200,000 or more, paid 26 percent of the taxes.
- The top one-twentieth of 1 percent of filers, those making $1 million or more—and Tom Wolfe's little demonstration in *Bonfire of the Vanities* notwithstanding, nobody's going to tell me *those* guys aren't rich—paid 10 percent of the taxes. That's a mere 67,000 households, who on average paid income tax of $707,000 apiece.

OK, but what about Marilyn's second point—namely, that the rich pay big with "virtually no exceptions"? In their entertaining 1994 book *America: Who Really Pays the Taxes?*, investigative reporters Donald Barlett and James Steele note that the number of filers reporting incomes of $200,000-plus who paid *no* tax, presumably through outrageous but legal tax dodges, has risen steadily, from 155 in 1966 to 1,081 in 1989, despite numerous attempts to plug the loopholes. That sounds pretty bad, but let's put it in perspective: the number of people making $200,000-plus shot up dramatically during the same time, from 13,000 in 1966 to 787,000 in 1989. The proportion of rich tax dodgers has dwindled from 1 percent of the $200,000-plus class to one-tenth of 1 percent in recent years.

The purpose of this exercise is not to make you feel sorry for the poor rich people. Quite the contrary. Barlett and Steele make the point that most efforts at tax "reform" are really attempts to reduce the tax burden on the wealthy. The most blatant recent example of this was the tax act of 1986. Between 1986 and 1987 the effective tax rate on millionaires fell from 40 percent to 29 percent, and as a result they paid $3.6 billion less in tax. Meanwhile, people making from $50,000 to $75,000, a reasonably prosperous but hardly rich crowd, paid $7.6 billion *more*. Some reform.

The flat-tax scam is more of the same. Nobody's sure what the actual flat-tax rate would be, but let's suppose it was 20 percent. Based on the 1992 returns, if this inane proposal were implemented, *taxes on*

everybody making $200,000-plus would go down and those on every-body else would go up. Malcolm Forbes Jr., one of the richest men in America, was the leading backer of the flat tax during the 1996 presidential campaign. Now do you see why?

Flat Liners For The Flat Tax

Re your column on taxes, I was curious about some of your conclusions. You say "people making $50,000 to $75,000 . . . paid $7.6 billion more [after the 1986 tax reform]." What was the average increase per person? Or was there an increase in the number of people in this bracket, which would have increased the total collected? How much was the tax increase on these people as a percentage of income? You don't say.

In your conclusion you start with a supposition of a flat 20 percent rate (higher than any I've heard proposed) without any mention of the automatic exemption of the first $20,000 to $30,000, which would result in the poor paying no tax at all. I assume this was a lapse and not an act of deliberate mendacity.

Yes, Forbes wants his taxes to go down. I want mine to go down too. Under every flat-tax proposal I've heard (except yours), mine would go down dramatically. Doesn't mean I'm going to vote for Forbes, but right now I find him more honest than you.

Can you explain why we should have a graduated tax system in the first place? Is it to make sure that everybody ends up with the same amount, regardless of effort? Isn't that called socialism?

Following this logic, shouldn't rich people also pay more for every-thing else? Why not a sliding scale for bus fare, Big Macs, movie tick-ets, etc.? After all, the rich can afford more.

Why do we need an income tax in the first place? Why don't you consider the merits of the "Liberty Amendment," which would abolish the IRS?—Jim MacQuarrie, via the Internet

Way to go, Jim, defend the rights of the rich! Shows you what a great country we've got here. Also shows you that whereas left-wingers are jerks, right-wingers are nuts. To be fair, though, the flat tax is like a date with Julio Iglesias. It takes you a while to realize you've been screwed.

Let me explain. Following the 1986 tax reform, the average income tax paid by somebody in the $50,000–$75,000 bracket indeed went down, and I mean way down: $1,100. The total tax take for that bracket went up $7.6 billion because there were many more taxpayers in that range in 1987.

Ha, you say, Cecil was using statistics to lie! Uh-uh. Fact is, taxes for virtually all tax brackets went down. Yet the total tax collected went up. How was this miracle accomplished? By eliminating many popular tax deductions. This forced millions of Americans into higher brack-ets, so they paid more tax. Example: elimination of the IRA deduction. If you and your spouse 1) both worked, 2) made a total of more than $50,000, and 3) had previously both taken the maximum IRA deduc-tion, in 1987 your taxable income increased $4,000 *even if your real income stayed the same.* Assuming two kids, $53,000 in joint income, and $9,000 in deductions in both '86 and '87, your taxes went up $862.

Taxes went up for most affluent Americans. In 1987 they reported an additional $300 billion in income, of which maybe two-thirds stemmed from closed loopholes. As a result, people making from $50,000 to $1 million paid an extra $24 billion in tax. OK, nobody's bleeding for a $500,000-a-year lawyer. But look who paid less tax: those making under $50K (average tax cut: $5 to $867) and those mak-ing $1 million and up (average cut: $214,000). Like I say, some reform. Other points:

1. Forbes claims his flat tax rate will be 17 percent. Most knowledgeable observers say if that happens the government will go broke. The real flat tax rate will have to be at least 20 percent. The working

poor will get screwed because they will lose the earned-income credit, which lets them collect a tax "refund" greater than the amount of taxes withheld. You don't have to be a genius to figure out that if taxes for the Forbes crowd go down, they have to go up for somebody else.

2. The income tax is progressive for several reasons, the cynical one being that there are a lot more poor voters than rich ones. The practical reason is that a progressive income tax overcomes the regressivity of the sales tax, which falls most heavily on the poor, and the property tax, which falls most heavily on the middle class. Some analysts say total taxes as a percentage of income are about the same for all income levels.

3. No income tax at all? Fine. When the guys in the military come looking for their pay, we'll tell them to see you.

From The Straight Dope Message Board

(Collected by OpalCat, keeper of the Straight Dope "Page o' Flames")

The first computer class I took in college was on punch cards. This wasn't before the earth's crust cooled, it was only 1979. Anyway, it's probably why it took me so long to sit down at a computer again; I had nightmares about those °&^% cards.

Oh yeah? The first programming I learned, we saved our programs on spools of paper tape. We didn't even have a CRT, just a Teletype machine. (This would have been in 1975 or '76). We eventually got a 9½-inch floppy drive and a CRT, and were some happenin' dudes. I've still got some of the spools, and the enormous floppy disk.

You had a Teletype machine? We would have KILLED for a Teletype machine! Once I had to write an entire operating system using nothing but a wall full of toggle switches! Keyboards . . . HA! You had it easy! ;-)

You all had electricity? All we had was a bunch of gears that had to be rotated by hand. . . . Took years just to get the thing to add 1 + 1.

You had gears???? All we had was rocks and sticks. Rock = 0 and stick = 1. You'd get a line of code all written and then a dog would come and carry off your 1's and you'd have to start all over. You guys had it easy.

You had rocks and sticks?? Jeez, try growing up in the desert. . . . Grains of sand made the coding damn near impossible!

Chapter 8

Words And Lyrics

Being a Native American, I was wondering why people and cartoon characters yell "Geronimo!" when they parachute from an airplane. To the best of my knowledge Geronimo never skydived.—Michael, southeast Texas

The other day a guy asks me why I love the Internet. Two reasons, I told him. First, you can come up with the definitive answer to seemingly inscrutable questions like this one in three days max. Second, the BS answers from the goofballs in the newsgroups are a riot. Example: Paratroopers yell "Geronimo!" because it beats screaming "Mommmyyyy!"

As it turns out, this isn't far from the real answer. The custom of yelling "Geronimo!" is attributed to Aubrey Eberhardt, a member of the U.S. Army's parachute "test platoon" that demonstrated the feasibility of parachute troop drops at Fort Benning, Georgia, in 1940. To speed up the drops, the brass decided to try a mass jump, in which the chutists would jump from the plane in quick succession. The men were nervous about this, and to relieve the tension a group of them went to see a western at the post movie house the night before the jump. The movie featured the cavalry mixing it up with the famous Apache chief Geronimo. None of our sources said exactly what movie this was, but one supposes it was *Geronimo* (1939) with Andy Devine and Gene Lockhart.

After the movie the men went to the post beer garden to further calm their nerves, and after a few hours were feeling pretty courageous. Strolling back to camp, Private Eberhardt announced that he expected the next day's jump to be no different from any other. His friends immediately began to razz him, saying he'd be so scared he'd barely remember his name. This ticked off the six-foot-eight Eberhardt, who was known for his confidence and powers of concentration. According to Gerard M. Devlin, author of *Paratrooper!* (1979), he declared, "All right, dammit! I tell you jokers what I'm gonna do! To prove to you that I'm not scared out of my wits when I jump, I'm gonna yell 'Geronimo' loud as hell when I go out that door tomorrow!"

Next morning half the platoon strapped on their chutes and boarded planes, while the other half sat by the edge of the jump field to watch the drop. By now everyone had heard about Eberhardt's promise. The lead plane flew over the field at low altitude and the men began spilling out as planned. As the chutes popped open, the guys on the ground could clearly hear a shout of "Geronimo!" followed by an Indian war whoop. Eberhardt had made good on his boast and the unofficial yell of U.S. airborne troops had been born.

Some people claim that jumpers yell "Geronimo!" because if their main chute hasn't opened by the time they're done, they know it's time to deploy the reserve chute. Not true. Official U.S. Army practice is to count out loud "one thousand, two thousand, three thousand, four thousand" (or higher, depending on the type of aircraft). If you're still dropping like a rock after that, deploying your reserve chute is strongly advised. Regardless of what you say, yelling on exit is a good way to calm the jitters and stay focused on what you're supposed to do.

My assistant Jane, always pondering the big picture, wonders if the course of history might have been different had Eberhardt and his friends seen a movie other than *Geronimo* before the big jump. Another notable 1939 release was *The Wizard of Oz*. Would the enemy have quaked with terror had jumping U.S. paratroopers shouted "And Toto tooooooo"? Thinking the same thought, one Usenet wag inquires, What if they'd seen *Rocky*? Jumpers everywhere today might be shouting, "Adriiiiaaaan!" For that matter, what about *The Terminator*? Think of the loss of credibility if they shouted, "I'll be baaaaack!"

The song "Blinded by the Light"—I have no idea who wrote it or sang it, but it's your job to know these things. I was wondering what the male vocalist says after the title phrase of the song. Is it "revved up like a deuce" or "ripped off like a douche" or some other phrase? —IMSMRTRTNU, via AOL

URSMRTRNI? DLUR, TRKE.

"Blinded by the Light" was written by a New Jersey musician named Bruce Springsteen. Maybe you've heard of him. It was on his *Greetings From Asbury Park, N.J.* album.

Bruce's lyrics were no paragon of clarity, but at least you could understand the words: "Cut loose like a deuce another runner in the night." Some claim the "deuce" being referred to is the 1932 Ford Coupe beloved of hot-rodders (cf. the Beach Boys' "Little Deuce Coupe"). Maybe, but when you're talking about a song whose opening line rambles on about madman drummers, bummers, Indians in the summer, etc., I'm not making any definite claims.

Manfred Mann's Earth Band ("Quinn the Eskimo") did a cover version of the tune in 1976. It became a hit, no doubt because the band made the lyrics even more opaque than they already were. They changed the line in question to "wrapped up like a deuce."

What's it mean? I'm barely on speaking terms with my own subconscious. Don't ask me to explain someone else's.

The Mosquitoes Swarm

AHA! I've been reading and enjoying your column for many years, and I finally caught a goof. In your explanation of the lyrics to "Blinded by the Light," you parenthetically implied that Manfred Mann's Earth Band was known for "Quinn the Eskimo." Nope! It was the group Manfred Mann that had the 1968 hit with this Bob Dylan song, not Manfred Mann's Earth Band. The Earth Band emerged following the dissolution of Manfred Mann (the group, not the guy).— Nick DeBenedetto, via AOL

Nick. Suppose my group Cecil had a monster hit with the Dylan tune "Nick the Nitpicker." And suppose a few years later I formed a new group called Cecil's Terrestrial Musical Organization. And suppose finally that I did another arrangement of "Nick the Nitpicker," and we sang it all the time because everybody expected us to, and we put it on two of our albums, including "Live in Hungary Right After Manfred Mann's Earth Band Played There." You think I would object if some twenty-first-century Einstein said my second band was "known" for the song, even though it had been made famous by my first?

People who can't see are blind, and people who can't hear are deaf. What is the term for people who lack the sense of smell or taste? Smell-less? Taste-less?—Bob, Dallas

No question, these would be handy terms to have in these trying times. Let me consult the files. Ah, here we are. The technical term for the inability to smell is *anosmia,* and a person who is unable to detect smells is *anosmic.* The inability to taste is *ageusia,* and a (literally) tasteless person presumably would be an *ageusiatic.* These terms allow one to express oneself in an honest yet tactful manner. Thus:

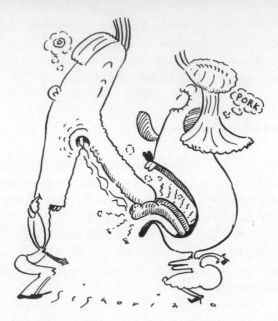

Vaguely Important-Looking Person at party: "I thought Demi Moore gave a compelling performance in *Striptease.*"

You: "Goodness, you must be an anosmic ageusiatic."*

VILP: "No, actually I'm a Presbyterian from Cleveland."

A related term is *dysgeusia,* the condition of having an abnormal, presumably bad, taste in your mouth. This word offers a range of uses. Basic application: "Marge, that velvet Elvis painting is the last word in dysgeusia." "Thanks, we're the envy of the trailer park." Or, more elaborately: "I know they pay me big money to be the president's press secretary, but spinning this Monica-gate thing leaves me feeling pretty dysgeusiatic." "Son, you work here long enough, you get used to being disgusterated." If you have an opportunity to use these words—and nowadays who doesn't?—feel free.

What does "Judas Priest" mean? Besides being the name of a bitchin' heavy-metal band, it was something my grampa used to exclaim every time the hated Philadelphia Phillies scored a run against

---

*"You have no taste and you can't tell when something smells."

the Giants. Was Gramps ahead of his time musically, or did the band rip him off?—Tommy Touhey, Augusta, Georgia

The truly great cusswords span the generations, don't they? The answer to your question is none of the above. Gramps was just trying not to scandalize Grandma. "Judas Priest" is a blasphemous-sounding but meaningless euphemism for "Jesus Christ."

I am sending you a copy of this letter I wrote to [San Francisco Chronicle columnist] Herb Caen at the urging of my husband. He says only a man of your intellect and discrimination can truly appreciate all its nuances.—Lisa Wells, Oakland, California

It's a classic, all right. You spend three pages kvetching to Herb about a grammatical error in his newspaper and in the process make about ten million mistakes yourself. Let me quote a few representative sentences: "As for the rapidly advancing era of illiteracy, sometimes it's funny to laugh and gaffe about, but other times it feels positively grievous, as though a huge chunk of literary and historical culture is dying. The specific incident which occasioned my writing today is a *faux pas* in today's *Chronicle* . . . The penultimate paragraph [of a certain story] states that Barbara Jeffers told police 'her son had been acting strangely recently and had threatened her safety.' I doubt very seriously that an agitated, frightened mother literally used the words

'acting strangely.' The only time I ever hear that expression, aside from newscasters in their embarrassingly misguided attempts to be 'correct,' is reverberating around my brain after reading it in the paper—oftentimes, I'm sorry to say, the *Chronicle*."

Cecil won't argue with your main point, which is that "act" in the sense of "appear" or "seem to be" is a linking verb properly followed by an adjective ("strange") rather than an adverb. However, in other respects your grasp of the mechanics could stand a little work. Thank God you've got me around to straighten you out.

1. "Funny to laugh about" doesn't make any sense. You either mean "funny," period, or "fun to laugh about."
2. "Gaffe" is not a verb. Perhaps you meant "chaff."
3. "Feels positively grievous" feels positively weird. Better to say "makes one positively grieve."
4. "Literary and historical culture"? Bag the meaningless adjectives.
5. "As though" generally introduces contrary-to-fact or hypothetical statements and so takes the subjunctive: "as though a huge chunk of our culture were dying." However, the sense of the rest of the sentence is not that the death of the culture is hypothetical but rather that it is advancing rapidly upon us. Let's start over and say, "As for the rapidly advancing era of illiteracy, sometimes it can be comical, but other times one positively grieves for our dying language."

    You are thinking: Cecil, I am unworthy of having my prose improved any further. Lavish your wisdom on some other chump. But I can't stand to leave a job unfinished.

6. "Specific incident" is redundant. "Incident" means "specific occurrence."
7. "Which occasioned" should be "that occasioned." Restrictive clause.
8. You can't say "the incident that occasioned my writing is a *faux pas*." It has to be either "occasioned . . . was" or "occasions . . . is." Sequence of tenses.
9. If the error appeared in today's paper, it's a good bet you're writing today too. Drop one instance of "today," which now appears twice in the same sentence.

WORDS AND LYRICS · 153

10. In the last sentence, "aside from newscasters" is shy a preposition (think about it). Let's say "other than from newscasters."
11. "Reverberating around my brain" cannot logically modify "the only time." Instead say "the only time I hear that phrase . . . is when it reverberates in my brain . . ."
12. "Reading," as in "after reading it in the paper," is a dangling participle. Say "after I read it in the paper."

Putting it all together, we have, "The only time I ever hear this expression, other than from newscasters who are misguidedly attempting to be 'correct,' is when it reverberates in my brain after I read it in the paper." Not perfect, maybe, but definitely improved. You appreciate my efforts, I'm sure. Just as Herb Caen appreciated yours.

Where did the word "Great" come from in the official title "United Kingdom of Great Britain and Northern Ireland"? When and why did Britain start calling itself great? Since the British Empire has disintegrated, shouldn't they change it to plain old Britain?—Wai Kong Lee, Montreal, Quebec

Well, I guess it's less of a mouthful than Formerly Great Britain or Still Pretty Good Britain, which are the other obvious choices. But the fact is, things will really have to go to pieces before the Brits will be obliged to drop the "Great" from their country's name. Originally the island was called Britain, period, but the name dropped out of common use after the masses coalesced into the separate kingdoms of England and Scotland and the principality of Wales. It was revived as part of efforts to unify the island in the sixteenth century. The "Great" had to be appended to distinguish the proposed kingdom from Brittany, a.k.a. *Britannia minor,* lesser Britain, the French peninsula that had been settled in the fifth and sixth centuries by Celtic immigrants from the British Isles. And Great Britain definitely had a classy ring to it, although I can't imagine the residents of Brittany were too happy. ("So, mes amis, eef you are Great Britain, what are we? Pissant Britain?") Suffice it to say, the name stuck. James I, who was also James VI of Scotland, unified the thrones of England and Scotland and had himself proclaimed king of Great Britain in 1604. The term became official with the Act of Union in 1707.

At one point in Walden, *Henry David Thoreau, having grown bored with making the reader feel grubbily materialistic if he cannot carry all of his belongings on his back, moves on to rub the reader's nose in his puny intellectual attainments: "I confess I do not make a very broad distinction between the illiterateness of my townsman who cannot read at all, and the illiterateness of him who has learned to read only what is for children and feeble intellects. We should be as good as the worthies of antiquity, but partly by first knowing how good they were. We are a race of tit-men, and soar but little higher in our intellectual flights than the columns of the daily paper."*

Assuming Hank Dave was not channeling Russ Meyer or Howard Stern, what the devil did he mean by "tit-men"? The context suggests he meant men preoccupied by life's inessentials—souls who lie in the gutter but fail to look up at the stars, or some such. Maybe he's comparing us with birds. But as I can't find the phrase in any old dictionaries, I can't be sure. Would you be good enough to shine the refulgent beacon of your nonesuch intelligence upon this umbrageous niche of Thoreauvia?
—David English, West Somerville, Massachusetts

Oh, David, I love it when you talk dirty like that. This is a topic I am happy to decrepusculate. I will even forgive Henry D.'s slighting reference to "the columns of the daily paper." Clearly he foresaw even then that truly mind-expanding journalism would be carried only in weeklies.

The reason you couldn't find "tit-men" in any old dictionaries is that you can't use just any old dictionary. For industrial-strength knowledge you want the *Oxford English Dictionary,* which tells us that a "titman" is "the smallest pig, etc., of a litter; hence, a man who is stunted physically or mentally; a dwarf, a 'croot.' "

So now you know. A tit-man (titman, whatever) is a croot. The phrase "soar but little higher" inclines one to think that Thoreau is also making a punning allusion to a similarly named species of bird.

Reminds me of a story. Two mice are in an English music hall watching a chorus line. "Lovely legs, haven't they?" says the first mouse. "Oh, I don't know," says the other. "I'm a titmouse myself."

My son says he has it on good authority that the phrase is "Feed a fever, starve a cold." I thought it was "Feed a cold, starve a fever." Can

you tell me who's right, what it means, and who said it?—Bob White,
Arroyo Grande, California

Your son thinks there's a better authority than dad? For shame. Although I realize the only way to make kids understand sometimes is to reason with them really loud.

Your version of the proverb is the traditional one, but you can find citations in the literature that have it the other way around. The idea, if not the exact wording, dates back to 1574, when a dictionary maker named Withals wrote, "Fasting is a great remedie of feuer."

You're thinking: This guy wrote a dictionarie? His medical advice wasn't so hot either. Doctors have been trying to stamp out the above piece of folklore for years. Current medical thinking is that you want to keep an even strain when you're sick with either a cold or a fever, and you certainly don't want to stress your system by stuffing or starving yourself.

Nobody's sure where the notion of feeding colds and so on arose. (It surely didn't originate with Withals.) One somewhat dubious explanation has it that the proverb really means, "If you feed a cold now, you'll have to starve a fever later." A more plausible interpretation is that the feed-a-cold idea arose out of a folk understanding of the disease process, namely that there were two kinds of illnesses, those caused by low temperatures (colds and chills) and those caused by high temperatures (fever). If you had a chill, you wanted to stoke the interior fires, so you pigged. If you had a fever, you didn't want things to overheat, so you slacked off on the fuel.

Bottom line: tell your kid to chill. But I can relate. When I had

sniffles as a kid the feed-a-cold thing was usually good for a few extra Twinkies. So you'll just have to forgive me if, in the delirium of a 99-degree temperature, I used to imagine it was feed a fever too.

What is the origin of the phrase "in like Flynn"? I have heard it alludes to the sexual exploits of the actor Errol Flynn but have a difficult time believing a reference so graphic could have become a common catchphrase.—Joe Lubben, Oberlin, Ohio

Oh? Consider the common expression "we're screwed." You think the true meaning of this phrase is "we're attached with rotary fasteners"?

The real question is whether people would have used phrases having a sexual connotation in the 1940s, when "in like Flynn" became common. To determine this, we apply the MOM test. This consists of asking ourselves, "Would my mom consciously use an expression meaning, 'In as surely as Errol Flynn gets his Buick parked in some young innocent's garage'?"

Maybe your mom would. Mine would sooner die. For that matter, I've never heard her say "we're screwed."

Let us review the evidence.

The earliest known use of "in like Flynn" in print is in the December 1946 issue of *American Speech*. Penn State prof Ed Miller reported that students of his who had served in the army air force during World War II used the expression to mean " 'Everything is OK.' In other words, the pilot is having no more trouble than Errol Flynn has in his cinematic feats."

From this we learn several things: 1) The expression was of recent origin. Had it been widely used in the 1930s, Miller would not have included it in a list of World War II slang. 2) The term was generally understood to refer to Errol Flynn. 3) It didn't necessarily refer to Flynn's success with women. 4) Then again, maybe Miller's students just didn't feel like proclaiming otherwise in the middle of class.

No question, a lot of people think the phrase means in like Flynn's you know what, and with good reason. Flynn, a popular film star in the 1930s, became notorious in November 1942 when he was charged with two counts of statutory rape. Though acquitted, he was the butt of jokes ever after.

One film bio none too subtly comments, "Warner Brothers . . . found [Flynn's] popularity not only had held but had a new spurt of interest. A new phrase was added to the English language: 'In like Flynn' " (Tony Thomas et al., *The Films of Errol Flynn,* 1969).

Another says the post-trial Flynn became a "wild man of the mattress. The slogan 'In like Flynn' rose like smoke from the trial and ran laughingly around the globe" (Earl Conrad, *Errol Flynn: A Memoir,* 1978).

An Australian playwright (Flynn was born in Australia) even claimed the expression "in like Errol" was current in his country for a time (Alexander Buzo, *Rooted,* 1973).

But still. These guys were writing after the sexual revolution of the 1960s. In like Flynn's schwanz? In the 1940s?

An alternative interpretation comes from *A Dictionary of Catch Phrases* (Eric Partridge, 1986). Edward J. Flynn (1892–1953) was a New York City political boss who became a campaign manager for the Democratic party during FDR's presidency. Boss Flynn's "Democratic Party machine exercised absolute political control over the Bronx. . . . The candidates he backed were almost automatically 'in,' and he himself permanently so," Partridge comments.

Now we have the beginnings of a theory. "In like Flynn" starts as rhyming slang in New York, helped along by the prominence of Boss Flynn. NYC draftees spread it among the troops nationwide with the start of World War II. The phrase gets a boost when the well-publicized travails of Errol Flynn in 1942 give it a double meaning. But its innocent origin allows Cecil's mom to use it without being scandalized.

Just one thing. We have no evidence that "in like Flynn" was used anywhere prior to November 1942.

So I appeal to the Teeming Millions. OK, so you pretty much made hash out of "the whole nine yards." Here is a chance to redeem yourselves. I know of the Straight Dope's abiding popularity among septuagenarians. If you have personal knowledge of "in like Flynn" having been used prior to 1942, or even better if you have written proof, send it in.

I'm not saying this ranks with the search for the quark. But human knowledge is human knowledge, and we all have to do our part.

In Like Flynn: The Sinful Truth

At the end of your column about the "Flynn flap" you invited us seventysomethings to offer what we could to the pool of human knowledge. Born in the Bronx in 1926, I lived there until age 16, which coincides with your critical year, 1942 [when Flynn was tried for statutory rape]. I never heard, or at least I don't remember, Boss Flynn's name coming up. But I and all my friends freely bandied about "in like Flynn." There is no doubt in my mind that it referred to his success with women.—Murray Lefkowitz, Merion Station, Pennsylvania

I [was] 70 in October, so I hope my recollections will carry some weight. . . . It was the double entendre involved that accounted for the phrase's popularity. Young males could smirkingly use it in front of females, who then started applying it to other situations without necessarily knowing its original meaning. As I recall, my brothers and I even got our mother to use it, which was especially amusing since she hated Errol Flynn with a passion. I was in the army air corps in World War II, and we all knew the phrase had nothing to do with Flynn's cinematic feats.—G. R. Niles, Honolulu, Hawaii

Jeez, when even Grandpa is arguing for the risqué interpretation, it's time to throw in the towel. Apparently, "in like Flynn" really does refer to Errol's success in the sack.

Whenever I watch an old Tarzan movie on TV, right when Tarzan and a few of the intruding white guys are worried sick and looking high and low we suddenly hear the drums. Tarzan stiffens, puts a hand

to one ear, and announces, "They have the girl. She is well, but they will not give her back unless you shut down your mines. They are 200 men strong and have guns. They will be here before dark tonight." Huh? How did he get that from a few drumbeats? Is there really a way to communicate any message besides "I'm beating a drum" across the jungle like this? And while you're at it, what's the story with those smoke signals the Indians were always sending?—Lying Awake in Wonder, Anna Banana, Olney, Illinois

You don't believe everything you see in the movies? In the age of Oliver Stone, this is comforting news. But there really are such things as talking drums.

First, let's kiss off Indian smoke signals. Some Native American tribes did use smoke signals, particularly on the plains or in the southwest, where the sky was usually clear and the view unobstructed. But the message was pretty basic. An army captain in the 1860s writes: "Apache smoke signals are of various kinds, each one significant of a particular object. A sudden puff, rising from the mountain heights . . . indicates the presence of a strange party upon the plain below. If these puffs are rapidly repeated they are a warning that strangers are well armed and numerous. If a steady smoke is maintained for some time, the object is to collect the scattered bands of savages at some designated point, with hostile intention, should it be practicable." Other means of signaling included fires (at night), gesticulating with blankets, or reflecting the sun off mirrors.

For your chattier Western Union–type communication you have to go to central Africa, where the Bantu family of languages is spoken. Many Bantu languages have drum equivalents, which work like Morse code except that the fundamental message unit is words rather than letters. Drum language is based on the fact that a key determinant of meaning in Bantu words is high versus low intonation. In the Bantu language Kele, for example, *liala* means "fiancé" if the syllables are intoned low-high-low and "rubbish pit" if pronounced L-L-L. You will appreciate, therefore, the importance of keeping Bantu intonations straight.

Drum telegraphy is accomplished using two-tone drums that duplicate these tonal patterns. You are thinking you see a fatal flaw in this approach—like there's only one three-syllable word in Kele that's intoned L-H-L? Of course not. To provide unique tonal combinations common words are replaced by stock phrases. Thus, *songe* (moon, H-H) is distinguished from *kaka* (fowl, also H-H) by stretching out the former into *songe li tange la manga*, "the moon looks down at the earth," H-H-L-H-L-L-L-L, and the latter into *kaka olongo la bokiokio*, "the fowl, the little one which says 'kiokio,' " H-H-L-H-H-L-L-H-L-H-L.

This procedure gives drum messages a somewhat discursive quality. The English sentences "The missionary is coming upriver to our village tomorrow. Bring water and firewood to his house" parses out to the drummed equivalent of the following: "White man spirit from the forest / of the leaf used for roofs / comes upriver, comes upriver / when tomorrow has risen / on high in the sky / to the town and the village / of us / come, come, come, / bring water of lakaila vine / bring sticks of firewood / to the house with shingles high above / of the white man spirit from the forest / of the leaf used for roofs." Such a message, combined with stop and start signals, repetition, parity bits—wait a sec, wrong technology. Anyway, it might take ten minutes or more to pound this baby out, and the idea that Johnny Weissmuller could get the drift in two seconds is strictly Hollywood. But eventually the drift could be gotten, and in fairly precise terms. For more, see J. F. Carrington's *Talking Drums of Africa* (1949), from which all the above examples are drawn.

I graduated from high school in the class of '71. Now I have a daughter, and it dawned on me recently that she will graduate from high school in June 2000, which, as I have learned from your book

More of the Straight Dope, *is pronounced "June of the year two thou-sand." My question is, what will her class be called? I know how they will* write *it, of course: Class of '00. But how will they say it? Class of Zero-Zero? Class of Oh-Oh? (Hmm.) Please hurry with your answer; she may be valedictorian and I don't want her to say the wrong thing in her speech.—Jeff Greenberg, New York*

I've been banging the gong about the pending crisis in decade names (of which your question is merely the latest reflection) for more than 20 years—so far, I am obliged to say, without noticeable result. What will we call the decade after the '90s, I have patiently inquired—the Nothings? The Nixies? The Voids? Later, say the nation's leaders. Right now we're worrying about war, genocide, and national decline. It's always something, says I.

Meanwhile, the clock keeps ticking, and as your question indicates, it's our children who will pay the price. My research so far, which con-sists of tossing this out to the Teeming Millions on the radio, has turned up the following: judging from somebody's grandfather's col-lege yearbook, last time this problem arose (in 1900), they called it the Class of Aughty-Aught. Do you want your daughter to get up in front of her classmates and have to say that? I didn't think so. If she can't avoid being valedictorian any other way, tell her to take a dive on that last physics quiz and let this particularly icky cup pass to someone else.

Speaking of the next decade, how did the people who lived in Theodore Roosevelt's America refer to the decade they were going through? I suspect they called it "the 1900s" or "the hundreds"—a natural sequel to "the 1890s" or "the nineties"—but I wasn't around then. They must have called it something, and it seems odd that no record of this has emerged as we approach another double-0 decade. You know everything, Cecil, even about the past. How'd they handle this the last time?—VCRogers, via AOL

You want to know what they called it? They didn't call it anything. At least nothing short and catchy, unless your idea of short and catchy is "the 1900s," in which case I don't want you writing any soap jingles for me.

It's not that folks a hundred years ago didn't have nicknames for the

decades they lived in. The 1890s, for example, were known as the Naughty '90s. You know, because they rode bicycles and stuff.

As far as I can tell, however, the 1900s had no such nickname. Even "the 1900s" was used only infrequently. Either it was a period of global monotony, or else they discovered what we're about to: there is no suitable term, and cumbersome locutions are your only recourse.

I can speak with confidence about this because I've applied technology to the problem. This consisted of running every nickname I could think of through the "search quotations" feature of the electronic *Oxford English Dictionary,* which has zillions of literary citations of English usage dating back to the time of Ethelred the Unready. Granted, the *OED* is skewed toward British English, but still. Results:

> Hundreds, aughts, aughties, naughts, naughties, zeroes, zeds, zips, zilches, ohs, double-Os, nothings, ciphers—no relevant citations.
>
> 1900s—5 citations.
>
> First decade [of the century]—9 citations.
>
> Opening/first/early years [of the century]—19 citations.
>
> Beginning of the/this century—20 citations.
>
> Turn of the century—38 citations.

Here's a typically convoluted construction: "A popular fashion of the 1890s and the first decade of the twentieth century." OK, that appeared in 1970. But try these: "In Canada alone in the first decade of this century" (1936). "The opening years of the twentieth century" (1917). "In the first years of the eighteenth century" (1907)—OK, different century, but you see my point.

Is this pathetic or what? In his discussion of this subject years ago, Cecil half seriously cited "turn of the century." Now we find it's the default usage, judging from the *OED*.

At least people are starting to wake up to the fact that we've got a problem. Combing through the data banks, I find anxious discussions of the subject in the *Atlantic,* the Norfolk *Virginian-Pilot,* and the *Dartmouth* ("America's Oldest College Newspaper"). The *New York Times* has written editorials urging that we call it the "ohs." Oh? Sorry, can't see it.

The *Virginian-Pilot* advocates the Aughties, on the dubious grounds that we will refer to the year 2006, say, as "twenty-aught-six." The paper credits the term to one J. William Doolittle, who was cited in a 1989 William Safire column. This shows you what passes for investigative prowess at the provincial press these days—Cecil joshingly proposed the Naughty Aughties in 1988. Though if somebody wants to pin it on Doolittle, no beef here.

At any rate, the unignorable fact is that we've been flailing at this for ten years and haven't produced anything that can be said without embarrassment. And people think "the year 2000 problem" refers to computers! Little do they know. If Bill Clinton wants to build a bridge to the twenty-first century, here's where he'd better start.

Naming The Coming Decade: Still Flailing

This begs the question of how to refer to 2000–2009 as a unit, but there is a cool way to reference the individual years. In the novels of Patrick O'Brian, the characters refer to dates in the early 1800s as "the year zero," "the year three," etc. This has a certain ring to it. I am certain O'Brian's references are historically correct in all respects because I have heard him speak on NPR. No one with an Oxbridge accent like his could be wrong about anything.—Yr ob'd't servant, David Light, via the Internet

The puzzle of how to refer to the opening years of the next century is pretty easy. Just look to the metric system, specifically the K in kilo. Piece of cake to write checks—September 21, 2K (or KK), for instance. Later in the century just add another digit, 2K7 for 2007. A graduate would be class of 2K, 2K1, 2K2, etc. [Further mildly amusing specula-tion deleted.] However, the ones who will enjoy this system most are conservative southerners, because 1,004 years from now will be the year KKK.—Mikey, via the Internet

The natural name to me would be "the singles."—Julian Ross Braver, Honolulu

Perhaps a reason why the first decade should remain nameless can be found in the old Hawaiian custom of waiting until a baby reaches one year before celebrating the event. One hesitates to assign a name too early as it may put an unwanted spin on all that follows. By leaving that first decade unnamed, do we not foster the hope of a Wondrous Age to come?—Guy Archer, Honolulu

Maybe, but I've pretty much given up hope of a Wondrous Name. Now, if you'll excuse me, I'm going upstairs for a little nap. Wake me in 2010.

Ever heard the expression mono e mono? *I thought it meant "one on one." My brother and his wife vehemently argue that it's spelled* mano e mano *and means "hand to hand." I think I'm right, but then again I'm only going by what the villain said to James Bond in* The Man With the Golden Gun. *The bad guy challenged Bond to a duel "mono e mono, one-on-one." Who's right? My brother and his wife or me?—Richard A. Galichon, Chicago*

None of you, which is par for the course. But they're closer than you, since all they did was misspell it. *Mano a mano* is Spanish for "hand to hand." Since hand-to-hand combat typically pits two indi-viduals against each other, the expression is often understood to, but doesn't literally, mean one-on-one. My assistant, Little Ed, made a similar mistake. Having read about the testosterone-driven naming of Grand Teton mountain (look it up), he had for years a giddy idea of the meaning of *tête-à-tête*. Imagine his disappointment upon discover-ing it merely meant "head to head."

They Thought Of The Word For When You Can't Think Of The Word. Unfortunately, They All Thought Of A *Different* Word

For two months I've faithfully watched the Straight Dope TV show every Sunday night on the A&E channel. Through the great hosting of Mike Lukas, I have vicariously experienced the mystery and wonder of your oh-so-reclusive genius. So imagine how surprised I was when you got something wrong!

On one program there was a question about what the word is for not remembering a word. Then the show said there wasn't a word, according to the folks over at Merriam-Webster.

Guys, the word is lethologica. It is in a dictionary of obscure words called Weird Words *by Erwin Berent and Rod L. Evans (1995).*

A more precise term is anomia, which according to the experts "is a deficit in finding words and is the most conspicuous feature of aphasia."—Jim Benjamin, via the Internet

[The proper term is] dysnomia. . . . The most common time for the condition is while taking medicinal antidepressants.—Elbert H. Seymour, Carnesville, Georgia

Psychologists refer to this as the tip-of-the-tongue phenomenon.—Joseph G., via the Internet

Ah, the marketplace of ideas. I'm just glad I'm not asking you guys for directions to the interstate.

This issue has been nagging Cecil for a long time. In the first Straight Dope book I said the word for when you couldn't think of the word was "aphasia." Actually, this is the term for a language impairment due to brain damage, but I figured one might use it metaphorically to mean the "I've-got-it-on-the-tip-of-my-tongue" syndrome. Or at least I might use it that way, being the kind of guy who thinks of dictionary definitions as a good start.

But let's face it, I was winging it. So when we did the TV show I told Mike to say, yeah, there's this word "aphasia," but it's not *really* the word for when you can't think of a word. Fact was, I couldn't think of the word for when you can't think of the word, presumptive proof in my mind that there wasn't one.

Still, one recognizes that in science new information is always coming in. Of the submissions above, anomia and dysnomia, which are more or less synonymous, are closer to what we're after than aphasia. But they're pretty much confined to the clinic, and in any case they don't really get at the guts of the thing, which is the experience of *almost* knowing a word, not drawing a complete blank.

Lethologica has the required meaning but, from what I can tell, is found strictly in books that have words like "lethologica" in them. In addition to *Weird Words*, cited above, it also turns up in Paul Dickson's *Words* (1982).

The truth seems to be, judging from a collection of journal articles cited by Joseph G., that the real, or at least commonly used, term for "tip-of-the-tongue syndrome" is "tip-of-the-tongue syndrome" (or phenomenon or experience or what have you).

One hopes this is a trend, but frankly I don't see it. You tell your shrink, "Doc, I've got this problem where there's a word on the tip of my tongue," and the doctor says, "Hmm, you've got tip-of-the-tongue syndrome." You're going to pay a hundred bucks an hour for that? Whereas if he says you've got dysnomia you think, Wow, maybe I can form a support group and get on *Oprah*. It's human nature to want to know things, and also human nature to think they're not very interesting when you find out.

From The Straight Dope Science Advisory Board

What about the National Hockey League makes it national? Whose "nation" are we talking about anyway? There are teams from both Canada and the U.S. in the league. In baseball there are two token Canadian teams in a U.S.-dominated sport. Why isn't the NHL called something like the "North American Hockey League"?—Dianne Jones, Fremont, CA

No such thing as a "token" Canadian team in the National Hockey League, Dianne.

As a matter of fact, according to the *Encyclopedia of Hockey*, the NHL started in 1917 with four Canadian teams: the Toronto Arenas, the Montreal Canadiens (yes, that's how they've always spelled it), the Ottawa Senators, and the Montreal Wanderers. This means the "nation" referred to in "National Hockey League" is none other than our neighbor to the north, Canada.

Of course, they've been playing organized hockey longer than that in Canada. The Stanley Cup, the award given to the championship team following a best-of-seven-games series between professional ice hockey conference champions, was first awarded to the Montreal A.A.A. in 1894. Until 1910, amateurs and professionals were permitted to play on the same teams, but since 1910, the cup has been presented to entirely professional teams—and the cup wasn't awarded to the NHL champion until 1926. (That same year, the NHL actually split into a Canadian division and an International division, but put them back together twelve years later.)

So celebrate the nation upon which the NHL was founded by hoisting a cold Labatt's or Moosehead, eh?

—*SDSTAFF Songbird*
Straight Dope Science Advisory Board

9

Technobabble

I recently cut open a golf ball to show my nephew Jason the rubber band wrapper and liquid-filled rubber ball in the center that I remembered from my childhood. Imagine my disappointment to discover a solid white interior made of who knows what, with no rubber bands and no secret center. There was nothing to do but reminisce. I remember as a kid it was common knowledge that the liquid in the center of the golf ball was a deadly poison and should never touch the lips. As an adult, however, I'm wondering . . . could we have been wrong? Did we miss anything? Was it the kids who tasted the stuff that went on to Yale? I must know!—Dave, via AOL

When I was a kid, I heard two stories. One was that the center of a golf ball was filled with compressed air and if you tried to cut it open it would explode. The other was that the center contained a deadly poison. Either way, I figured: Wow, golf is *exciting!* Obviously I had a lot to learn.

I have now established that 1) the compressed air thing was total bunk; 2) you can still get liquid-filled golf balls, although the solid-core ones dominate the market; but 3) the liquid isn't and wasn't poison. Titleist, the leading maker of liquid-filled balls, says it has always used a nontoxic solution of salt water and corn syrup. I suppose it's possible some fly-by-night outfit in the dim past might have used something less innocuous, but I'm betting they didn't. Apart from being safe, salt water and corn syrup have the big advantage of being cheap.

Years ago, most golf balls were of "wound" or three-piece construction. They either had 1) a small, hollow rubber core filled with liquid, a middle layer of tightly wound rubber thread, and a rubber cover, or 2) a solid rubber core, the wound middle layer, and a plastic cover. Things changed in 1968 when Spalding, now the largest golf ball manufacturer, introduced "solid-core," two-piece construction, the two pieces being the large, solid rubber core and the plastic cover. Solid-core balls tend to travel farther, which is mainly what duffers are interested in, and now account for 70 percent of the market. But three-piece balls have better control and feel, and for that reason they're preferred by pros. If you want to relive your youth and convince Jason you weren't hallucinating that "secret center" thing, get a Titleist Tour Balata, Titleist Professional, or Hogan 428 Balata. All have liquid cores.

Why a liquid core? Mainly because it helps regulate the ball's spin. Three-piece balls in general have high rates of backspin. High backspin = more lift = ball stays in the air longer. It also makes the ball stop faster when it hits the ground. (Control-oriented pros like that; duffers don't.) Too much backspin, though, and the ball tends to go straight up and straight down. Golf ball engineers use liquid cores (which act as a brake) in balls that would otherwise have too much spin, and solid cores in balls that would otherwise have too little. Liquid centers also provide a softer feel when one hits the ball. I could go on, but it gets too complicated, what with your launch angles, your ionomer resins, and your icosahedral dimple patterns. People think rocket science is, well, rocket science? Bah. Rockets are for guys who can't cut it in golf.

I love fountains—especially the fact that they were installed in very old homes and public places before the advent of electricity. We all know modern fountains recirculate water with the aid of electric pumps, but how did these fountains of yesteryear operate?—Joel Hazan, via the Internet

Conceptually, it was easy. Of course, I guess conceptually the creation of the universe wasn't all that complicated. Take the fountains of Rome, probably the most famous in the world. In ancient times someone realized there were lots of water sources outside Rome that were at a higher elevation than the city itself. Ergo, if one could convey the water from the sources to the town, one would have water pressure (and, if desired, fountains) galore. One then had the mere technical detail of building ten miles of more or less watertight aqueduct with a constant slope of 1 in 320 using the resources available in 312 B.C. Plus ten more aqueducts in later years, the longest extending 56 miles, bringing in a total of 38 million gallons of water per day. Plus an elaborate municipal plumbing system in which the runoff from one fountain fed others downhill from it and ultimately wound up in the sewers. Result: 1,200 fountains (and 800 baths) that couldn't be shut off. (Engineers to Roman senate: Get it to stop? We had enough trouble getting it to start! It's only 312 B.C.! You want freaking miracles, wait till the birth of Christ!) Your poet says, Ah, the fountains, the gushing water, they are so beautiful! To which your plumber says, Yeah, bub, it was either that or burst the pipes.

Cecil, you are my hero. My ultimate goal in life is to be the polymath you are. My question concerns a mythical "chicken gun" used for testing jet engines. I have heard tales of store-bought poultry being shot out of a gun at 500 mph into a running jet engine to test the engine's mettle should a pigeon or some other fowl have the misfortune to cross

paths with a 747. Does this gun exist, and how does it shoot a roasting hen at that speed without said bird disintegrating?—NoraPatric, via AOL

One problem with researching this question is that everyone thinks he has to tell you the chicken joke. Seems the French borrowed the chicken gun from an American aircraft company to test the windshields of their high-speed trains. After the first test they called the American engineers and said, "*Sacrebleu*, ze chicken destroy ze windshield and dent ze back wall! What gives?" Having asked a few questions, the engineers replied, "Next time let the chicken thaw first." Talked to two different guys who swore this really happened. Bet they believe in the $250 Mrs. Fields cookie recipe, too.

One of the main users of the chicken gun (also known as the chicken cannon or turkey gun) is Pratt & Whitney, the jet engine manufacturer. The "chicken ingestion test," as it's called, is one of a series of stress tests required by the Federal Aviation Administration before a new engine design can be certified. The tests take place in a concrete building large enough to enclose an entire jet engine. With the engine operating at full speed, the cannon uses compressed air to shoot chicken carcasses (or sometimes duck or turkey carcasses) into the turbine at 180 mph (not 500 mph). This is the approximate speed a plane would be traveling if it encountered a bird during takeoff or landing, when most such incidents occur. The chickens are bought not from the corner grocery but from a game farm; the engineers apparently figure that for maximum realism they'd better use birds with feathers. Bird disintegration occurs only after the chick hits the fan. If the turbine disintegrates too, or if the engine can't be operated safely for another twenty minutes after impact, the design fails the test.

Other stress tests involve water and ice. The most pyrotechnic test of all requires that dynamite charges be strapped to the compressor blades and detonated while the engine is going full blast. (Needless to say, this is the last test of the day.) If the exploding blades aren't completely contained by the fan case, it's back to the drawing board. Better to have pieces of engine embedded in the concrete walls of the test building than in some poor passenger's skull.

When wrapping your baking spud in aluminum foil, should you wrap shiny side in or shiny side out? I could swear I was taught in school that shiny side in will help it retain heat better, making it cook faster. However, I know a guy who says that you should always keep the shiny side away from your food, the reason being that the shiny side is shiny because it's treated with a dangerous chemical, and you don't want the chemical getting into your edibles. When I asked him why on earth they'd cover one side of the foil with a dangerous substance, he replied that shiny foil sells better than dull foil, and the only reason they don't coat both sides is that they want one side to be safe enough to put next to food. Personally I think the guy's nuts, but then again he's got a Ph.D. in engineering while I am just a humble product of the Louisiana public school system. Still . . . dangerous shiny chemicals? Come on.—Ray Shea, via the Internet

Makes perfect sense to me, Ray. Big corporation markets product used mainly in food preparation. Coats one side with poison to boost sales. Leaves other side uncoated so product can be used safely but—here's the best part—*doesn't tell anybody.* Half of uninformed consuming public wraps spuds wrong side in, eats toxic result, dies horribly! Big corporation conceals shocking death toll for 50 years! And I'm queen of Romania!

The truth is that the shiny side is not treated with a dangerous chemical. Mineral oil is used as a lubricant during the rolling process, some trace of which may remain on the finished foil—but it's not dangerous. The shiny side is shiny because of the way foil is made. During the last pass through the rolling mill, a double thickness of foil is run between the rollers. The side of each sheet that comes in contact with the polished steel rollers comes out shiny. The other side has a matte finish.

Having dispensed with the paranoid rumors, let's get down to the heart of the matter. Are you supposed to wrap stuff shiny side in or shiny side out? (We'll pass over the issue of whether you ought to be wrapping spuds with foil in the first place, a practice that many regard as folly.) The official word from the Reynolds aluminum people is as follows: "It makes little difference which side of the Reynolds Wrap aluminum foil you use; both sides do the same fine job of cooking, freezing, and storing food. There is a slight difference in the reflectivity of the two sides, but it is so slight that laboratory instruments are required to measure it."

However. When I first called up Reynolds I got Terry, who was filling in for Joe, the regular foil guru. Terry had the idea you were supposed to wrap food shiny side in. The quote above came later from Mary, by fax. Cecil loves PR people and believes everything they tell him, but when they contradict each other he's suspicious. I resolved to conduct an independent test.

I considered calling my brother-in-law the physicist at Oak Ridge National Laboratory, figuring maybe they could fire up the cyclotron. But I decided that wasn't in keeping with the do-more-with-less tradition of Straight Dope kitchen science. Instead I went out and got two baking potatoes, which I determined were the same size by digital measurement (felt 'em). I also bought two identical meat thermometers and a roll of Reynolds Wrap aluminum foil and wrapped the aforementioned vegetables therein, one shiny side in, the other shiny side out. Finally, I stuck a meat thermometer an equal distance into each spud, placed them in the Straight Dope Oven of Science, and cranked her up to 450 degrees Fahrenheit (232 Celsius).

Result: the shiny-side-in potato heated up more slowly than the shiny-side-out one and after 40 minutes was less thoroughly cooked.

Having been criticized in the past for generalizing from inadequate data, I repeated the experiment with another pair of potatoes. This time the shiny-side-*out* potato heated up more slowly. The statisticians out there will no doubt inform me that I should test another 15,000 spuds before drawing any firm conclusions. Given the cutbacks in federal funding for basic research, I wouldn't hold my breath. For now, however, my opinion is as follows: Shiny shminy. Put the foil on any way you want.

Not to ask a stupid question, but . . . why are covered bridges covered? It can't have been just because they look good that way in the postcards.—Laura Wargo, Naperville, Illinois

Why not? Looking good has always been prized over functionality in our society. Consider the thong bikini. But you were asking about bridges. You realize, first of all, that covered bridges are wooden. Excuse me if I spell this out in excessive detail, but these days one can leave nothing to chance. The uninformed believe covered bridges are covered to protect the wooden flooring from snow. Ha! Who cares about the flooring? Flooring is cheap. (Except when it's in your kitchen, I mean, but that's a paradox we'll take up another day.) Truth is, one of the jobs of a bridge tender in the old days was spreading snow on the floor of a covered bridge in winter so sleighs could get across. A few characters say the bridges were covered to prevent horses from getting spooked when they realized they were above flowing water, but about this theory we will not even speak.

What you're really trying to protect in a covered bridge are the structural members—the trusses. Made of heavy timber, these are the expensive part of the bridge, and if they fall apart due to exposure to the elements, so does the bridge. An unprotected wooden bridge will last maybe ten years. Put a cover over it, however, and it'll last for centuries. Or at least until some birdbrain adolescent decides to burn it down, the fate of quite a few covered bridges in recent years. But I digress.

Covering a wooden bridge is easy. The trusses already form a boxlike framework. Tack on some rafters and shingles and siding, and there you go. OK, it's not brain surgery, but somebody had to think it up, and the somebody usually credited is Timothy Palmer, who built the prototypical American covered bridge in Philadelphia between 1800 and 1804. Over time there have been anywhere from 3,000 to 16,000, depending on who's doing the estimating. Today fewer than 800 remain. Be assured, however, that this dwindling number is the result of progress, heavy trucks, and teenagers, not exposure to the rain.

Often when you put your clothes in the dryer you discover they stick together because of static electricity. But if you put a sheet of Bounce or Cling Free in the dryer, somehow it neutralizes the static electricity. Maybe I should just be glad my clothes don't stick together, but I'm curious. How precisely do Bounce and Cling Free work? —Michael T. Preston, Washington, D.C.

They, uh, lubricate. I know, doesn't seem like a very direct approach to the problem. That's the way science is. From the point of view of drama what you want is New and Improved Cling Free with Antimatter, in which the static electricity particles are annihilated by the antistatic antielectricity antiparticles, leaving only a hint of April freshness. In your dreams. What really happens is that static electricity is created when your clothes rub together. As much as 12,000 volts' worth, in fact. If only we could harness this resource! I'll get on it as soon as I perfect the wintergreen Life Savers reading lamp.

Anyway, if you can create static electricity by rubbing, you can not create it by not rubbing. (Work with me on this.) Assuming (a) not drying the clothes or (b) hanging them on the line to be dried by God's healing sunlight aren't viable options, you can eliminate rubbing by means of strategically applied lubricants. A quart of 30-weight during the rinse cycle? Don't be an amateur. Better to use the waxy compound impregnated in sheets of Bounce or Cling Free and liberated by the dryer's heat. You wax skis, you wax floors, you wax poetic (well, I do), so why not clothes?

Here's why not: after a while you get dingy wax buildup. In the oh-what-a-tangled-web-we-weave way of high technology, you can try to minimize this latest problem by means of "optical brighteners." This is not a new idea. You ever hear of bluing? You know what the idea behind it was? You made your clothes whiter than white, or at least not yellow, by dyeing them blue. The sophisticated version available today involves adding chemicals that fluoresce under the ultraviolet light of the sun, giving the colors a vibrant glow. Of course, it's an illusion, but Buddha teaches us that everything is an illusion. Some may see only laundry; I see a metaphor for life.

Why do broadcasting call letters start with certain letters depending on what part of the world the station is in, e.g., K in the U.S. west of the Mississippi, W east of the Mississippi, C in Canada, D in parts of Asia?—Eddie DiLao, Los Angeles
P.S.: Try to give me a straight answer, smartass.

Don't worry, Eddie, I'll explain this so even you can understand. The easy part of the answer is that the starting letters of radio call signs were parceled out to the countries of the world by the Berlin International Radio Convention of 1912. Canada got C, France got F, and so on. The letters assigned to the United States were W, A, N, and K—"wank," in other words. Surely this means something, although one shudders to think what. Actually, two of the letters are no great mystery. A and N are used by Army and Navy radio stations. Persons having some familiarity with the armed services will now say, Hmm,

I'll bet Navy stations have A and Army stations have N. But no. You can probably guess which Navy ships have the call letters NFDR and NJFK. A slightly tougher one is NJVF. Time's up: the *James V. Forrestal.*

W and K were used by other types of stations, eventually including commercial stations. At first there was no distinction between east and west. The first commercial station, in fact, was KDKA in Pittsburgh, established in 1924. But most eastern radio stations chose call signs starting with W. In order to help persons who otherwise could not tell whether they were in Los Angeles or New York, the Federal Radio Commission in 1927 decreed that henceforth west would be K and east would be W.

The remaining question is what W and K stand for. Nobody really knows. Demented theories vouchsafed to this department include: 1) They stand for "watt" and "kilowatt." Watt? 2) W stands for "watt" and K is from the Spanish *que*, what = watt. I have notified the police to have the author of this picked up. 3) Recalling W-A-N-K, we note that in Morse code A is dot-dash, while N is dash-dot. Add a dash to dot-dash and we get dot-dash-dash: W! Add a dash to dash-dot and we get dash-dot-dash: K!! It tires me just to think about it; I must go home and rest. Maybe it will come to me in a dream.

How on earth can the Chinese and Japanese use computers, given that their writing uses thousands of different characters? The keyboard must look like something off a Wurlitzer pipe organ.—Nora Krushoc, Knoxville, Tennessee

Nah, it looks pretty much like any keyboard, and using it is a piece of cake. All you have to do is adhere closely to the following six hundred steps. You might want to pack a lunch.

1. Figure out which of the 50,000-plus Chinese characters you want to use. It should not be necessary to point out that each character stands for a word or concept (usually) rather than a sound, as in English. However, I did have one guy recently who thought Chinese had 50,000 different sounds and wondered why we English speakers felt we had to scrape by with a few dozen. Also, lest 50,000 characters seem a little extreme, I should point out that you can get by with about 3,000–4,000.

2. Try to remember how to pronounce said character. This is fairly simple. Each Chinese character has one syllable, and in Pinyin, the official pronunciation system used in mainland China, there are 403 possible spoken syllables. Syllables can be pronounced with one of four tones (level, rising, falling, and falling-and-rising), each tone giving the syllable a different meaning. The tones account for what many westerners regard as the singsong quality of East Asian speech.

3. Enter the syllable into the computer phonetically, using Roman (i.e., our) letters. This takes up to six keystrokes plus, in some programs, one more keystroke for the tone. Typically this pops up a menu of possible characters, six characters or so at a time.

4. Page through the characters looking for the one you want. With 50,000 possible written syllables but only a few hundred possible spoken ones, each spoken syllable can have as many as 131 different meanings (average: 17), each with its own character. You could be paging quite a while, and you still might not find the character you want—no program includes all 50,000. (Answer to obvious question: in speech you figure out the meaning from the context. Never let your attention wander during a Chinese conversation.)

5. Hope like hell you speak Mandarin, the most important of the seven or eight major Chinese dialects. Although written Chinese is pretty much the same throughout China, spoken Chinese can vary dramatically and some dialects are mutually unintelligible. The Pinyin pronunciation system and Pinyin-based word proces-

sors are geared toward Mandarin. If all you speak is Cantonese, you'll have to use an alternative input method, which can involve stroke analysis, numerical codes, or other matters even more frightening.

6. Having found the character you want, tap one more key to enter it into your document.

Net result of steps 1 through 6: one syllable. That's all you need for some simple words, but many modern terms are multisyllabic compounds. For example, one Chinese news service renders "World Wide Web" as "Ten-Thousand-Dimensional Web in Heaven and Net on Earth." Mercifully, this condenses a bit in Chinese. Nevertheless, if I were typing a letter to Mom in Shanghai, I think I'd allow most of the day. Some programs do let you use abbreviations and other shortcuts to speed up the process.

So, if you're Chinese, do you hate computers? On the contrary, you think they're great, because the alternative is to write out your damn language longhand. Although educated Chinese pride themselves on their calligraphy, the process does not lend itself to speedy communication, since one Chinese character can have as many as 36 strokes. (Max per English character: four.) You could try a Chinese typewriter, but they're clunky and expensive. A computer with decent Chinese word processing software, in contrast, lets you achieve a reasonable approximation of touch-typing, assuming you use the same program long enough. (Every program is different, needless to say.)

This is just Chinese we're talking about. Japanese, now . . . they say Japanese is *really* complicated. Sad to say, we do not have space to discuss it here. Just get down on your knees and thank G-O-D for the A-B-Cs.

Chinese Characters

Regarding your column on Chinese word processors, you can't really get by with only 3,000 to 4,000 characters [for basic literacy in Chinese]. . . . My own estimate is that a vocabulary of 10,000 to 15,000 characters is required to read ordinary materials without needing a dictionary every few minutes.—James Brock, Honolulu, Hawaii

Although I don't want to split hairs, I feel that one can actually get by with even fewer than "about 3,000 to 4,000" Chinese characters. I recall reading of a study . . . where it was discovered that only a few hundred characters were normally used in Chinese-language newspapers published on Taiwan.—Damien P. Horigan, Honolulu, Hawaii

Damien, meet James. When you guys figure this out, let me know.

From The Straight Dope Message Board

How did the number 69 come to be associated with oral sex?

Pretty straightforward. The head of the six is down, the head of the nine is up. You can figure out the rest.

I think I related before how back before AOL became all-you-can-eat, I took advantage of a free month of service using the screenname "Bermuda969." All of a sudden I began getting messages asking if I was looking for three-way sex.

I still can't figure out what the first "9" is getting except, perhaps, a good back rub.

10

Pillow Talk

Did medieval lords really have the "right of the first night"—that is, the right to be the first to bed the local brides? This figured in the movie Braveheart, *and I know I have seen other references to it. I'm not saying the big shots didn't take advantage, but I have a hard time believing this was a generally accepted custom, much less a law.—Paul S. Piper, Honolulu, Hawaii*

My feeling exactly. It's one thing to have your way with the local maidens. It's something else to persuade society as a whole that this is a cool idea. "Sure, honey, we can get married, but first you have to do the rumba with some old guy with bad teeth." Also, once the element of surprise was lost, don't you think this policy would present some risks? Granted, women were supposed to be the weaker sex and all, but they did know how to fillet fish.

The right of the first night—also known as *jus primae noctis* (law of the first night), *droit du seigneur* (the lord's right), etc.—has been the subject of locker-room humor and a fair amount of scholarly debate for centuries. Voltaire condemned it in 1762, it's a plot device in Beaumarchais' *The Marriage of Figaro*, and various old histories refer to it.

The sixteenth-century chronicler Boece, for example, says that in ancient times the Scottish king Evenus III decreed that "the lord of the ground sal have the maidinhead of all virginis dwelling on the same." Supposedly, this went on for hundreds of years until Saint Margaret persuaded the lords to replace the *jus primae noctis* with a bridal tax.

Not likely. Skeptics point out that 1) there never was any King Evenus, 2) Boece included a lot of other stuff in his account that was clearly mythical, and 3) he was writing long after the alleged events.

The story is pretty much the same all over. If you believe the popular tales, the *droit du seigneur* prevailed throughout much of Europe for centuries. Yet detailed examinations of the available records by reputable historians have found "no evidence of its existence in law books, charters, decretals, trials, or glossaries," one scholar notes. No woman ever commented on the practice, unfavorably or otherwise, and no account ever identifies any female victim by name.

It's true that in some feudal jurisdictions there was something known as the *culagium,* the requirement that a peasant get permission from his lord to marry. Often this required the payment of a fee. Some say the fee was a vestige of an earlier custom of buying off the lord so he wouldn't get physical with the bride.

Similarly, ecclesiastical authorities in some regions demanded a fee before a new husband was allowed to sleep with his wife. Some think this means the clergy once upon a time exercised the right of the first night too. But come on, how many first nights can one woman have? What did these guys do, take a number?

The more likely interpretation is that the *culagium* was an attempt by the nobles to make sure they didn't lose their serfs by marriage to some neighboring lord. The clerical marriage fee, meanwhile, was apparently paid by newlyweds to get out of a church requirement for a three-day precoital waiting period. (You were supposed to pray during this time and get yourself in the proper frame of mind. Guess they figured a leather teddy wouldn't do it.)

Did the *droit du seigneur* exist elsewhere in the world? Possibly in some primitive societies. But most of the evidence for this is pathetically lame—unreliable travelers' accounts and so on.

A few holdouts claim we don't have any definite evidence that the right of the first night *didn't* exist. But I'd say most reputable historians today would agree that the *jus primae noctis*, in Europe anyway, was strictly a male fantasy.

None of this is to suggest that men in power didn't or don't use their positions to extort sex from women. But since when did some creep with a sword (gun, fancy office, drill sergeant's stripes) figure he needed a law to justify rape?

Is there a biological reason for men to feel sleepy after orgasm? My girlfriend says there is some scientific basis for this. If so, is there any hypothesized rationale for this occurrence in terms of human evolution?—Chuck R., Chicago

Before we drag Darwin into it, Chuck, we'd better make sure we have a genuine phenomenon on our hands. It's true everybody thinks men get sleepy after sex. Pioneer sex researcher Alfred Kinsey wrote, "A marked quiescence of the total body is the most widely recognized outcome of orgasm." One might object that the most widely recognized outcome of orgasm is the one you have to put diapers on. Still, when Kinsey goes on about "a [postcoital] calm, a peace, a satisfaction with the world," coupled in some quarters with a desire to set fire to tobacco, most men and, for that matter, most women know what he's talking about. It's just that whereas women see this tranquil state as a chance to cuddle and talk, guys tend to look at it as a cure for insomnia—sometimes literally. When a man over 40 talks about trying to sleep with women, he's not necessarily using a figure of speech.

But let's get down to the physiological facts of the situation. While sex might mellow you out, does orgasm really make men (or anybody) sleepy? The medical literature on the subject is not voluminous, but I did turn up one study conducted, fittingly, by ze French (Brissette et al., 1985—from Quebec, actually). The researchers signed up five male and five female volunteers to engage in sexual activity. This wasn't as much fun as it sounds. Number one, the sexual activity to be engaged in was masturbation. Number two . . . well, let me quote from the report: "At 11:00 P.M., after placement of the electrodes and thermistors, subjects retired to their room and the anal probe was inserted. . . . The anal probe transmitted pressure changes in the anal canal to a transducer connected to a DC amplifier. . . . The use of this anal probe gave an objective account of the orgasm in both men and women." The electrodes and thermistors, meanwhile, recorded heart and respiratory rate. The things one does for science.

Anyway, on successive nights the test subjects performed one of the following procedures: 1) Read "neutral material" while sitting in bed for 15 minutes, "after which the probe was withdrawn and the lights turned out." 2) Masturbate for 15 minutes without reaching orgasm. Yank probe, douse lights. 3) Masturbate for 15 minutes, reach orgasm. Decide you like probe, ask that voltage be turned up. Told to bugger off, experiment over. Results tabulated. Conclusion: sex or the lack of it made absolutely no difference in how soon and how well you slept afterward.

The researchers concede that the experimental design was open to criticism on various grounds, the most telling in my opinion being that it was incredibly stupid. Suppose you were one of the male subjects on night three. Having on the previous night been subjected to a severe case of cyanotic spheroids, you're now lying there postejaculatively in . . . well, let's say you're in a state of disarray. In comes some guy in a white lab coat to roll you over and extract a hot-wired turkey baster from your sphincter ani. Does this put you in a state of mind conducive to sleep? On the contrary, you're expecting them to tell your folks to come take you home from summer camp. So maybe these results shouldn't be taken with 100 percent seriousness. But right now they're all we've got.

What's the Straight Dope on Charles Lutwidge Dodgson, known to millions as Lewis Carroll, and his unusual interest in prepubescent girls? Was he a . . . well . . . you know? What can you tell us about his relationship with Alice Liddell, the real-life inspiration for Alice in Wonderland? And what was going on with those photographs he took, anyway? Does Newt Gingrich know about this?—Paul H. Henry, Lawrence, Kansas

If you're asking whether Lewis Carroll was a . . . well . . . Republican, I confess I do not know. He was shy, eccentric, and seemingly incapable of having a mature relationship with a woman, but that can't be said of all members of the GOP. Newt sure wasn't shy.

But perhaps what you are asking is whether Dodgson was a deve. His interest in little girls was such that he probably would not be the first guy you would think of to put in charge of your daughter's Brownie troop, but for the most part he seems to have been harmless. A lifelong bachelor with a stammer, he was uncomfortable among adults and could relax only with little girls, who were amused by his stories and games.

Dodgson's biggest crush was on Alice Liddell, daughter of a dean at Oxford, where the author of "Jabberwocky" taught mathematics. Dodgson saw her often over a ten-year period but drifted away after she reached puberty—a typical pattern for him. Some believe he asked her parents for permission to marry her and was rebuffed, but it seems out of character, like a proposal from Mister Rogers. Whatever his intentions, on the surface he was always the proper Victorian gent.

Then again, we do have those nude photographs. An enthusiastic amateur photographer, Dodgson took thousands of pictures, many of them portraits of his little friends. Everybody was clothed at first, but in the late 1870s, when Dodgson was in his mid-40s, he tried to shoot some of the girls in the buff—not an easy thing to arrange. He did a few nude studies of young female models and went prospecting among the families of his friends and acquaintances.

In 1879 Dodgson sent several curious letters, republished a while back in *Harper's,* to the family of Andrew Mayhew, an Oxford colleague. He asked permission to take nude photographs of the three Mayhew daughters, ages 6, 11, and 13, with no other adults present. When the parents nixed the idea of no chaperone, Dodgson lost interest. He did succeed in doing nudes of other girls, but usually by agreeing to let their moms hover nearby.

In 1880 Dodgson gave up photography forever. Too much heat? Nobody knows, although around the same time he got flak for kissing one of his girl friends. At any rate, the nude photos and plates were returned to the families of the subjects or destroyed on his death. It was long thought that none survived.

But then four turned up. For this we can thank Morton Cohen, who unearthed the photos and published them in his *Lewis Carroll: A Biography* (1995). One is of a little girl named Evelyn Hatch in a pose that, were Evelyn older or Cecil weirder, would be seductive. As it is, I can imagine Evelyn's parents' thinking: That Rev. Dodgson, he is one amusing fellow. But he'd better keep his mitts to himself.

There's been a lot of talk in the last few years about subliminal advertising, sexual words and phalluses in Disney movies, etc. Another rumor I keep hearing is that a part of the male anatomy was pictured unintentionally in a Sears catalog underwear ad in 1975. Let me put it this way: a penis is peeking out under somebody's boxers. Naysayers claim that advertising photographers scrutinize their work and would never let something like that get by, that it could be just a drawstring. But wouldn't they have noticed something like a drawstring, too? Could it be an intentional joke on the part of a wacky or disgruntled photographer or editor, to make a job taking pictures of undies for Sears more interesting? More important, where can I get a copy of this picture?—Jill Gatwood, Albuquerque, New Mexico

You think getting a picture of a penis is difficult? I get X-rated E-mail spam offering shots of just about every part of the human anatomy you'd care to see, and some you wouldn't. (I haven't actually seen a Web site for appendectomy scar fetishists, but I expect one any day.) Naturally, we at the Straight Dope feel we have to post saucy photos ourselves, just so we can . . . well, when I first started working on this I wrote, "hold our own." But when the topic is the male organ, you definitely have to watch what you say.

Anyway, you'll find the infamous Sears page on our Web site at www.straightdope.com. We've also posted a computer-enhanced 200-percent enlargement for those who can't see anything in the original. Warning: if you can't see anything either, it's not necessarily a sign of an underpowered libido; it may just be your crummy monitor. I've seen the original, and there's definitely something there.

The object in question appeared in the Sears catalog for fall/winter 1975 in a photo of two guys modeling underwear. It's extremely faint; Sears clearly had a lot of customers who scrutinized those underwear ads. (Probably the same people you'd see in the Craftsman section looking at the big tools.) Once you do see it, you don't have much trouble believing it's a penis. A circumcised penis. This last detail is pointed out by Jill, with whom I've communicated via the magic of cyberspace. Jill obviously scrutinizes underwear ads too.

The photo created an uproar at the time, although contrary to popular belief the catalog was not recalled. Sears has consistently denied that you're seeing what you think you're seeing. One explanation for many years was that it's a drawstring, but Sears says not so. Rather, says spokesperson Jan Drummond, it's a blemish that was introduced during the reproduction process. (Cecil's copy editor notes here, "Isn't that how many women would describe a penis?" Everybody wants to get into the act.) Drummond's explanation is easy to believe. No disrespect to Sears, but what with all the bleed-through from adjacent pages, I've seen better printing jobs done with a stamp pad and a potato. Ms. Drummond, though, says the whatsit was introduced at an earlier stage—it's visible on the film used to make the printing plate. She described it as a "hickey," the term used in printing to describe a certain type of defect (honest). Having spent some time in print shops, I don't think that's what it is. But it may well be a water stain.

Of course, one can never entirely rule out the possibility of sabotage. But let's get one thing straight (sorry—*you* try writing a column like this): it's probably not a penis. Ms. Drummond says the same photo ran in the preceding catalog (spring/summer); no penis is visible. She denied my request to visit the Sears archive and inspect this earlier catalog—sometimes in this business one longs for subpoena power. But she says she's personally inspected it and is certain there's nothing there.

I'm confident she's telling the truth, in part because I had the following unworthy thought: it can't be what it looks like because (a) the model's member would have to be at least eight inches long in its detumescent state, and (b) the guy ain't Secretariat. If you've had a chance to look at the photo, don't tell me you didn't think the same thing.

From The Straight Dope Message Board

I can't for the life of me figure out how those "card counters" do so well at blackjack. Every time I count the cards, I come up with 52. What gives?

Chapter **11**

Science News

Is it true cats always land unharmed on their feet, no matter how far they fall?—A D DOO, via America Online

I love this question. I love it because 1) it seems completely wild; 2) it nonetheless appears to have some scientific basis; 3) on examination the scientific basis is open to serious question; and—this is the best part—4) the Teeming Millions figured this all out by themselves. I may be able to retire from this job yet.

Here's the EP version of the story you heard, related to me by AOL user Bmaffitt: "There was a Discovery Channel special on this a while back. The truth is, after a few floors it doesn't really matter [how far the cat falls], as long as the oxygen holds out. Cats have a nonfatal terminal velocity (sounds like a contradiction in terms, but most small animals have this advantage). Once they orient themselves, they spread

out like a parachute. There are cats on record that have fallen 20 stories or more without ill effects. As long as the cat doesn't land on
something pointy, it's likely to walk away."

You're thinking: No freaking way. But the believers trot out a 1987
study from the *Journal of the American Veterinary Medical Association*. Two vets examined 132 cases of cats that had fallen out of
high-rise windows and were brought to the Animal Medical Center, a
New York veterinary hospital, for treatment. On average the cats fell
5.5 stories, yet 90 percent survived. (Many did suffer serious injuries.)

Well, we know cats have exceptional coordination and balance, so
maybe that contributed to the high survival rate. One cat, for example,
is known to have survived a 46-story fall. (It apparently bounced off a
canopy and into a planter.)

But here's the weird part. When the vets analyzed the data they
found that, as one would expect, the number of broken bones and
other injuries increased with the number of stories the cat had
fallen—up to seven stories. Above seven stories, however, the number
of injuries per cat sharply declined. In other words, the farther the cat
fell, the better its chances of escaping serious injury.

The authors explained this seemingly miraculous result by saying
that after falling five stories or so the cats reached a terminal velocity—
that is, maximum downward speed—of 60 miles per hour. Thereafter, they hypothesized, the cats relaxed and spread themselves out
like flying squirrels, minimizing injuries. This speculation is now
widely accepted as fact.

But there's a potential fatal flaw in this argument, which emerged
from a discussion on—I can't suppress a grin—alt.fan.cecil-adams on

the Usenet. (In fairness, the objection may have originally been raised on alt.folklore.urban.)

The potential flaw is this: the study was based only on cats that were brought into the hospital. Clearly dead cats, your basic fell-20-stories-and-looks-like-it-came-out-of-a-can-of-Spam cats, go to the Dumpster, not the emergency room. This may skew the statistics and make falls from great distances look safer than they are.

I called the Animal Medical Center to see if this possibility had been considered. The original authors were long gone, so I spoke to Dr. Michael Garvey, head of the medical department and current expert on "high-rise syndrome."

Dr. Garvey was adamant that the omission of nonreported fatalities didn't skew the statistics. He pointed out that cats that had fallen from great heights typically had injuries suggesting they'd landed on their chests, which supports the "flying squirrel" hypothesis.

I suggested this merely meant that a cat landing in this position had a chance of surviving long enough to be brought into the hospital, whereas cats landing in other positions were so manifestly dead that the hospital was never notified. Dr. Garvey didn't buy it, but said this was a matter about which reasonable people might disagree.

We await the formation of a committee of New York high-rise doormen to compile truly global statistics on the fate of falling cats. Meanwhile, don't believe something just because it was on the Discovery Channel—or, for that matter, in the Straight Dope.

Curiosity Killed The Cat

Back when I was a kid, we used to take the cat up on the roof and toss it off. It was just a one-story house, so the cat didn't have far to fall. That little bugger would spread out his arms and legs and glide on down, just like a flying squirrel. He never seemed to mind it in the least. He'd let us drag him up there again and again. It seems cats have a natural ability to protect themselves from falls. Now, that's science! —Dave, via AOL

No, that's stupidity. I got another note telling about some moron who dropped (a) a cat and (b) a chicken out of a Cessna at 800 feet to see

what would happen. The cat survived. The chicken didn't. While that might seem to validate the flying-squirrel hypothesis, what it really tells me is that the teenage sadists of the world have gotten the idea that cats are immortal, so anything goes. Nonsense. Let's review the facts:

1. Nobody says that cats will survive any fall *uninjured*. Of the 132 cats brought to New York's Animal Medical Center after accidental falls, two-thirds required treatment, and half of that number required lifesaving treatment.
2. The flying-squirrel hypothesis may well explain why *some* cats survive extremely long falls. No one has demonstrated that *all* cats will survive long falls. On the contrary, from anecdotal accounts we know that at least some cats are killed—the deaths just aren't reported.

Cecil's assistant Little Ed got into a big on-line argument with a young fellow who was enamored of the flying-squirrel hypothesis. After Little Ed patiently explained the difference between *some* and *all*, the young fellow conceded Cecil was right to make point number two above.

"But so what if Cecil was right?" the young fellow said by way of a parting shot. (I'm paraphrasing here.) "Cecil's point was boring. The flying-squirrel hypothesis is *interesting*."

OK, fine, it's interesting. The ditz pitching the kitty out of the Cessna thought *that* was interesting. Now, get your hands off that cat.

I am getting married later in the year and to do so must get a blood test. What is the purpose of this? What kind of information could the

government possibly be looking for? Is this test to ensure that Americans aren't running around marrying their kin?—Engaged but Confused in Los Angeles

Got news for you, kid. Premarital blood tests haven't been required in California since 1994. The test used to be required to ensure that you and your betrothed were free of venereal disease, chiefly syphilis. The tests were a holdover from a New Deal–era anti-VD campaign and were once required in virtually all states. But maybe a third have now repealed the requirement, on the grounds that the handful of cases detected doesn't justify the exorbitant expense.

Venereal disease was one of a handful of maladies (tuberculosis was another) that were deemed to have such horrible public-health consequences that they justified compulsory testing and other drastic measures. According to medical historian Allan Brandt (*No Magic Bullet,* 1985), a 1901 study claimed that 80 percent of New York City men had been infected with gonorrhea and 5 to 18 percent had syphilis. These numbers were probably exaggerated (then, anyway), but maybe not by much. In 1909 VD afflicted nearly 20 percent of army recruits and accounted for a third of all sick days. In the 1920s, 500,000 new cases of syphilis and 700,000 cases of gonorrhea were reported each year. Some experts believed VD was more widespread than all other infectious diseases combined.

The first effective treatment for syphilis had been discovered in 1909 but wasn't widely used, partly because of side effects, but also because of reluctance to deal with the subject openly. Moralists viewed the situation with growing alarm, fearing that men would all get the clap from hookers (who, in fact, had high infection rates) and subsequently infect their brides. The women would then pass the disease along to their babies or become sterile, and *poof*—there goes the human race, or at least the white, middle-class part of it. To this day, newborns get eyedrops to prevent eye problems due to sexually transmitted disease. (Maternal gonorrhea at one time accounted for 25 percent of all blindness in the United States.)

During the late 1930s Surgeon General Thomas Parran was able to overcome national squeamishness and crank up an anti-VD crusade similar to that surrounding AIDS 50 years later. One result of his efforts was the requirement of premarital VD testing by the states, starting with Connecticut in 1935.

The only problem with these tests was that they didn't turn up many cases of venereal disease. Even in New York City, that pesthole of promiscuity, the positive rate for syphilis during the first year of compulsory testing was only 1.34 percent. In part that was because many couples sought to avoid the expense by getting their marriage licenses in neighboring states that didn't require testing. And, of course, it's possible the prevalence of the disease was exaggerated. But probably the main reason was that the respectable types who got marriage licenses were at low risk for sexually transmitted disease (or at least for the STDs being tested for).

Some anti-VD measures were more successful. VD testing of pregnant women, for example, greatly reduced the incidence of congenital syphilis. But premarital testing has largely been a waste. A study in California found that of 300,000 persons tested in 1979, just 35 cases of syphilis (0.012 percent) were found—at a cost of $240,000 per case.

The ineffectiveness of premarital VD testing deterred most states from requiring tests for today's sexual scourge, HIV. Only two states, Illinois and Louisiana, enacted premarital HIV testing laws, and both repealed them when, predictably, few new cases turned up. Illinois repealed its syphilis testing requirement at the same time. A lot of people apparently are unaware that California repealed its requirement as well—even the folks at the state Department of Health Services were surprised when we inquired about this. If some local county clerk

196 · TRIUMPH OF THE STRAIGHT DOPE

gives you grief, tell him to look up Assembly Bill 3128, approved by the governor July 15, 1994.

Why The Government Wants Your Blood

In a recent column you advised a young Los Angeleno on the real reason for premarital blood testing. Although you hit the nail on the head about venereal disease, you left out an important fact. Premarital blood tests are done for another reason as well—namely, to test for blood type, including Rh factor.

Rh factor was first isolated from rabbits inoculated with rhesus (hence Rh) monkey blood. It turns out that 85 percent of the population tests positively for the Rh antigen in their red blood cells (i.e., they're Rh-positive). The other 15 percent are Rh-negative. If you are an Rh-negative female and your husband is Rh-positive, as revealed by your premarital blood test, you run the risk of having an Rh-positive child. If so, you would produce antibodies against your own child's blood. The first child might be anemic, and a second or third might well die in utero or soon after birth (erythroblastosis fetalis). If you are planning to have children, it is important to know if you are Rh-positive or -negative so the proper precautions may be taken.—G. Dellaire, Department of Medicine, McGill University, Toronto

Rh testing is not the reason most states require premarital blood tests. According to the most recent list I have, Rh testing is required only in Colorado. No question it's a good idea, though.

When I was in sixth grade in 2972 I remember reports of the discovery of a tenth planet located beyond Pluto. This planet was referred to as "Planet X." I have heard nothing further about it. Are there ten of us in the solar system, or was there a dust mote on the telescope?—Alice in Chicago, via AOL

Um, 2972? You *are* ahead of your time. I'll assume it's a typo, although with AOL users one never knows.

The story of Planet X starts in 1846 with the discovery of Neptune. Neptune was the first planet whose discovery had been predicted based on irregularities in the motion of nearby bodies, in this case Uranus (which in this squeamish age we've agreed to pronounce YOOR-uh-nuss).

Scientists guessed these "perturbations" were due to the gravitation of an unknown planet and calculated where said planet could be found. Sure enough, when astronomers looked in the indicated direction, there was Neptune.

Naturally, all the other astronomers wanted to duplicate this extremely cool feat. As it happened, Neptune's orbit wasn't precisely as predicted. Within days of its discovery one astronomer was speculating about the existence of yet another planet. Many others chimed in with their own predictions in the following decades.

Some of the most famous predictions came from astronomer Percival Lowell, best known for his belief in the canals of Mars. Lowell dubbed the mystery body Planet X. He never found it, but after his death Clyde Tombaugh, an astronomer at Lowell's observatory, did. Or so he thought.

The new planet, dubbed Pluto, jibed pretty well with Lowell's predictions for Planet X. Just one problem. It was way too small to cause the observed perturbations in the orbits of Uranus and Neptune. (We now know Pluto's mass is only 1/500th that of earth.) Tombaugh's find was a result of luck and his own doggedness. Back to the telescopes.

More Planet X predictions surfaced periodically. The one you remember was made in 1972 by an astronomer who shall remain nameless, who predicted a Saturn-size (i.e., huge) planet that took 500 earth years to revolve around the sun and whose orbit was tilted at a cockeyed angle to the earth's. Not surprisingly, within a year other scientists had determined no such planet could exist.

Finally, in 1993, someone recomputed the orbits of Uranus and Neptune using more accurate data gathered by space probes. Guess what? Once you got the slop out of the numbers there weren't any perturbations—never had been. So no Planet X. All that time and brainpower spent on the chase, and at the end there was squat to show for it. I can relate.

In 1996 IBM came out with an ad that made a remarkable claim. It said an IBM scientist and his colleagues had discovered a way to make an object disintegrate in one place and reappear intact in another. Beam me up, Scotty! Was this a publicity stunt? Is it true? They said there was a teleport exhibit on their Web page at http://www.ibm.com/news/ls960202.html and gave a phone number as well. Couldn't get through. Can you?—Charlene McKee, Orleans, Massachusetts

Publicity stunt? What makes you think somebody placing full-page ads in the *New Yorker* could possibly be interested in publicity? The more pertinent question is whether the bit about teleportation is true. The answer is, well, sorta. But don't sell the moped yet.

We look up the ad. After a bit of nonsense about Margit telling her E-mail pal Seiji she's going to teleport him some goulash, the ad says their plans are "a little premature, but we are working on it. An IBM scientist and his colleagues have discovered a way to make an object disintegrate in one place and reappear intact in another. It sounds like magic. But their breakthrough could affect everything from the future of computers to our knowledge of the cosmos."

The IBM Web page refers us to an article titled "Teleporting an Unknown Quantum State via Dual Classical and Einstein-Podolsky-Rosen Channels" by Charles Bennett et al. Ideally you want an article like this to start, "Get two D-cell batteries and some string . . ." However, that's never the way. The abstract begins, "An unknown quantum state . . . can be disassembled into, then later reconstructed from, purely classical information and purely nonclassical Einstein-Podolsky-Rosen (EPR) correlations."

OK, so maybe a practical guide to teleportation was too much to hope for. Still, as we read on, the suspicion forms in our mind that perhaps the ad copywriters didn't read the article before writing the ad, or if they did, didn't understand it. On page 2 Bennett and company write, "It must be emphasized that our teleportation, unlike some science fiction versions, defies no physical laws. In particular, it cannot take place instantaneously. . . . The net result of teleportation is completely prosaic: the removal of [a particle having a certain quantum state] from [one person's] hands and its appearance in [someone else's] hands a suitable time later." In other words, you could accomplish the same thing with Federal Express—except that FedEx lets you transport more than one particle at a time.

Don't get me wrong. Bennett and company's quantum teleportation (Q-TP) is subtle and ingenious (way too subtle and ingenious to explain in a 600-word column—check out their article if you need to know more). But there's no necessary connection between Q-TP and science fiction TP. Q-TP lets you transmit quantum (i.e., unbelievably detailed) information about particles and conceivably a large-scale assemblage of particles (e.g., Captain Kirk) to a remote location. However, unbelievably detailed information may be unnecessary—and if sci-fi teleportation is to be feasible, it damn well better be.

See, the fundamental problem is one of, how shall I say, bandwidth. Physicist Samuel L. Braunstein points out that a fairly coarse scan of the human body (one atomic length in each direction) would require 10^{32} bits of data. Using today's best fiber-optic technology, this would take a hundred million centuries to transmit. Even allowing for technological progress, it's going to be a long time before teleportation as a mode of transportation compares favorably with such none-too-challenging benchmarks as the U.S. mail.

Even if we get over the bandwidth hurdle, consider this. Suppose we could actually sci-fi-TP you somewhere. Even sci-fi writers figure this would entail disintegrating the original and re-creating it elsewhere. The result would be someone who believes she is, and to all appearances would be, you. But is she you—or a copy?

Why are there high tides twice a day when the earth rotates beneath the moon only once a day? In diagrams it appears the moon's gravity causes the earth's oceans to bulge (creating a high tide) not only on the

side toward the moon, but also on the side away from the moon. I've heard some unconvincing explanations for this, including: "the water on the far side is flung away from the earth" (why?); "the moon attracts the earth, and the water on the far side is left behind" (why isn't the water on the far side attracted too?); and "the earth and the moon both revolve around a common point" (I know that, but what does that have to do with the question?). Please help.—Kathleen Hunt, Brookline, Massachusetts

Not to discourage you, Kathleen, but this makes 22 questions from you in three months. Think quality, not quantity. This isn't a scrap drive.

The following homely metaphor is sometimes used to explain why there are two tides: The earth and moon, which are really dual planets, are like two figure skaters spinning around one another while holding hands. Centrifugal force naturally tends to pull them apart, but their clasped hands (i.e., their mutual gravitational attraction) keep them together. Similarly, centrifugal force tends to fling the ocean outward on the side of the earth away from the moon. On the near side, the water is tugged moonward by lunar gravity.

There's just one problem with this explanation. It's wrong. Cecil has consulted with the physics division of the Straight Dope Science Advisory Board and is satisfied that centrifugal force (OK, inertia, if you want to get technical) has nothing to do with why there are two tides.

The real reason is this. The pull of gravity drops off rapidly with distance. Lunar gravity tugs on the side of the earth facing it a *lot*, on the earth itself a *medium* amount, and on the opposite side of the earth relatively *little*. In short, the far-side tide is a result of the moon attracting the earth, leaving the ocean behind. Which, looking back at your letter, I guess you already knew and didn't find convincing. If so, Kathleen, come on. Would I lie to you?

My high school physics teacher gave us this problem once, but I forget what the answer was. Suppose you've got a bullet in one hand and a pistol in the other, aimed so it's perfectly level. You drop the bullet and fire the pistol at the same time. Which bullet hits the ground first?—L., Indianapolis

I know this is a lot of physics for one day, but this one is so twisted you gotta love it. The average mope reasons like this: The dropped bullet falls only a few feet, whereas the fired bullet travels hundreds of yards. Ergo, the dropped bullet hits the ground first. The average mope with a college education (e.g., a physics teacher) is a little more sophisticated. He figures, Hey, the force of the gun propels the fired bullet strictly horizontally. The only *downward* force is gravity, which acts equally on both bullets. Therefore they both hit the ground at the same time. (We assume a vacuum throughout this discussion.)

Then we have the answer given by those who have achieved spiritual awareness as a result of regular reading of the Straight Dope. This may be summarized as follows: It depends. If the fired bullet travels only a short distance, then yes, both bullets hit the ground at the same time. However, if the fired bullet travels far enough, the earth, being round, *curves away from it*. (Remember Newton's first law of motion: moving objects tend to travel in a straight line.) Since the fired bullet has farther to fall, it takes longer to hit the earth, so the dropped bullet hits the ground first.

What's more, if the fired bullet travels fast enough (roughly five miles per second—a practical impossibility given atmospheric friction, but never mind), it goes into orbit around the earth and *never hits the ground at all*. Amazing, no? Try this one out in your next physics class and you'll kill the whole hour, guaranteed.

When will average people feasibly be able to afford a commercial trip into orbit?—Mike, via AOL

What's your idea of average? If it's "people who have $98,000 they can plunk down for a 2½-hour ride in 2001 aboard a spacecraft that isn't even built yet," there's a company that'll take your money right now. It's called Zegrahm Space Voyages, based in Seattle. They probably figure they'll get a lot of business from Microsoft execs cashing out on their stock options.

I had two basic questions when I called up Zegrahm, which made its name offering trips to exotic locales like Antarctica and Botswana: 1) Is this a scam? and 2) what are the chances it will actually, you should pardon the expression, fly? Having talked to Zegrahm vice president Scott Fitzsimmons at length, I'm willing to believe these people are sincere. Whether they'll succeed remains to be seen, but if it were me contemplating the trip I'd definitely have some backup vacation plans.

What Zegrahm and its partners propose (design is being overseen by a company called Vela Technology Development) is an update of the old X-15 rocket plane from the 1950s and '60s. As with the X-15, which was launched from a B-52, two vehicles are involved. The Space Cruiser is a vaguely Space Shuttle–like craft that will carry six passengers and two pilots. It'll be borne aloft by the Sky Lifter, a larger aircraft along the lines of the British Vulcan bomber.

The Cruiser will remain suborbital, reaching an altitude of 100 kilometers. The passengers will be weightless for only about 2½ minutes, but they'll be able to float around the cabin, and one supposes they'll experience a reasonable approximation of orbital space flight. (Possible drawback: when the astronauts did weightless training in a jet transport flying in a parabolic arc similar to that proposed for the Space Cruiser, they nicknamed it the Vomit Comet.) Interestingly, the Cruiser's rockets will burn a combination of propane and nitrous oxide, the well-known dental anesthetic. So even if the rest of project goes bust, the fuel will be good for a few laughs.

One obvious problem is that although the projected launch date is December 1, 2001, Zegrahm and Vela have yet to start building the two vehicles. Engineering work is complete, Scott says, and a rocket engine has been tested. He optimistically believes construction can be completed in a year and a half, allowing another year and a half for certification by the Federal Aviation Administration.

All of this is expected to cost about $150 million. Scott wouldn't say how much money they'd raised yet, but my guess is it's a lot closer to $1 than $150 million. Not to worry, he says; negotiations are under way with unnamed heavyweights. I was led to believe these were established aerospace or aircraft companies for whom the development of a suborbital craft would have potentially profitable spin-offs—for example, for long-distance commercial air travel from New York to L.A., say, or New York to Tokyo. Scott thinks (well, hopes) something may pop soon.

On the face of it the economics of commercial passenger space flight don't add up. Even at a hundred grand a head, the proposed spacecraft would have to make 250 voyages to recover the development cost, and that's allowing nothing for operating expenses. Sure, there might be some money in spin-offs, but supersonic craft such as the Concorde have been less than a resounding financial success.

What seems to keep the whole thing going is the surprisingly widespread conviction that passenger-carrying commercial spacecraft are an idea whose time has come. The X Prize Foundation, backed by business leaders in St. Louis, is offering $10 million to the first private venture to carry passengers into space. (You have to do it at least twice, to prove it wasn't a fluke.) The foundation has already raised half the prize money; author Tom Clancy pitched in $100,000. So far 15 teams including Zegrahm have registered their interest, many with considerable aerospace expertise.

There's a space-hungry public out there, too. Scott says Zegrahm has had inquiries from 6,000 prospective passengers in 42 countries, and 40 true believers have put down all or part of the $98,000 fare. (There's a $5,000 minimum deposit, in case you're a little short this week.)

Will they get this thing off the ground? I'd say the chances of it happening by December 1, 2001, are pretty slim. (If there's a delay of more than a year, the Zegrahm passengers can get their money back.) But someday, who knows? Twenty years ago I scoffed to think I'd ever be balancing my checkbook on a personal computer, and guess what I do it on now.

From The Straight Dope Message Board

Subj: Amusement Park Barf
From: GFHH
This is gross, I know, but since the town I live in is having its Labor
Day carnival this weekend, I got to thinking. How often do people
throw up while on the puke-o-whirl, or whatever, all over everyone
else?

Isn't walking around a carnival or amusement ride park dangerous?
Besides all the junk food, aren't the pedestrians fair game for airborne
barfers?

From: JILLGAT
Wow. Finally a question I have had personal experience with. I was
once the victim of an airborne barfer. It was on one of those Ferris
wheels with the little cages that roll you upside down (what was I
thinking?). It stopped to let someone get off, and while it was still, the
guy above me barfed and it dripped through the cage all over me. Not
like there was anywhere I could go to get away from it, either. Amazing what we will pay money to do.

From: LilethSC
As a child, I once puked on the "Hustler" after eating lasagna. The
same weekend, my friend puked on the "Salt and Pepper Shaker,"
which I think is the same ride that JILLGAT had an experience with.
One year, my (different) friend was on the "Rotor," (the one where
you stick onto the wall when the floor drops), and a girl puked, sending vomit everywhere to stick onto the walls. In that situation, you cannot escape, and dare not scream. These all had dire consequences to
the fellow riders.

From: Toy Drone
Not a puking story, but . . .
When I was about 14 I went to the local amusement park with my
dad and my four-year-old sister. It was summertime, and I was wearing
baggy "jams"-type shorts, as was the style then (circa 1985). The only
cash that I had handy, and therefore brought along, was a roll of quar-

ters which I had gotten for returning a bunch of soda cans to the market earlier that day. Okay: baggy shorts, roll of quarters. I go on the Rotor while Dad and Sis waited. The other six or seven people on the ride were all drunken college-age kids. The ride starts, my body and clothes are pinned to the wall, leaving the outline of this . . . this . . . this cylindrical form—of the quarters—on my upper thigh. The college kids across from me were hysterical, and I couldn't figure out what was so funny until one guy took pity on me and told me, "Don't worry about it; we've all been there . . . It used to happen to me a lot before I could control it."

I was totally embarrassed and unable to explain or convince them that it was indeed a roll of coins.

Chapter 12

Animal Stories

We request your wisdom to investigate a story (fact or fiction) regarding exploding mosquitoes. Many years ago I was told that when a

mosquito is engaged in dinner one should flex or tighten the muscle [of one's body] in the general vicinity. This would trap the hapless female, along with her proboscis, causing her to overfill and explode. Recently I read an article on the same subject, with the only exception being one should pull taut the human skin around the offending wench, which would also trap her, causing her the same fate as fable number one. Any insight from the Straight Dope would be appreciated.—Louis Oniga, via the Internet

Some might say we're dwelling excessively on the subject of EFOs (exploding flying objects), but I feel this question has been shamefully neglected in the popular press. First thing we did was review the scientific literature. This consisted of going down to the drugstore and getting a copy of the August 1997 *Discover* magazine, which contains the article you undoubtedly saw, headlined "Why Mosquitoes Suck." Sounds like our kind of journalism. Unfortunately, most of the article was about how mosquitoes may be attracted to your body by the same odor found in Limburger cheese, whereas exploding mosquitoes, a topic that truly elevates the human spirit, gets kissed off in 3.5 paragraphs—which, moreover, do not resolve the question! I quote:

"Here's the trick: Once a mosquito has landed and begun feeding, you stretch the skin taut on either side of it. *Supposedly*, if you're deft, you can trap the proboscis in your skin in midfeed. Stuck in the blood vessel, unable to pull out, its anticoagulants working overtime to keep its blood meal coming, the mosquito sucks until it pops.

"*Maybe* this method of entrapment works. *Maybe* it works only for small boys. *Maybe* it's just a stupid pest trick or one of those urban legends that shouldn't be put to the test" (my emphasis).

"Maybe"! "Supposedly"! What kind of baloney is that? Our job as journalists is to ascertain the facts! Although there *is* such a thing as delegating responsibility. I sent out a bulletin to the Straight Dope Science Advisory Board asking for volunteers to have the blood sucked out of their bodies. The Teletypes fell silent. After some moments the Colorado division inquired whether it would be possible to substitute different bodily fluids. Denied. Finally, we got this dispatch from Lileth:

"No need to try; I've done this many times. (I am easily bored.) It's cool, because you can see its belly filling up. This takes a lot of patience, and nerves of steel, because it takes a while, and is kinda un-comfortable. Anyway, if you leave the muscle tensed enough, she can-not pull out, and then she—well, explodes is a little graphic. Ruptures, maybe? It's not that gruesome, but it is strangely satisfying."

I cabled back: "IF YOU TENSE OTHER MUSCLES ARE OTHER CRITTERS UNABLE TO PULL OUT?" This was not well received. Other members of the panel were blunter. "Lil is lying," commented the ever-tactful JillGat. "Or she's recounting what she heard her neighbor's son's roommate's sister told her." Bitter words ensued. The term "pie hole" was used. (I didn't ask.) This was fol-lowed by a period of alarums and excursions during which the follow-ing facts emerged:

- The female members of the SDSAB did all the work, while the men didn't accomplish squat. (CK says he tried, but no mosqui-toes would bite him. Sure.) We note that only female mosqui-toes drink blood, so maybe there was some kind of sisterhood thing going on here.
- Katherine trapped some skeeters by stretching the skin. They ruptured rather than exploded, but good enough for me.
- Songbird apparently got an entire concert audience to try this. (One assumes it was some kind of John Cage deal and they thought it was part of the performance.) One participant said the mosquito "swoll up so big I could see his brand."
- Iowa State University entomologist John VanDyk, to whom Lileth appealed for support, confirmed the thing could be done.

OK, it can be done. The unanswered question is why you would do it. Looking at the big picture, you wouldn't call this a cost-effective method of mosquito abatement, and the entertainment value of watching a mosquito leak has got to be down there with watching your sunburn peel. But if it helps you pass the time on a dull summer eve-ning, have at it.

Wait a sec. The Teletypes are clattering again. It's JYDog from Hoboken: "This disturbs me. Are we doing tapeworms next?"

Fine, Dog. Be a pup. But when I want volunteers for sex in space, don't let me see *you* at the front of the line.

I've just begun reading your latest book, The Straight Dope Tells All. *On page 2, while ruminating on the subject of "questions . . . that give you pause," you write, "The other day someone writes in and says, 'If making a robot limb is so hard but other types of machines are easy, how come no animal species has ever evolved wheels?' Had to think about that for a while." You then go on to answer a completely unrelated question. Could I trouble you to answer the question you were asked?—Marie Hansen, Saint Augustine, Florida*

At first I didn't answer this question because I thought it was too, you know, out there. Then I thought, Twenty-five years I've been doing this, and I'm worrying about being out there *now*?

For starters, let's concede the original writer's premise. Robot limbs that faithfully duplicate animal motion are a design nightmare. Coordinating multiple limbs, maintaining balance—if you think that's easy, try it after you've had a few brewskis. Remember the walking war machines in the Star Wars movies? One reason they were so striking is that no one would ever make such machines in real life. We use wheels for our vehicles because rolling is so simple. Why doesn't nature?

You might say: Because it's impossible. How would such a wheel evolve? Many intermediate steps would be required, but until the proto-wheel became functional (semi-techie talk coming up here), it would be useless baggage offering no selective advantage.

Just one problem. Some critters already *have* evolved wheels, sort of. Take the mother-of-pearl moth, *Pleurotya ruralis*. While in the larval stage, this bug is generally content to amble along in the we'll-get-there-when-we-get-there manner of all caterpillars. However, when sufficiently startled, *P. ruralis* hoists itself into a wheel shape and rolls out of harm's way—up to five full revolutions at 40 times its normal walking speed. (OK, so I previously denied there were hoop snakes. Who said anything about hoop caterpillars?)

You're not impressed. "Armadillos, tumbleweeds, freaking *rocks* roll," you say. "What I want to see is a creature with a wheel and *axle.*"

Coming right up. The bacterium *Escherichia coli*, among others, moves by spinning whiplike filaments called flagella like tiny propellers. The typical flagellum is rotated up to several hundred times per second by what is basically an organic electric motor. We know it spins (rather than, say, twisting back and forth like a washing machine agitator) because researchers glued down an *E. coli* flagellum and the critter's body spun around like an eggbeater. If this thing isn't a wheel, it's pretty darn close. For an illustration, see:
id-www.ucsb.edu/fscf/library/origins/graphics-captions/flagellum.html.

(Note: This illustration is used to support a creationist argument about "irreducible complexity." Pay this no mind.)

You object: "Who cares about a germ? A more complex creature couldn't evolve the wheel. Every time the thing turned, the nerves and blood vessels serving it would get hopelessly twisted." Science writer Stephen Jay Gould makes essentially this argument in his book *Hen's Teeth and Horse's Toes.*

But this may not be an insurmountable obstacle. A flesh-and-blood wheel might use the umbilical hookup found on some merry-go-rounds. Tape one end of a piece of ribbon to a tabletop and the other to the bottom of a compact disc. Turn the CD over so that the ribbon drapes over the side. Now move the CD so that it "orbits" the ribbon clockwise, at the same time rotating the disc clockwise, two rotations per orbit. (Not the easiest thing to explain without diagrams, but think of it as an IQ test.) The wheel turns, but the ribbon doesn't twist.

Would it be easy for a living wheel to evolve something along these lines? Maybe not, but who's to say it's impossible?

"I give up," you say. "Why *didn't* animals evolve wheels?" Best guess: no interstates. Wheels are fine if you've got roads but next to useless on rough terrain. For quick starts, stops, turns, climbing, etc., legs are hard to beat. (For more, see McGeer, "Principles of Walking and Running," in *Advances in Comparative and Environmental Physiology*, volume 11, 1992.) We've got plenty of roads now, though, and natural selection presumably continues apace, for us as well as our forest friends. Aeons hence, who knows? There may be a whole new meaning for the expression "Hey, nice wheels."

Many people have tried to convince me chocolate is toxic to dogs. I even heard a news report warning people to keep dogs out of the Halloween candy for that reason. However, my four dogs have stolen chocolate cakes, pies, and candy bars without ill effects. What gives?
—Jason Eshleman, Berkeley, California

Either you're in serious denial—the mutts, they moved much lately?—or you and they got lucky. Chocolate is the third most common cause of poisoning in dogs. Certain chemicals in chocolate, notably caffeine and theobromine, can cause erratic heartbeat and in large enough doses can kill your pup. While you're getting used to that idea, consider this: the second most common cause of canine poisoning (after rat and mouse poison) is ibuprofen, the well-known pain reliever. Dogs apparently love the smell and taste, so they chew through the bottles, eat the contents, vomit their guts out, and die. ODing on

chocolate and Advil might seem nutty to us, but it's pretty serious to the dogs.

Sick Of Chocolate

I was intrigued by your column on chocolate poisoning in dogs, but don't you think we have an overeating problem here rather than one of poisoning per se? You mention a toxic threshold of two ounces of milk chocolate per kilo of body weight. For my Jenny, who weighs 20 kilos (44 pounds), that's 40 ounces of chocolate! Let's put the issue in human terms. I'm a big boy at 100 kilos. If I ate 200 ounces (12.5 pounds) I think I'd get mighty sick, and I don't think we could blame it on the chocolate.

By the way, what the hell is theobromine and what does it do?
—Roger Strukhoff, via the Internet

You ever watch your dog eat? Dogs will make pigs of themselves if they get unlimited access to a food they like. Vets at the National Animal Poison Control Center say it's not uncommon for a 10- to 15-pound dog to eat a pound of chocolate, wrappings and all. The bigger breeds, proportionally speaking, are almost as bad.

It's true that at extreme doses the sheer volume of fatty food can cause problems such as pancreatitis, which is often the culprit when a dog gets sick after eating garbage. But chocolate alone is plenty toxic. This is more apparent in the concentrated forms of chocolate. I cited the toxic threshold for milk chocolate because, being sweet, it's what dogs gorge on most often. But where milk chocolate contains 65 milligrams of caffeine and theobromine per ounce, semisweet chocolate contains 165 milligrams and baking chocolate has 300 to 400. A dog who eats a package of baking chocolate isn't necessarily overeating but could still wind up dead.

Theobromine is one of a class of chemical compounds called methylxanthines, which also include caffeine and theophylline (found in tea). They're all stimulants and not good for your pooch (or for you, for that matter) in excess.

In cartoons bulls are always depicted with rings through their noses. Being a city kid whose idea of farm life mostly comes from watching Green Acres, *I have never had the opportunity to inspect a bull up close. Do they really have nose rings? If so, why? I have a hard time believing it's all due to teenage rebellion.—Phil Gemperl, Elk Grove Village, Illinois*

Well, I guess I better not try that line of humorous development, then. How about this: the ring represents, not rebellion, but . . . discipline! It does, too. You've heard the expression "led around by the nose"? You were thinking maybe this was just a figure of speech? Uh-uh. Even if you're a mighty hunk of rock 'em, sock 'em bullflesh, if some little slip of a farm girl comes along and hooks a rope to your nose ring, you're going to go where she wants you to go. Male humans understand this concept too, even if what you're being led around by is not necessarily the nose.

Now, your animal rights type of person might think putting a ring in a bull's nose is cruel. I'm not saying it's a day at the racetrack. Usually it's done when the critter is six to eight months old. You put the bull in a restraining device called a head gate, then you get a long pointed steel rod and possibly some local anesthetic. The anesthetic is for the bull, of course, but I think if I were about to pound a nail through some bull's schnozz I'd want a little stiffener for myself, too. The ring, which is brass, can be as big as six ounces and three inches in diameter for larger bulls. (There's a hinge in it, in case you were wondering how they got it on.) So we're definitely talking a major fashion statement.

The question is whether it bugs the bulls. My personal feeling is no, because not every bull gets a ring. It's reserved for animals that are going to be handled a lot, typically those shown in livestock exhibitions or else used for breeding. So a ring, to a bull, means: 1) I'm a stud, 2) I'm dangerous, and 3) I look good. You think he's going to be ticked?

Every so often I read about certain prehistoric reptiles not being true dinosaurs. A trip to the encyclopedia yielded the statement that at the same time there were dinosaurs there were also pterosaurs, crocodiles, etc., who were not dinosaurs. But it never actually defined what a dinosaur was. So what exactly differentiates a dinosaur from other lizards?—Rob Wintler, Santa Monica, California

I understand your confusion. When I was a kid my idea of a dinosaur was that it was big, ugly, and dead. Not the most scientific definition, but no book or museum exhibit ever offered a better one. Now I know why: until the 1970s paleontologists believed, in their heart of hearts, that there weren't *any* true dinosaurs. "Dinosaur" was an informal term used to describe two distinct groups of animals, the Saurischia and the Ornithischia. The two groups were related, but

they were equally related to the crocodiles and the pterosaurs (flying reptiles), all of whom were thought to have descended from a common ancestor. There was no real justification for saying tyrannosaurus (a saurischian) and stegosaurus (an ornithischian) were dinosaurs but a pterodactyl wasn't. Nevertheless, the term "dinosaur" had been around for a long time and the public had gotten used to it. So a definition of sorts evolved: dinosaurs were (a) landbound but (b) nonflying (c) reptiles who (d) lived between 230 and 65 million years ago and (e) had upright legs like mammals rather than splayed-out legs like lizards. But the definition was arbitrary, and scientists knew it. So they didn't go out of their way to explain it to anybody else.

Just as well. Though the old definition still turns up in books, it's pretty much out the window. For one thing, many experts now agree modern birds descended from saurischians—in short, birds are dinosaurs. This kills (b) and (d) above. A few heretics say dinosaurs weren't reptiles either, which shoots (c). Definition-wise, you may conclude, we're back to big, ugly, and dead.

Not to worry. A new, and this time scientifically grounded, definition of dinosaurs has emerged. Having reexamined the fossils in light of a relatively new approach to classification called cladistics, paleontologists have decided the Saurischia and Ornithischia were more closely related than previously thought and together constitute the Dinosauria, a true order—that is, they and only they were descended from some yet undiscovered Big Mama Dinosaur, their common ancestor.

Unfortunately, that's not going to help you explain to Junior why some critters are dinosaurs and others aren't. In the inevitable way of science, the experts haven't worked out all the details. For example, the majority view at the moment is that pterosaurs weren't dinosaurs because they split off from the protodinosaurian lineage before the Big Mama Dinosaur appeared on the scene. However, Robert Bakker, whose brilliant but controversial work has done much to shake up orthodox paleontology, argues to the contrary—that pterosaurs descended from Big Mama and so really are dinosaurs. The fossil record is too spotty for the question to be settled now, but lots of folks are out digging, and new specimens and species are discovered all the time. The question probably won't be settled in time for you to explain it to your kids, but maybe they'll be able to explain it to theirs.

In the meantime, let 'em chew on this. Pterosaurs flew. Birds fly. Birds probably are descended from dinosaurs. Pterosaurs maybe are dinosaurs. However . . . birds didn't descend from pterosaurs. What's more, bats didn't descend from either one. In other words, the ability to fly, that most magical of nature's gifts, evolved among the vertebrates not just once, not twice, but three times. Don't know about you, but I say: huh.

From The Straight Dope Science Advisory Board

Why is Popeye's nemesis sometimes called Brutus, and other times called Bluto?—Mike Hutson

The short answer: lawyers. For the long answer, we need to look at some history.

E. C. Segar was assigned to draw Thimble Theater for King Features Syndicate in 1919. Popeye was introduced in 1929, and quickly became the protagonist. Bluto, introduced in 1932, was one of many villains Popeye faced, but had the good fortune to appear in the strip at the time that Max Fleischer, riding the success of Betty Boop, made the decision to animate the strip. The first cartoon, "Popeye the Sailor" (1933), featured Bluto as the heavy (with a cameo by Betty Boop herself), in the now-familiar "Bluto harasses Olive until Popeye, under the influence of spinach, whomps his butt and saves the day, then sings his song" formula.

Forward to 1956. Fleischer Studios, later Famous Studios (under the auspices of Paramount Pictures), having produced 234 films, began to realize that they had really played out the formula. They decided to cease production, but, trying to squeeze some blood from the Popeye stone, sold the syndication rights to Associated Artists Productions. To their amazement, the TV ratings went through the roof in most major markets. King Features, which owned the print rights to Popeye et al., did not make any money from the syndication of the Popeye films, so they decided the best way to capitalize on Popeye's TV popularity was to produce a new series of cartoons, and fast. In 1960–61, King Features produced 220 new shorts, in five separate studios. In these new cartoons, the tall, heavy villain with the beard was called Brutus.

Why? Well, King did some sloppy research. They were operating under the misapprehension that Bluto was created for the Fleischer cartoons, and that Paramount had exclusive rights to the name. The first King cartoons, in fact (e.g., "Barbecue for Two," 1960), had the character referred to only as "neighbor." Hastily, they issued a press release, claiming they were "going back to the original . . . in the first newspaper comics the villain was Brutus." False, as we've seen. In any case, it was soon decided that Brutus was actually a whole new character, and his appearance and demeanor were altered, albeit not enough that anyone would notice.

Brutus was around for only two years onscreen. When Hanna-Barbera produced "The All-New Popeye Show" in 1978, the character's name reverted back to the original Bluto. It remained so for the short-lived "Popeye and Son," 1987–88. And, of course, in the Robin Williams film *Popeye* it was Bluto, not Brutus. In print, Brutus lingered for some time, primarily under the direction of Segar apprentice Bud Sagendorf, who drew the strip, comic books, and designs for merchandise until 1986. Bill London, who took over from Sagendorf, preferred Bluto, but sometimes reverted back to Brutus, even within the confines of a single story (cf. "Witch Hunt," 1992).

Really, a fascinating tale, even if it is ultimately the result of boneheadedness. As an aside, most aficionados think of the King episodes as hastily thrown together, and inferior in quality to the earlier Fleischer (now Associated Artists Productions) films. In other words, if you've got a Brutus episode, it's probably not top of the line, but if you're seeing Bluto—now, that's good watchin'! For further reading, see *Popeye: An Illustrated History*, by Fred Grandinetti, 1994.

—*SDStaff Ian*
Straight Dope Science Advisory Board

Chapter **13**

The Marketplace Of Ideas

The other day at work we were sitting around (on our coffee break, of course) telling stories about our middle-school days. We discovered that although we grew up in different parts of the country (Atlanta and Dallas), the students in both our middle schools believed you could tell the quality of a necktie by the number of golden threads running through the lining inside.

When we graduated to high school and our parents began to equip us with nicer neckwear, we noticed that some expensive ties such as Hermes and older Brooks Brothers models did contain the much-sought-after golden stripes, confirming our beliefs. However, other quality ties, such as newer Brooks Brothers and Perry Ellis, were stripeless.

Is there any basis for the belief that gold threads mean quality? Or

have we been prying open perfectly good ties all these years for noth-
ing?—Paul White, Wally Ingram, Austin, Texas

This is what guys talk about nowadays? Whatever happened to cars, sports, and girls? Contrary to common belief, the number of gold stripes in a tie's inner batting (the "interlining") does not indicate its quality. We might have guessed this. You really think a manufacturer would use a lining proclaiming that it made crummy ties?

Gold stripes indicate that the lining 1) was made by the Ack-Ti Lining company of New York City, the world's largest maker of interlinings and holder of the gold stripe trademark; and 2) contains some wool. Wool's resiliency helps the tie hold its shape and shed wrinkles hanging in the closet overnight.

The number (as opposed to the mere presence) of gold threads indicates not the quality but the *weight* of the interlining. One stripe indicates the lightest material, six stripes the heaviest. Tie makers generally use light interlinings with heavy "shells" (the outer part of the tie) and heavy interlinings with light shells. This ensures that ties of varying materials all have roughly the same "hand"—i.e., bulk or feel.

Years ago Ack-Ti was quite successful in promoting the idea that gold stripes = wool = quality, and Joe Citizen naturally but erroneously concluded the more stripes the better. Interlinings without gold threads aren't necessarily bad; they may simply have been made by a different manufacturer (or else they're one of Ack-Ti's nonwool varieties).

So now you're asking: If the gold stripes are no guide, what does indicate a tie's quality? While I haven't made a detailed study of the subject, my guess is that if the tie has little lights that spell out "SHRINERS," this is not a good sign. One might, I suppose, deduce that a tie with a light shell (silk, say) *and* a light interlining was on the cheesy side, but even that's not certain because of the trend toward ties with a lighter hand, which make a smaller knot. My advice is to check with the one font of wisdom that's never let you down. If Mom's in Vegas this weekend, you can always fall back on *Esquire* magazine, America's main textbook on the art of manliness. The March 1988 issue covers the topic in abundant detail.

What is the meaning of PEZ?—NgCarolyn, via AOL

Glad you put it that way, Carolyn. Your unimaginative type of person might have asked, "What do the letters PEZ stand for?" The answer to which is, they're an abbreviation of the German Pfefferminz, peppermint. Excuse me while I stifle a yawn. But the meaning of PEZ—whoa! Give me a minute and I'll drag in Plato, deconstructionism, and the World Bank.

The PEZ story is one of triumph over unexpected setbacks. It all started in the 19th century, when Eduard Haas, an Austrian doctor, invented a baking powder to lighten up the leaden baked goods of the day. But he was unable to capitalize on this discovery, writes PEZ historian David Welch, because, "as a result of medical experiments upon himself with the then up-and-coming injections," he died. Yow. Unexpected setback number one.

Setback number two occurred soon after: Son Eduard II had to drop out of med school for financial reasons. (One suspects this may have been related to setback number one.) Instead, he went into the wholesale grocery business. Wisely avoiding freelance medical experiments, he pioneered in preweighing and packaging goods. His business thrived.

By and by, Eduard III arrived. As a teenager in the World War I era he mixed up baking powder according to Grandpa's recipe and sold it in Dad's shop. Continuing the family tradition of innovation, he advertised the stuff in the newspaper, an uncommon practice at the time. Sales took off.

You're wondering when I'm going to get to PEZ. Patience, I'm building up to a big finish. Ed III liked peppermints. In the 1920s he and a chemist came up with a cold-pressing process to permit peppermints to be made inexpensively. Another innovation—we owe so much to these guys—was to make the candies rectangular so they could be more readily machine wrapped. PEZ was born. Marketed as an alternative to smoking, or at least a good way to disguise tobacco breath, the candies were a hit.

At first PEZ was sold in pocket-size tins. But in the late 1940s the Haas company introduced the "PEZ box," a little plastic gadget that dispensed candies one at a time. The dispensers were unadorned, looking something like a disposable lighter.

In the early 1950s Haas decided it was time to introduce North America to PEZ. Here we get to setback number three. In Europe PEZ had been marketed as a sophisticated adult treat. Unfortunately the New World, and in particular the United States, suffered from a lack of sophisticated adults. The product went nowhere. Casting about for a new strategy, the head of PEZ's U.S. operations, Curtis Allina, proposed marketing PEZ to kids, with new flavors and, more important for future collectibles connoisseurs, new kid-oriented designs for PEZ dispensers. Old Man Haas reluctantly agreed. The first new dispensers, introduced in 1955, were the Santa Claus and Space Trooper models. Sales were huge. Haas was mortified, but since he was making millions, I guess he coped.

Santa and the Trooper, as well as the PEZ Space Gun, introduced the following year, were "full-bodied" designs, with the dispenser fully enclosed by the toy. (The Space Gun ejected PEZ candies when you pulled the trigger.) But full-bodied designs were a pain to manufacture, and subsequent dispensers in the North American market featured decorative heads only.

Hundreds of designs—no one is quite sure how many—have been issued over the years, including Mickey Mouse, Bullwinkle, and Popeye. (My personal fave, issued during the psychedelic '60s, was a hand holding an eyeball.) Unauthorized knockoffs include Hitler, Pee-wee Herman, members of the band Kiss, even—ahem—a penis. One blushes for Papa Haas.

One last setback. Peppermints had always been nearest to Ed III's heart. Even after new flavors were introduced in the mid-50s, peppermint was still part of the mix, along with lemon, orange, anise, eucalyptus, lime, and chlorophyll. (Yeah, I'd forgotten about chlorophyll too. Kind of a minty flavor.) But despite being made with the world's finest peppermint oil, the peppermint flavor—the source of the PEZ name, don't forget—stank up the marketplace and was soon withdrawn.

PEZ Candy, which is now independent of the Austrian company and sells two billion PEZ candies annually in the United States alone, recently reintroduced peppermint in hopes that the public had grown sophisticated enough to appreciate an adult PEZ. PEZ Candy president Scott McWhinnie tells me they even make non-character-headed dispensers for it. In the land of Beavis and Butt-head, appealing to mature tastes is always a dangerous proposition. But I guess you gotta dream.

In your book The Straight Dope *you state that Coca-Cola will dissolve aluminum. My question is this: How is it that this beverage is sold in aluminum cans without oxidizing them?*—PARACELSUS, *via AOL*

According to Coke, the cans are "coated with a very thin layer of a type of light, food-grade plastic material approved by the FDA." This prevents the highly corrosive contents from dissolving the containers. The unanswered question is, What keeps them from dissolving you?

I have never understood why Circus Peanuts (orange, gooey, diabetic coma-inducing, peanut-shaped candy) are still available. I have never known anyone who actually likes this candy, and I have asked everyone I know. So, Cecil, can you give me a little information about who invented this candy treat, why they are colored orange, and any other interesting tidbits you could provide?—Margaret Husfelt, Houston, Texas

Cecil has mixed feelings about this. On the one hand, it's not like we're trying to put second-tier candy makers out of business. On the other hand, if you've sampled much Brand X candy, you can see why this stuff is no threat to Snickers. Based on our informal survey, consumer reaction to Circus Peanuts falls into three categories:

1. Fear and loathing. Sample comments: "Ewwwww! I tried one once. It was like eating a dead finger." "They taste like they're stale even when they're fresh." "Like orange-flavored Styrofoam." "I think they are the horror that is the circus, that flat tin taste of fear and clowns and little lost children amid the cotton candy stink and the piles of elephant doo-doo and the clamor of the midway and the tinny sound of the circus band endlessly wheezing its way through yet another soulless circus fanfare." You get the idea. My assistant Jane found that the few stray Circus Peanut molecules escaping from an unopened package made her gag.
2. Grudging acceptance. Sample comments: "Yeah, I like them. When they get hard enough you can use them for building material." "It wouldn't be my first pick, but if there was a bowlful at Grandma's, I'd take a couple." Cecil personally falls into this category. Having done this job 25 years, I can put up with anything.
3. Don't like 'em, but have an older/younger relative who thinks they're great. Sample comment: "The only reason I would buy them is for my nieces and nephews. I could have them in the house without temptation."

No one we heard from would admit to a personal enthusiasm (as opposed to tolerance) for Circus Peanuts. Wait, I take that back. We did get this comment: "Circus Peanuts! Nature's perfect food!" But I wouldn't take that too seriously; the guy is obviously sick.

Despite a public response that can charitably be described as tepid, Circus Peanuts are available from several companies. In other words, people compete to sell them! So apparently what we've got here is a product that survives not because anybody is genuinely fond of it, but because less than 100 percent of the populace is totally repelled. Strange, but people have used the same principle to become president of the United States.

Circus Peanuts are a traditional candy that's been around since the nineteenth century. Until the advent of polyethylene packaging in the 1940s they were sold in bulk at the penny-candy counter. For some reason they were considered a seasonal product, available chiefly in the spring. This might explain their somewhat dense consistency. If you're trying to sell a bulk candy that's going to be sitting in the bin for months, you want something with the shelf life of a brick.

What accounts for Circus Peanuts' unusual taste and appearance? Even the makers of the product can't explain it. Here's the sum total of what Spangler Candy, "a producer of superior Marshmallow Circus Peanuts," has to say on the subject: "Over the years the best-selling item has been orange in color, banana in flavor, and peanut in shape."

Peanut Lovers

I just read your column about Circus Peanuts. In all seriousness, I happen to like Circus Peanuts. I really do. I'm not kidding. Just thought you should know that there was someone in the world who actually likes the things.—Brian, via the Internet

I wholeheartedly (and proudly) love Circus Peanuts! Can't keep them in the house. Can't say there is a rational reason why, but stale or fresh (not that you really can tell the difference), I can't get enough of them.—Christopher Leeds, assistant professor, Rush University, Chicago

I truly and honestly like Circus Peanuts. Circus peanuts are yummy. Mmmm, Circus Peanuts. Good, good, good. I seem to be the only person willing to admit my enjoyment of the orange banana things (I know not what they are, nor do I care), thus I must defend them when they are under such an attack as was waged in your column. I do not eat them very often, but since reading your column I have developed a craving. Mmmm.—Mary K., Chicago

Hand me a plate with a Godiva chocolate, a Dove bar, and a half-dozen Circus Peanuts to choose from and I'll take the third.—Mark Furlong, via the Internet

I'll be damned.

I guess I shouldn't be surprised. If Marv Albert gets his kicks dressing in women's underwear, what's so weird about liking Circus Peanuts?

Don't get me wrong. As I said before, I'm not one of those people who gag at the mere thought of Circus Peanuts. I've eaten them without throwing up. But to say that you are genuinely fond of this candy . . . I dunno. I think it bespeaks a serious mental disturbance.

Granted, it's a mental disturbance that's widely shared. We got letters from dozens of people proclaiming their love, or at least their serious like, of Circus Peanuts. Many of them seem to realize this is strange, even if they don't explicitly say so. Take Mary K. above. "Yummy. Mmmm. Good, good, good." Laying it on a little thick, wouldn't you say? Clearly, Circus Peanuts are a way for her to flaunt her rebelliousness, like a drug habit or a scuzzy boyfriend. One can only hope she'll outgrow it.

Other people are more upfront. John Morrison writes: "Do gays coming out of the closet have this problem? Probably not. They're greeted with either unreasoning hatred or friendly acceptance. Us Circus Peanut lovers are met with blank-faced bewilderment, as if we had avowed a love of fingernail clippings. Yes! I'm the one who buys 'em, although thanks to the rather unhip image of Circus Peanuts they're hard to find. Worse yet, perhaps as a result of this incredible media pressure, new strains of CPs have come out: different colors, different flavors, same shape. The connoisseur will accept none of these modern abominations, of course. I might point out that, like chili, CPs gain something by being other than perfectly fresh. The slightly crusty outside of a properly aged Circus Peanut gives it a texture that is far superior to the mushiness of a fresh one."

JYDog: "Like heroin, they are subtly addictive. Then you gorge yourself, and that orange dye looks so much different when they come rumbling back up."

Dave Boersema: "Do I remember them??? How could I (or anyone) ever forget them? Much like the mashed potatoes at Kentucky Fried Chicken or some former girlfrends, there was an unexplainable attraction to them followed by a mystified sense of self-doubt bordering on self-loathing. (Why did I eat that? And, I know I'm going to do it again.) Did I like them? Yes and no. It was a love/hate kind of thing. At times I would want them and nothing else would satisfy. It was always the case upon first opening the bag that that strange aroma would hit and I would think, 'Yes! Circus Peanuts! Who's your daddy?!' And the first gentle squeeze—and they had to be gently squeezed—was wonderful. But then, after eating two or three, I started getting that slightly nauseous feeling, though, of course, I would still eat another one or two, so that by the time I stopped I felt gross."

I close with this thought from Rob Atkinson: "Circus Peanuts are only the beginning of a long list of 'Who buys this stuff?' items. At the top of my list at the local supermarket is kraut juice, in little five- or six-ounce cans, six to a pack. I never see anyone buying them, but someone must or they wouldn't stock them. Can you picture someone relaxing with a nice tall glass of kraut juice? Gross."

Kraut Juice: When Circus Peanuts Aren't Enough

At the risk of dragging out an already idiotic discussion (Circus Peanuts suck, period), I just wanted to provide reader Rob Atkinson with some interesting information. A few years back, I worked in a grocery store as a night stocker. A fellow night stocker, we'll call him "Wayne," started a stupid morning ritual of trying some bizarre new product at the end of each shift. One morning, his choice was a fine can of kraut juice. We weren't sure if you were supposed to drink it by itself or what, but the packaging showed a mouthwatering WINEglass full of the green sludge.

Anyway, Wayne popped the cap open and took a big swig. He then began gagging and spitting out as much as he could. His first words after tasting the kraut juice were "How can this be a marketable product!?!"

After calming down and quelling the desperate attempts of his stomach to return to sender, Wayne sat down, looked at the can, and then chugged the rest of it. After he nearly vomited once again we asked him why he did it. With a face nearly as green as the juice, he replied, "Well, I didn't want to waste it."—John Lamberth, Arlington, TX

We know of Absorbine Jr.; whatever became of Absorbine Sr.? Are there any other family members of which we should be aware? —Donarita and Wally, via the Internet

You say there are eight million stories in the Naked City? Forget it. For real drama, walk down the aisles of the supermarket. We called up W. F. Young, Inc., maker of Absorbine Jr., and asked what the deal was with Absorbine Sr. The following amazing tale emerged.

The Absorbine family of health care products was the brainchild of Wilbur Fenelon Young of Connecticut. In 1892, after eight years

selling pianos, he decided to go into the business of making liniment. You may think: Here's a guy who moved a few too many pianos. Not at all. Young's product was meant for horses, not people. It was called Absorbine Veterinary Liniment—Absorbine Sr. to you.

The other topical pain remedies of the day were harsh or blistering, the prevailing medical theory apparently being that it couldn't be good for you unless it felt bad. Young's revolutionary concept: a pain reliever that relieved pain! He mixed up the first batch of herbs and "essential oils" in a tub in his farmhouse kitchen. Absorbine "would help keep a horse from going lame while gently reducing the swelling and stiffness," the company says today. It caught on with farmers, some of whom were soon struck with the thought: If it works on horses, why not me? Sure enough, they found if they rubbed the stuff on their own aching muscles, it would ease pain and reduce swelling and discomfort. Eventually Young heard about this, and in 1903 he developed a version of his product for humans that he called Absorbine Jr. Antiseptic Liniment.

Demand for Absorbine liniment soon outstripped the capacity of Young's small factory. To finance a move, he went to his father, Charles, and asked for a loan of $500. Charles, not one of your great visionaries, thought Wilbur had been silly to abandon the respectable life of a piano salesman for a career in liniment. He did not, however, tell his son to forget the whole thing. Instead, acting on some twisted impulse that makes you think Oedipus was right, he made the loan contingent on Wilbur signing his advertising "Wilbur F. Young, P. D. F.," which stood for "Pa's Darn Fool." And you thought *your* old man was weird.

Absorbine products went on to become an essential component of American life and remain so today. Among its many other claims to fame, W. F. Young coined the term "athlete's foot" in the 1930s. Today a fifth generation of Youngs continues to sell Absorbine liniment as well as "a host of other equine and human products." Not that I have anything specifically in mind, but I hope they don't get 'em mixed up.

We've been having a heated discussion in the office, and we need to know how Spam luncheon meat is really made. Also, how come they never released a chicken or turkey version (i.e., Spurkey or Spicken)? Finally, what is Monty Python's true relationship with Spam?—Steve Tolin, Sudbury, Ontario

In the interest of thoroughness I thought that somebody here at Dopecorp should actually eat some Spam before we wrote about it. You'd think I was asking these guys to throw themselves on a grenade. "Cecil, I ate a damn Circus Peanut," wailed my assistant Jane. "I did

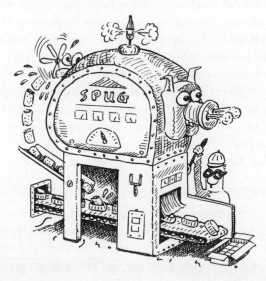

230 · TRIUMPH OF THE STRAIGHT DOPE

laundry. Hell, I even sniffed out sperm trees. This is where I draw the line." Little Ed was likewise unwilling, the pup. So it was up to me.

I bought a tin and popped it open, fully expecting to be bowled over by who knows what awful aroma. Didn't happen. The smell was . . . surprisingly mild. Moreover, the stuff was edible, if salty. Granted, I ate Circus Peanuts without ill effects, and I've had a couple of airline meals that I considered tasty, so maybe I just have a high threshold of disgust. Still, when I see the reaction some people have to this stuff— come on, folks, get a grip. Our ancestors ate meat they'd just killed with a rock. What's so bad about Spam?

What does make you a bit queasy is the nutritional labeling on the side of the can. A single serving—two thin slices—contains 30 percent of your daily saturated-fat quota, 31 percent of your sodium, and 13 percent of your cholesterol. If people ate Spam exclusively, we'd solve the Social Security crisis in a generation. Nobody would live long enough to collect.

On to your questions. The common assumption is that Spam is made of stuff even pigs don't like to admit they've got. Not so, says the nice lady at Hormel Foods, which manufactures Spam. It contains a mixture of ham and chopped pork shoulder. (Ham is the pig's thigh; pork is everything else.) Ham is Hormel's top-of-the-line product, and Spam was created in 1937 partly to use up what was left of the pig after the ham had been removed. But only the wholesome parts.

The name Spam, dreamed up by the actor brother of a Hormel vice president, is short for "spiced ham." (Cute story: Said brother supposedly had this brainstorm at a name-the-product party, in which you had to contribute a possible name in order to get a drink. It took a few rounds, so nobody is sure whether the guy was inspired or just drunk.) It should be recognized that Hormel is in Austin, Minnesota, so these are Minnesota spices: sugar and salt. If you want to go crazy and add pepper, don't blame Hormel.

As for what Monty Python saw in Spam, one supposes they were celebrating the ineffable, I dunno, pinkness of it all. (The Brits, like so many others, had been introduced to Spam during World War II.) Their famous Spam sketch, in which the dialogue is periodically drowned out by the chorus "Spam, Spam, Spam," was the inspiration for the Internet term "spam," meaning the junk E-mail that now floods the net. Presumably, a similar sort of artistic impulse animates the annual Spam sculpture contest as well as a Web site for users' Spam haikus (pemtropics.mit.edu/~jcho/spam/). Samples from the more than 10,000 currently on file:

The color of Spam
Is natural as the sky:
A block of sunrise

Pink tender morsel
Glistening with salty gel
What the hell is it?

Old man seeks doctor
"I eat Spam daily," he says
Angioplasty

Pink beefy temptress
I can no longer remain
Vegetarian

Thanks to aggressive marketing, worldwide Spam sales have grown substantially over the past few years, with well over 150 million cans sold annually. Previously, Hormel marketers concede, people thought of Spam as something you kept in the basement in case the refrigerator went out during a nuclear war. To change this perception, Hormel boss Joel Johnson promoted concepts such as the Spamburger, sold Spam merchandise (e.g., Spam-can earrings—check 'em out at coyote.co.net/spamgift/), and even made a concession to the current interest in not dying young by introducing a low- (well, lower-) fat Spam. Which brings us to your question about chicken Spam: they do make it, sort of—chicken is one of the things that go into the aforementioned low-fat Spam, known as Spam Lite. Some may find the taste a little funkier than that of the regular version. But what the heck, it's still pink.

The Secret Of Spam

Regarding Spam, is it true, as travel writer Paul Theroux claims, that the people of the South Pacific love their Spam because it tastes so much like . . . people?—Mary E. Sage, via the Internet

Marketing Spam must present some unique challenges. Imagine the conversation in the boardroom:

Spam product manager #1: I've got some good news and some bad news. The good news is that Spam is hugely popular among the people of the South Pacific. The bad news is that, according to the famous travel writer Paul Theroux, the islanders dig it because they're ex-cannibals and they think Spam tastes like human flesh.

Spam product manager #2: Hmm. Is this a problem . . . or an opportunity?

Let's start with the facts, then segue to the rumors. Spam is one of the favorite foods of Pacific islanders, including Hawaiians, who consume it in vast quantities and consider it a delicacy. This offends the upper-middle-class sensibilities of some writers, who consider Spam emblematic of all that is vile about Western culture. For example, in *The Island of the Colorblind*, Oliver Sacks writes about the fare served during his visit to the island of Pingelap:

We were all revolted by the Spam which appeared with each meal—invariably fried; why, I wondered, should Pinge-lapese eat this filthy stuff when their own basic diet was both healthy and delicious? . . . How was it that not only the Pin-gelapese, but all the peoples of the Pacific, seemingly, could fall so helplessly, so voraciously, on this stuff, despite its intolerable cost to their budgets and their health? I was not the first to puzzle about this; later, when I came to read Paul Theroux's book *The Happy Isles of Oceania*, I found his hypothesis about this universal Spam mania.

Theroux writes:

It was a theory of mine that former cannibals of Oceania now feasted on Spam because Spam came the nearest to approximating the porky taste of human flesh. "Long pig" as they called a cooked human being in much of Melanesia. It was a fact that the people-eaters of the Pacific had all evolved, or perhaps degenerated, into Spam-eaters. And in the absence of Spam they settled for corned beef, which also had a corpsy flavor.

Nowhere does Sacks say he actually believes Theroux's theory, and it seems clear enough that the often peevish Theroux is exercising his tongue-in-cheek . . . uh, perhaps not the best choice of words. His ironic sense of humor. So far I haven't been able to get him on the phone to confirm this, but what's he going to say?

1. Yes, it was a joke.
2. No, it wasn't a joke. I have personal knowledge that human flesh tastes like pork and corned beef.

Still, these things have a way of taking on a life of their own. Lest our great-grandchildren find this wacky story circulating on the Inter-galactinet in the year 2098, let it be known that:

1. There is no correlation between alleged prior cannibalism and love of Spam. As Sacks notes, the Spam-craving Pingelapese had no tradition of cannibalism. More important, Hawaii, epicenter of

Pacific rim Spamophilism, has been more or less cannibal-free since the arrival of Christianity in the early nineteenth century.

2. The popularity of Spam among Pacific islanders can be readily explained by the scarcity and expense of other types of meat and the lack or unreliability of refrigeration. Fresh meat is stored primarily in a self-propelled biounit known as "a pig," which is slaughtered only for major occasions. If you're looking for a spicy bit to have with your breadfruit you can't beat the convenience of Spam.

Still, let's concede one point to Theroux. Does Spam taste corpsy? Of course it tastes corpsy—it's meat. We're just arguing about the identity of the deceased.

Toldja

Cecil, my man!
You were right the first time. Yes, it is a joke. In spite of my solemn

declaration in The Happy Isles of Oceania, *the voracious Spam consumption in the Pacific is not conclusive evidence of a cannibal past.*

And I enjoyed seeing my laborious joke cleverly adumbrated in yet another of your witty, wide-ranging and inexhaustibly erudite columns.

But also, speaking as a vegetarian, all meat-eating looks to me like the first step down the road to anthropophagy.—With good wishes, Paul Theroux

I've been plagued with a problem for years. With the coming of the Internet I thought I might be spared the anger and bitterness, but no answer has yet been found. Please help. What are the six flags of amusement-park fame that have flown over Texas?—David Sauerwein, Durham, New Hampshire

You know, Dave, a shrink would have you in therapy for years trying to work this out. Me, I'm not even going to fill a whole column. Here are the six flags:

1. *France.* Robert Cavelier, Lord de La Salle, established a colony at Matagorda Bay on the gulf coast in 1685. This was a bit of a fiasco—by 1688 everyone, including La Salle, had been killed or captured. But Bob had been authorized by Louis XIV of France, and one presumes he brought a flag with him.
2. *Spain.* Spain had established effective control over Texas by the early 1700s with its HQ in San Antonio.
3. *Mexico.* Mexico, including Texas, became independent of Spain in 1821.
4. *Republic of Texas.* Texans declared independence in 1836. Alamo, Sam Houston, etc.
5. *United States of America.* Annexed in 1845.
6. *Confederate States of America.* Seceded from the United States in 1861. Unfortunate events ensued. Readmitted in 1869.

Count 'em, six flags. But then a nagging thought: What about Six Flags Over Mid-America near St. Louis? What are they including, that 1944 St. Louis Browns pennant? But one suspects the truth is Two Flags Over Mid-America didn't have the same ring. For the record, the nice lady in St. Louis informs me that the six Mid-America flags are Spain, Britain, France, USA, Missouri, and Illinois. Spain, Britain, and Missouri are a stretch, but Illinois? I don't think so. To forestall embarrassing inquiries, the park was recently given the unobjectionable (because meaningless) name Six Flags St. Louis.

From The Straight Dope Message Board

Is there a difference between Circus Peanuts and regular salted Planters peanuts?

Yes. Circus Peanuts are a marshmallow-type candy. Regular salted Planters peanuts are peanuts. That are salted. In a Planters jar.

My turtle doesn't eat at all. He just lies on his back. He doesn't move, either. And he's starting to smell. But I still love him.

Chapter **14**

Getting Religion

Is there anything to the phenomenon known as "stigmata," i.e., when people inexplicably develop the same type of bloody wounds inflicted on Jesus on the cross?—R.T. in NYC

Maybe I shouldn't tell you this, but I have these scaly patches on my palms that have been known to bleed. At first I thought they were caused by winter dryness. But now I know. They're stigmata.

As you might guess, Cecil is pretty dubious about this stigmata

JOCK
ITCH
SALVE

thing. The first definite case (there may have been a couple of earlier ones) was Saint Francis of Assisi in 1224. As of 1894, 321 cases had been recorded, and there have been many more since. The Italian stigmatic Padre Pio died in 1968; in 1997 he was declared "venerable," a step on the road to sainthood. In 1992 a stigmatic Catholic priest turned up in, of all places, suburban Washington, D.C. Not only did Father James Bruse have wounds, but religious statues wept and changed colors in his presence, and several people he blessed were said to have been healed.

Lest you get the wrong idea, stigmata aren't some wacky variant on getting your ears pierced. The wounds supposedly just appear. And sometimes keep on appearing. One of the classic cases of the nineteenth century, Louise Lateau, got them every Friday for 15 years.

The question isn't whether the stigmata are self-inflicted. Of course they're self-inflicted. Even if I were disposed to believe in divine intervention, the variety in the appearance and location of the wounds on different stigmatics argues strongly that this is a matter of, how shall I say, human handiwork. In some cases the wounds have duplicated those of Jesus as depicted at the stigmatic's local church.

The real issue is whether the wounds are psychosomatic—that is, a physical manifestation of the stigmatic's tortured psyche—or else got there by more conventional (i.e., fraudulent) means. Plenty of cases have been shown to be hoaxes, but with others you can't be sure. Tantalizing evidence comes to us from the medical journals, which report numerous cases of "psychogenic purpuras." These are instances of nonreligious stigmata, in which patients with emotional disorders experience unexplained painful bruising and swelling and occasionally even bleeding through apparently intact skin. One theory blames "autoerythrocyte sensitization," in which individuals react pathologically to their own blood.

Stigmatics are often tormented souls. Many of the religious ones deny themselves to the point of masochism. The nonreligious ones are frequently on the operating table or the shrink's couch for a laundry list of ailments. Reading some of the accounts makes you think that if anybody were likely to get psychosomatic wounds, these would be the guys.

On the other hand, the fact that many stigmatics are emotionally unbalanced means you can't rule out the possibility that they're simply hurting themselves when no one's looking. It's virtually impossible to keep an eye on someone every second of the day, and observers are often naive about what they do see. One scientist thought he'd proved something when Lateau's hands bled even though he'd covered them with bandages and gloves. But he ignored the fact that the bandages were perforated with pinpricks. In 1973 doctors reported a ten-year-old girl in California who was briefly stigmatic. They thought the chances she was faking were "almost nil," but when they attempted to observe her, the bleeding appeared only when she was alone.

Whether you believe in psychosomatic wounds or not, nobody's arguing that even the most intense hysteric can make things happen from the other side of the room. That's what makes reports of multimedia miracles so suspicious, as in the case of the stigmatic Father Bruse and his weeping statues. Bruse had been something of a character in his youth, having three times gotten himself into the *Guinness Book of World Records* for most consecutive hours riding a roller coaster. In a time of declining church attendance, his ability to conjure up signs and wonders kept the pews packed every Sunday.

When we spoke, he told me nothing unusual had happened since he'd been made pastor of a rural Virginia parish in 1995. We had the following exchange:

> Me: Father, not to be melodramatic about this, but it seems to me that if I lied about something like this and deceived the faithful, I would be trifling with my soul. On your honor as a priest, did you fake this?
> Father Bruse: What?
> Me: Did you fake the stigmata and the tears?
> Father Bruse: No, no, no.

To which I can only say again: I'll be damned. Or he will.

Sticking It To The Stigmatics

In your recent column regarding stigmata you failed to mention one very important fact. In most cases the stigmata displayed by "stigmatists" manifest on the palms and the feet. It's well known that the

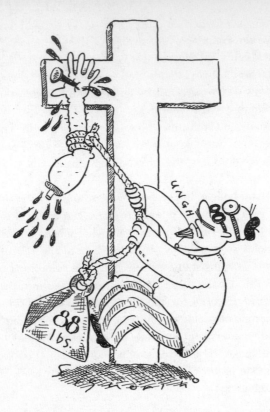

Romans discovered very early that nails through the hands and feet (especially the hands) would not support the weight of the body and would rip through the hands very quickly. Anyone with stigmata of the palms, therefore, would definitely be bogus. Seems to me that would be the quickest and easiest way to debunk these quacks. Whaddaya think?—Jeff A., Ashburn, Virginia

Jeff, you're absolutely right. I can't believe I overlooked an opportunity to describe nails ripping out of flesh. But I should tell you, the facts are more complicated than you think.

The Romans crucified people by the boatload, but exactly how they went about it is unclear, since crucifixion was not the kind of thing you wrote instruction manuals for. The gospels describe wounds in Jesus's hands, and most people (including most artists depicting the crucifixion) have assumed the nails went through the center of his palms.

But some modern researchers have disputed this. The most enterprising was the French surgeon Pierre Barbet, who nailed up freshly
amputated arms through the palms and tied weights to the other ends.
He found that the nail tore through when the weight was increased
to 88 pounds and the arm was given a good jerk. (Be grateful you
weren't this guy's lab assistant.) Since a human body would exert substantially more force, he concluded that nailing through the palm was
impractical.

Barbet believed the wrist was a more likely location. After more experiments with nails and amputated arms, he found that a nail could
be driven readily through an anatomical area known as Destot's space,
located near where the base of the hand joins the wrist. Because
Destot's space is surrounded by the wrist bones, a nail there could
easily support the weight of the body.

To buttress his thesis Barbet cited the Shroud of Turin, which appeared to have blood marks at the wrist. Shroud advocates were quite
taken with this notion and gave it wide currency. Barbet summarized
his findings in his book *A Doctor at Calvary*, published in 1953.

Barbet's hypothesis seemed to get a boost in 1968 when archaeolo-
gists in Jerusalem unearthed the first known skeleton of a crucifixion
victim. The guy's feet had been nailed to the cross sideways, through
the heel rather than the arch, as is commonly depicted. More to the
point, there was a scratch on one of the bones of the right forearm (the
radius), as though from a nail. In the minds of many people this
cinched the wrist crucifixion hypothesis.

In the biblical archaeology game, however, nobody ever gets the last
word. Among the objections raised: 1) In the Jerusalem crucifixion
victim, the nail didn't go through Destot's space in the wrist bones, it
went between the two bones of the forearm. 2) There might not have
been a nail at all. Two later researchers claim that scratches and inden-
tations are commonly found on ancient bones and have nothing to do
with crucifixion (Zias and Sekeles, *Israel Exploration Journal*, 1985).
They think the Jerusalem victim was tied to the cross with ropes. 3)
Destot's space, and for that matter the bones of the forearm, aren't the
only places you can nail a guy to make him stay up. In a 1989 issue of
Bible Review, Frederick Zugibe, a medical examiner for Rockland
County, New York, claims that there are at least two other possible
nailing locations, one of which is on the palm. (It's in the "thenar furrow,"

the deep fold where the base of the thumb joins the hand; touch your thumb to the tip of your little finger to see it.)

In short, we have no idea how Jesus was crucified, other than the fact that they nailed him somewhere. Even if we did, it wouldn't prove anything. Remember Father Bruse, the stigmatic Catholic priest who could make statues weep, heal the sick, etc.? His stigmata—you can see this coming—were on the wrist.

Thanks to the *Biblical Archaeological Review* for research assistance. Let me know when I can help *you* guys dig something up.

I'm one very disgruntled and estranged member of the Catholic Church—so disgruntled, in fact, that I really don't want to be counted as a member. How can I get excommunicated? I assume it's not as simple as writing a letter (though this probably only means the church is more bureaucratic than most mail-order CD clubs). How can I make my intentions known to the right offices?—Bobby Jo Wojtyla, Cary, North Carolina

I think you fail to grasp the concept here, bubba. The purpose of excommunication isn't to allow you to quit or make a political statement or pursue some other private agenda. It's to allow the church to throw you out. If you're already out—that is, if you don't partake of the sacraments or otherwise participate in Catholic activities (I assume this describes your situation)—excommunication is likely to strike church authorities as a waste of good holy water.

That's not to say you can't get excommunicated; on the contrary, canon law describes a number of situations in which excommunication is automatic. But these days formal proceedings are rare and reserved mostly for renegade clerics and such. Too bad you weren't around centuries ago, when they were bigger on this sort of thing. You could have gotten the old "book, bell, and candle" routine (more on this in a sec) or even been burned at the stake.

Strictly speaking, excommunication does not render you a non-Catholic. It merely means you're a Catholic who's been damned to hell. What's more, it isn't intended to permanently separate you from the church; rather, it's a "medicinal" procedure, meant to make you see the error of your ways. If in fact you do become reconciled later, you won't be rebaptized, just forgiven. In the eyes of the church, once a Catholic, always a Catholic. Irritating, I know, but as I say, this wasn't set up to accommodate you.

There's also a practical problem. You can't have your name stricken from the Catholic membership rolls, because there aren't any such rolls. Sure, some records may be kept at the parish level, and if you're the determined type I suppose you could get your name crossed off those. But the church maintains no central registry. They figure God can keep track.

Fine, you say, but I still want to get excommunicated. OK, let me get out my—whoops, *Buckland's Complete Book of Witchcraft*. Gotta get this library organized. Ah, here we are, the *Codex Juris Canonici*. As revised in 1983, there are nine grounds for excommunication: physical attack on the pope, "violating the sacred species," procuring an abortion, etc. . . . all a little drastic. Your best bet is "apostasy, heresy, or schism," canon 1364. Probably the simplest thing is to join the Presbyterians. Voilà, *latae sententiae* (automatic) excommunication.

But I think what you're after is an official pronouncement of excommunication (*ferendae sententiae*). Apparently, the only way to do this nowadays is to make a conspicuous pest of yourself. The ultraconservative French archbishop Marcel LeFebvre did this by consecrating bishops without authorization, which got him excommunicated in 1988. If he could get himself formally kicked out, so can you, though it may require establishing your own schismatic sect.

Who knows, maybe you could get the Holy See so ticked off they'd dust off the old "book, bell, and candle" ceremony referred to above.

First, a bishop and twelve priests appear holding lighted candles. The bishop then recites a bloodcurdling formula: "We separate him, together with his accomplices and abettors, from the precious body and blood of the Lord and from the society of all Christians; we exclude him from our holy mother the church in heaven and on earth; we declare him excommunicate and anathema; we judge him damned, with the devil and his angels and all the reprobate, to eternal fire until he shall recover himself from the toils of the devil and return to amendment and to penitence." The priests answer, "So be it!," whereupon the whole crew extinguish their candles by dashing them to the ground. Dunno about you, but if they threatened mé with this I'd never miss Sunday mass again.

Are there any jokes in the Bible? I look for humor in nearly everything, but I've never been able to find any in the Bible. I realize most current humor is either sexually oriented, scatological, and/or disparaging to some group or other, all of which is quite antithetical to the Bible's purpose. But no humor at all? It's a long book and theoretically speaks to every aspect of the human condition. I'm not a biblical scholar and thus look to you and your vast research abilities to explain the total lack of frivolity, humor, or gaiety in this book.—Willard Cloutier

Cecil must say that, vast though his knowledge is, yea, even of things biblical, he has never read the Good Book with a view to looking up the funny parts. Therefore, I have consulted specialists, who

have furnished several candidate jokes. I'm not saying that if these were on Christian TV you'd necessarily want to skip Letterman to hear them. However, they do employ the stuff of wit, such as wordplay, riddles, etc. Examples:

1. *Wordplay*. Told by the Lord that his 90-year-old wife Sarah will bear a son, Abraham laughs to himself. And what's more, continueth the Lord, obviously a little peeved at Abe's attitude, "you shall call his name Isaac," from Yitzak, "he laughed." Not a line that's going to kill them in Vegas, but I didn't claim these were going to score big on the laugh-o-meter.
2. *Riddles*. In Judges 14:14, Samson bets his bride's relatives they can't answer this riddle: "Out of the eater came something to eat. Out of the strong came something sweet." The relations are stumped, mainly because the riddle makes no sense unless you know Samson recently had seen honey deposited by bees in the carcass of a lion, which he had—urk—scraped out and eaten. The relatives pester the bride for the answer, and she pesters Samson, who finally breaks down and tells her. The newly clued relatives say to Samson, "What is sweeter than honey? What is stronger than a lion?" "If you had not plowed with my heifer," Samson ungallantly ripostes, "you would not have found out my riddle," whereupon he massacres 30 unlucky locals to raise enough swag to pay off the bet. Hilarious, eh?
3. *Subversive wit*. In Mark 5, Jesus asks a man possessed by devils, "What is your name?" The devils reply, "My name is Legion; for we are many." Conceivably this is a pun on legion in the sense of "a vast bunch of" and legion in the sense of a Roman military unit. The devils beg to be sent into a nearby herd of swine, which stampedes into the sea and drowns. One can construe this (not without some strain) as a sly prayer that the Romans, an unwelcome presence at the time, would all take a running jump.
4. *Bathroom jokes*. Scatological humor is beneath the Bible, eh? See what you make of 1 Samuel 4–6. The Philistines, having captured the Ark of the Covenant, are visited with twin plagues: mice and, depending on whose translation you accept, either tumors or hemorrhoids. Cecil naturally prefers the latter. Consider the ineffable poignance of the following: "There was a deadly destruction

throughout all the city . . . and the men that died not were smitten with the hemorrhoids: and the cry of the city went up to heaven."

The Philistines ask their priests what to do, and the priests say to send the Ark back to the Hebrews with a "trespass offering." What kind of offering? the Philistines ask. "They answered, five golden hemorrhoids, and five golden mice, [one each for the five] lords of the Philistines." My consultants caution that the author of this did not necessarily think it was funny, and I am confident this column's refined and sensitive readers will not think it is funny either. But nobody's going to tell me whoever wrote it didn't have his tongue stuck firmly in cheek.

More Biblical Humor

Regarding humor in the Bible, here are some jokes from the New Testament (John 1:45–51):

"Philip found Nathanael and said unto him, 'We have found him of whom Moses in the law and also the prophets wrote, Jesus of Nazareth, the son of Joseph.' Nathanael said to him, 'Can anything good come out of Nazareth?' (Joke!) Philip said to him, 'Come and see!' (Boom!) Jesus saw Nathanael coming to him, and said of him, 'Behold, an Israelite indeed in whom there is no guile' ('Hey, here's an honest Jew'—joke). Nathanael (not getting it) said to him, 'How do you know me?' Jesus answered him, 'Before Philip called you, I saw you yesterday, standing under a fig tree.' Nathanael said (losing his cool), 'Rabbi, you are the son of God! You are the king of Israel!' Jesus answered him, 'Because I said I saw you standing under a fig tree, believest thou?' (Big joke! Gets laughs!) 'You shall see greater things than these.' (Release.) And he said to him, 'Truly, truly I say unto you, you shall see the heavens opened and the angels of the Lord ascending and descending upon the Son of Man.' (Boom!)"

Preserving humor through translations from Aramaic to Greek to Latin to English is problematic, but with a little sympathy for the intent of the speaker, you can find a lot.—Del Close, Chicago

P.S.: I tried out these jokes on my improv class this afternoon, and after 2,000 years they still get laughs!

Del. You're a pro. (Close is the well-known improv pioneer and comic actor who once directed the Second City comedy troupe.) You could get laughs reading the phone book. Still, I'll admit the fig tree story is the closest I've heard to a Bible joke that's actually funny.

I have a friend who has a cross made of wood supposedly from a door in Saint Peter's Basilica. It was said that this door is only opened once every 100 years. What is behind the door, and why is it kept closed?—Blewick, via America Online

I know what you're thinking: A secret back door to the Vatican! Exactly, except that it's not secret, in the back, or to the Vatican. What you refer to is an odd tradition at St. Peter's involving the Porta Santa, or Holy Door. This door is in the front of the basilica to the right of the main entrance. Most of the time it's kept not merely locked but walled up. It's opened only during Holy Years, also known as Jubilee Years. Massive numbers of pilgrims descend on St. Peter's at these times, and I gather the door functions as a sort of a Holy Fire Exit.

Holy Years are an odd tradition in their own right. The first was proclaimed in A.D. 1300 by Pope Boniface VIII, not entirely voluntarily. The faithful somehow got the idea that centenary years were the occasion of a Great Pardon. Tens of thousands of them spontaneously embarked on a pilgrimage to Rome with the view of getting one.

So here's Boniface looking out the window, and he sees vast crowds of people who'd evidently done something bad enough that they figured

it was worth going to Rome to get a pardon for. Whoa, says Boniface, time to think fast.

He worked up a system whereby participants could gain a special indulgence (pardon from punishment for sins) in return for fulfilling various conditions, notably visiting certain Roman churches, St. Peter's being the most important.

The original plan was that Holy Years would occur every 100 years, but the interval was soon reduced to 25 years. Additional Holy Years are sometimes proclaimed for special occasions—e.g., in 1983–84, which marked the 1,950th anniversary of the Crucifixion and Resurrection.

A Holy Year starts on Christmas Eve, at one time considered the last day of the year. There's an elaborate ritual in which the pope strikes the Holy Door three times with a silver hammer. The door promptly collapses, no doubt inspiring at least one or two spectators to hope that the rest of St. Peter's was built by a different contractor. In fact, however, workers with ropes and pulleys nudge things along.

Considering all the buildup, one would suppose the Holy Door provided admittance to a garden of forbidden delights. But in fact it gets you into the back of the church just as the other entrances do. The door remains open until the following Christmas Eve, when it's again walled up.

One can appreciate that having a special door heightens the drama of the Holy Year, provides instructive symbolism, etc. But why the pope feels he has to wall it up as opposed to using a good dead bolt is a matter that remains obscure. Cynics will of course suggest that some cardinal's nephew probably has the plaster contract.

If you want to investigate personally, you won't have long to wait. The next Holy Year begins on Christmas Eve 1999.

Why is Jesus so popular? I mean, how did he become so incredibly well known after his death when up to that point he was a rebel and a heretic? His crucifixion is irrefutable evidence of his singular lack of popularity with the powers that be at the time. It can't be the miracle thing, as he'd already performed many before they nailed him to the cross. I don't understand the contrast between his infamy during his life and global superstardom still going strong 2,000 years later.—Alex Fleming, Montreal

Well, Jesus did found a successful religion, historically a good way to keep your name before the public eye. The question really is why Christianity went over so big. Considering some of the characters who've been connected with it over the past couple millennia, you've got to figure the only explanation is the hand of Providence. This is not a topic that lends itself to scientific inquiry, however, so let's stick to the human contribution.

Most historians give the major credit to Saul of Tarsus, better known as Paul, who converted to Christianity (although it wasn't called that yet) just a few years after the crucifixion. Paul was instrumental in taking an obscure Jewish sect, stripping away its parochial baggage, and positioning it to become a major world religion. In addition to being a tireless proselytizer, organizer, and propagandist, Paul was a creative theologian who played up the parts of Christianity with universal appeal, notably the belief in eternal life, popularly understood to mean an individual afterlife. At the Council of Jerusalem in A.D. 49 he also helped kibosh the idea that Christians needed to observe Jewish ritual, including (urk) circumcision, a major disincentive till then.

But it wasn't all Paul. Christianity succeeded because it showed up at the right place at the right time. The explanation usually given is that 1) the centuries-long Pax Romana that began around the time of Christ made it possible to spread ideas throughout the Mediterranean basin in a short time, 2) the old Greek and Roman pagan religions were by then completely out of gas, and 3) the imperial court was run by such a collection of cutthroats and lunatics that people were desperate for a religion promising a moral order.

All true, I guess, but none of it quite gets at the genius of the thing.

There were many competing cults at the time, in particular the so-called mystery religions, that vanished with scarcely a trace. What set Christianity apart was its sophistication. It was the West's first modern religion, coupling a coherent and attractive picture of how the world worked with a commonsensical moral code. Most Western religions prior to Christianity, Judaism included, were narrowly focused ethnic affairs, primarily concerned with placating a perpetually pissed-off godhead. (The Roman state religion was merely an amalgamation of such local beliefs.) Christianity, in brilliant contrast, offered the following propositions: God is good, God is universal, God wants you to live forever with him in paradise provided you . . . Well, exactly what you had to do to be saved was a matter of dispute. But the point was, you could be saved.

Many religions previously had had some notion of an afterlife, but, as in the Greek belief in Hades, it was often thought of as some sort of astral garbage can into which souls were pitched once stripped of flesh. Christianity turned this bleak idea into the positive concept of salvation and resurrection. (In the Church's earliest days it was believed the second coming would occur within the lifetimes of those then living, which made acceptance of Jesus all the more urgent.)

The idea of salvation was appealing enough in its own right, but it had an equally appealing subtext: the universe makes sense, you have a central place in it, and you can, up to a point, control your own fate. (I realize we get into the free-will-vs.-predestination argument here, but you see what I'm getting at.) The complexity and emotional power of this system of belief swept away the primitive religions that preceded it. Tellingly, Christianity made less headway against the religions of the East, which offered a worldview that was equally compelling.

Today a few skeptics feel Christianity itself has run out of gas, but I'm not seeing it. Assuming you're not merely going to switch to some other well-established religious tradition, or else take up with the Shirley MacLaine crowd, what else is there? Sure, I know there are some who profess to take solace in science. But who in his final hour rejoices at the thought, onward to the void?

From The Straight Dope Science Advisory Board

Is yeast infection yeast the same as cooking yeast? If I put my girl-friend in an oven the next time she has a yeast infection, will she rise? Have you ever heard of women using their own yeast in emergency cooking situations?—Love & Pastry, Brian Kelcher

I can see why Cecil declined to answer this one. Brian, just so it comes as no surprise, I am NEVER eating at your house.

As far as yeast goes, the stuff we traditionally use as a leavener in baking is a microscopic fungus from the *Saccharomycetaceae* family. Yeast multiplies quickly in certain situations, such as those that bread dough supply: warmth, moisture, and sugars to digest. This yeast causes alcoholic fermentation, converting the sugars and starches it digests into ethyl alcohol and carbon dioxide. This gas is what causes bread to rise. If you bust open a loaf of your favorite bread you'll find that it's chock-full of little holes—the bubbles caused by this process.

Yeast *infection* yeast, on the other hand, is a parasitic yeastlike fungus called *Candida albicans*. This is a fungus that normally lives in everyone's intestines, genital tract, mouth, esophagus, and throat. Normally it's not a problem, as it keeps some kind of balance going with the bacteria and other assorted wee beasties that also inhabit said spaces. It's when something upsets this balance and gives the *Candida* a chance to bloom out of control that we get the classic "yeast infection" that has plagued nearly every woman past the age of puberty. I won't go into the symptoms of this, or the other dozens of symptoms that can affect both men and women. I will note that it is the same fungus responsible for thrush in babies, that it can cause athlete's foot and jock itch, and that it's possible to get it so badly that you get "candida septicemia," a form of blood poisoning that affects every system in the body.

Yeast infections are often caused by taking antibiotics, which kill off some of the other bacteria present in the genital tract and allow the candida to overgrow, causing "candidiasis." A condition that can make someone susceptible to *Candida* infection is diabetes, so a good health care provider will test for diabetes any woman who has recurrent infections (though some women just do, and no one knows why).

Some believe cutting down on the sugar you eat will go a long way toward curbing the growth of this particular nuisance, although the experts tend to be skeptical of this. Others swear by yogurt. I can add as "notes from the field" that I stopped getting yeast infections (yep—got them every single time I had to take antibiotics) when I discovered liquid acidopholus (the live culture in yogurt). It's wayyyy nicer to use than that nasty over-the-counter-make-a-mess-in-your-panties stuff. Cheaper, too. But I doubt there's any proof it works. Except that I said so.

Suffice it to say that if you bake with this stuff you probably won't get any of the results you'd hoped for.

—SDSTAFF Lara, with assistance from SDSTAFF Jill
Straight Dope Science Advisory Board

Chapter 15

Horror Stories

My friends and I were discussing the great horror movies when someone claimed that The Texas Chain Saw Massacre *was based on a true story. I went to the video store, and sure enough on the back of the box it said the movie was based on real events. I rented it, and after my friends and I watched it we got to wondering just how true this story is. Cecil, help us out here. How loosely is the movie based on the real story? What are the facts?—Mike McGrory, via the Internet*

Coming right up, friend, but be warned. Gross-out danger: high.

If you're looking for me to tell you there really was a family of

backwoods weirdos, including a goon in a mask called Leatherface, and that a kid really went into their house and got hit with a hammer, and then his girlfriend went looking for him, and Leatherface impaled her on a meat hook while he butchered the boyfriend with a chain saw, and then a second guy went looking for the first two and got hammered too, and then Leatherface sawed up yet another guy in a wheelchair, and then one last woman got away and found refuge in a barbecue shop, only it turned out the barbecue was really human flesh, and the shop's proprietor was Leatherface's cousin or something, and they were really all cannibals . . . um, sorry, but this isn't a 100 percent accurate reenactment of actual events. The real Leatherface didn't use a hammer. Also, the chain saw was a whimsical creative touch. But I'm not telling you that director Tobe Hooper made the whole thing up.

The Texas Chain Saw Massacre was—well, I don't know that "inspired" is the word you want to use here, but at any rate Hooper got the idea from a sensational 1957 murder case involving Wisconsin farmer Ed Gein. Gein's exploits weren't quite the over-the-top carnival of crime depicted in the movie, but for an amateur he made quite a splash. Gein's mother was a domineering Bible-thumper who persuaded her son that all women were evil strumpets. He cared for Mom alone after she had a stroke, and when she finally died he nailed shut the rooms where she'd lived. He was fascinated by crime stories, anatomy textbooks, and embalming and liked to discuss them with folks in the nearby town of Plainfield. People found him a little odd but likable. Little did they know.

One day Bernice Worden, proprietor of the town hardware store, vanished under suspicious circumstances. Clues pointed to Gein, who'd been hanging around the previous few days. The sheriff drove out to Gein's farmhouse and found Worden's headless corpse hanging by the feet in the kitchen, "eviscerated and dressed out like a deer," according to one press account. The head was in a cardboard box, the heart in a plastic bag on the stove. Elsewhere in the cluttered home authorities found ten skins from human heads, bracelets and chair seats made from human skin, a box of noses, the skin from a woman's chest rolled up on the floor, and more.

Under questioning Gein admitted to two killings—Worden plus Mary Hogan, a 54-year-old saloon keeper who'd vanished in 1954. He said he'd gotten the other body parts from robbing women's graves. Later accounts painted Gein as a cannibal and a necrophiliac, but a 1957 *Time* story specifically denied this, saying he preserved the remains "just to look at." I mean, lest you think the guy was a kink. Gein's story made headlines all over the country, including an eight-page spread in *Life* magazine. After a hearing, he was committed to a Wisconsin state hospital for the criminally insane.

So let's check off these parallel motifs from the Gein and chain-saw sagas: grave robbing (oops, I forgot to mention this in my summary of *TCSM*), butchering of victims, use of human body parts as an element in the home-decorating scheme (this was in *TCSM* too). The great literary themes. But wait, you say. Mild-mannered bachelor murderer, lonely rural setting, obsession with dead mother. There's another classic horror movie this reminds me of, and it doesn't have anything to do with gasoline-powered garden implements. You got it, babe: Alfred Hitchcock's *Psycho*. Gein was also the source for a character in *The Silence of the Lambs* and gave rise to some lesser-known movies as well. I ask you, how many movies has Mother Teresa inspired? Of the high-profile flicks, *TCSM* is undoubtedly the stupidest (I'm telling you, it doesn't play as well as it reads), but they say it launched the slasher genre. Way to go, Ed. Shows you what a man can accomplish if he won't settle for upholstering the seats in leatherette.

Greetings, Master. I've checked the archives and found no reference to the following story, which is supposed to have come from the Daily Texan, *the University of Texas newspaper. Is there any truth to it?*

"This guy went out last Saturday night to a party and had a couple of beers. Some girl seemed to like him and invited him to another party. He quickly agreed. She took him to a party in some apartment and they continued to drink, and even got involved with some other drugs (unknown which). The next thing he knew, he woke up completely naked in a bathtub filled with ice. He was still feeling the effects of the drugs but looked around to see he was alone. He looked down at his chest, which had 'CALL 911 OR YOU WILL DIE' written on it in lipstick. He saw a phone was on a stand next to the tub, so he picked it up and dialed. He explained to the EMS operator what the situation was and that he didn't know where he was, what he took, or why he was really calling. She advised him to get out of the tub and look

himself over in the mirror. He did, only to find two nine-inch slits on his lower back. She told him to get back in the tub immediately, and they sent a rescue team over. They found his kidneys were stolen. They are worth $10,000 each on the black market. . . ."—MLScola, via AOL

Dozens of folks have written me about this. My initial reaction was, Well, at least now we know where they found the people for the first O.J. jury. Who could possibly believe this absurd urban legend? Then again, you did send the story to me first. Many goofs instead would have spammed it to everybody they know via E-mail, thereby proving that the missing organ we should really be worried about is the one between the ears. The facts:

1. There are no documented cases of kidneynapping, or for that matter any killing, abduction, or mutilation for purposes of organ theft. The National Kidney Foundation, which fears this persistent myth will scare off donors, has asked victims of organ theft to step forward. So far, no takers.

2. While I suppose it's possible to remove somebody's kidneys with a paper plate and an X-acto knife, as a practical matter it can't be done. The operation customarily takes a five-person surgical team working for three or four hours in a sterile operating room. Much of the equipment required (anesthesia machines, operating tables) is bulky and not the sort of thing you could readily sneak into an apartment, hotel room, etc. The tissue and blood types of the donor and donee must be precisely matched; you can't just grab the first mope you see in a bar.

3. None of the checkable details in the story pans out. The *Daily Texan* says it never ran the kidney-theft story, though it has run several denials. This is the third time the UT version of the legend has made the rounds.

4. The original version, in which a guy meets a woman in a New York bar and later wakes up kidneyless, dates back at least to March 1991. (See folklorist Jan Harold Brunvand's 1993 book, *The Baby Train and Other Lusty Urban Legends*.) It may have originated in a 1989 incident in England. A Turkish man told authorities he'd been lured to the U.K. by a job offer, only to have a kidney stolen. An investigation revealed that the man had advertised in a Turkish newspaper to sell his kidney, found a buyer, and evidently sought revenge after failing to collect full payment. (See the Urban Legends Reference Pages, www.snopes.com.)

The only thing that makes kidneynapping even slightly believable is the very real market for transplantable human organs, in which demand exceeds supply. (See David Rothman's March 26, 1998, piece in the *New York Review of Books*.) In India the desperately poor can sell a kidney for $1,000 to $1,500. The People's Republic of China doesn't even bother to pay; they extract organs from executed prisoners. Two men were arrested in New York in early 1998 for offering to sell kidneys and other organs of executed Chinese. A related legend, common in some developing countries, has babies being kidnapped by rich westerners so they can be stripped for parts. In 1993 in Guatemala, one American tourist was beaten to death and another was jailed after they were falsely accused of babynapping. Stories of third-world babynappings aren't that far-fetched; black-market adoption rings allegedly do it. But nobody north of the border has that kind of excuse.

Going For The Kidneys

With reference to your column about losing a kidney after a party, check out this story from the San Francisco Examiner *headlined "Poor Robbed of Kidneys in India." Urban myth, heh?—Dave B., via the Internet*

Dave refers to a May 1998 Associated Press report from New Delhi telling of the arrest of 10 people, including three transplant surgeons and a hospital owner, after a patient claimed he'd been lured to the hospital and robbed of a kidney. Supposedly the hospital had promised the man a job in Singapore and told him a medical exam was needed to obtain a visa.

Aspects of this story strike me as fishy. What did the surgeons think, the victim wouldn't notice he'd had major surgery? Similar allegations in the past have turned out to be false. But even if the accusations are true, there are big differences between organ theft in India and the stories circulating in North America, in which guys meet beautiful strangers only to awaken kidneyless later in a bathtub of ice. In parts of India it's still legal to sell a kidney, and clinics openly remove organs from the poor and transplant them in the rich. (Maybe not for long, though. In 1995 the Indian parliament forbade organ sales except to close relatives, but this has not been ratified by all states.) In the United States and Canada, organ sales are illegal and the delicate business of stealing the organs, matching donors and recipients, and doing the transplants would have to be conducted entirely underground. That's highly improbable, and hasn't occurred as far as we know. Then again, you read about Jack Kevorkian removing kidneys from people he helped commit suicide and you think: Just wait.

Please settle a debate for us before somebody gets killed. Is there really such a thing as a snuff film?—snopes, Canoga Park, California

This is the weirdest urban legend of all: that there are underground movies in which people are literally murdered on camera for purposes of entertainment. The question is not whether there are people sick enough to traffic in such things (in a world containing Jeffrey Dahmer and Geraldo Rivera, there probably are), but whether they actually do. All we can say is that in the nearly 30 years stories of snuff movies have been circulating, no genuine example has ever come to light.

"The [snuff movie] rumor evidently originated in publicity circulated in the 1970s by Alan Shakleton of Monarch Pictures, a low budget sado-porn movie distributor," Penn State folklorist Bill Ellis tells me. Shakleton "bought up a Latin-American Manson family rip-off titled *Slaughter,* had it subtitled, added a scene in which a woman was murdered (cut out of another film), then marketed the film under the title *Snuff* in New York City. Rumor has it that he then incited women's groups to picket the film under the [erroneous] impression that the murder scene was an actual killing. Certainly the publicity Shakleton used implied that it was: 'Made in South America Where Life Is Cheap.' "

Every few years since then snuff movies have been back in the news, either because some nut is accused of trying to make one (never successfully) or the tabloids report some sensational claim—e.g., that the main centers for the snuff-movie industry are London, Amsterdam, and Bangkok. But pornography experts for the FBI and other law-enforcement agencies say they have never seen a genuine snuff film.

Many people are convinced snuff films are real, possibly because it suits their ideological bent. For example, in her book *Feminism Unmodified,* feminist legal scholar Catharine MacKinnon says flatly that snuff films exist. But when I asked her to elaborate she declined, and indeed was quite mysterious about the whole thing. She just knew.

That's not to say there aren't movies purporting to show people actually being killed. These fall into several categories:

- News footage and the like in which a death is filmed by happenstance. One commonly cited example is the Zapruder film of the Kennedy assassination. One underground video series, *Faces of Death,* depicts numerous grisly deaths, some of it apparently drawn from newsreel outtakes, with a lot of reenactments thrown in.
- Porn films gone wrong. Ted McIlvenny, director of the Institute for the Advanced Study of Human Sexuality and caretaker of

what is probably the world's largest collection of sex movies—289,000 films and 100,000 videos—says that in his 25 years of following the porn business he's seen exactly three films in which someone was killed on camera. In two cases the death was unintended: 1) a guy died of a heart attack while being beaten during an S&M scene; and 2) a man accidentally strangled himself during an autoerotic asphyxiation.

- Anomalous weirdness. McIlvenny says the third film involving an actual death was a bizarre religious number from Morocco in which a hunchbacked kid was torn apart by wild horses while men stood around and masturbated. Sick, but not intended as commercial pornography.
- Filmed executions from Southeast Asia, etc. McIlvenny says he saw a film showing these once.
- Realistic fakes.
- Home videos by psychopaths. A commonly cited case involves Leonard Lake and Charles Ng, who in the mid-1980s murdered at least 11 women in Lake's California cabin and made videos of several victims begging for mercy. I have not been able to confirm that anyone was actually killed on camera in this or similar cases, but I wouldn't be surprised.

None of the above constitutes a snuff movie as the term is usually understood. It's not out of the realm of possibility that one will yet turn up. But the notion that there is some sort of snuff-movie industry out there, complete with film crews, lab technicians, and, God help us, sacrificial actors; that these people film themselves committing capital crimes and sell the result to strangers; and that for nearly 30 years they've succeeded in concealing all traces of their handiwork, strikes me as absurd.

The other night I was sitting around with some friends discussing the sort of thing college students discuss at three in the morning while avoiding chemistry homework—namely, strange mutilations of the human body. Someone told a story that sounds like an urban legend to me, but he was so sure it was true. The story goes that an obese woman felt the call of nature while on an airplane. After relieving herself in the designated cubicle, she committed the unfortunate error of flushing while still on the commode. Since airplane toilets work by suction, and since her large girth covered the entire seat opening, creating a seal, a vacuum was formed beneath her behind. The resulting pressure differential proceeded to . . . partially suck out her intestines! Yet through the timely intervention of an onboard physician, her life was spared (though she is no doubt doomed to eat lots of food rich in fiber for the rest of her life).

Now, come on! Besides the fact that all toilets I've seen have little cushioning doohickeys between the seat and the bowl, thus creating an airspace, this story just seems a little far-fetched. Can you help us get to the bottom of this? Is there yet another reason why Mom was right in telling us never to sit on public toilet seats?—Bethany G., Ann Arbor, Michigan

No doubt many feel this is something they could stand not to know. However, I feel an informed public is the cornerstone of a democratic society. Like you, I initially thought this was purely an urban legend. To be on the safe side, though, I dropped a line to folklore guru Jan Brunvand. To my surprise, he referred me to a letter by Philadelphia osteopath J. Brendan Wynne in the *Journal of the American Medical Association* (March 6, 1987, page 1177). The letter related a, how shall I say, gut-wrenching tale:

It seems the doctor was on a cruise ship moored near Vancouver, British Columbia, when he responded to an emergency call over the ship's loudspeaker. He was asked to administer first aid to a woman who had sustained a serious pelvic injury.

"A 70-year-old, slightly obese woman was in her cabin lying on the

bunk in the right lateral recumbent position," the doctor writes. She was alert but moaning in pain. "Protruding behind her on the bed were several feet of small intestine with [connective tissue] attached."

The woman said she had flushed the toilet while seated. Evidently her bottom had completely sealed the toilet opening and the suction had "pulled everything out." The woman kept repeating, "Why didn't they warn me?"

The only warning was a sign near the toilet saying, "This toilet operates on vacuum system. Please do not throw any object except toilet paper."

Paramedics arrived in a few moments and took the woman to a local hospital. The doctor concludes with the modest observation that this type of thing "certainly bears further investigation."

Some have intimated that this account is a hoax, saying that if a toilet did in fact suck out somebody's innards, you'd see the large intestine, not the small one. Not so. While I'm not about to go into detail, accounts in the medical journals of similar accidents (for example, when a toddler sits on a suction-type pool drain) suggest Wynne got it right. A United Press International story at the time confirmed the essential details of Wynne's letter and included a telephone interview with the doctor in which he said, "I realize this almost defies belief." I'll say. Momma always said not to sit down on rest-room toilet seats, and boy, was she right.

In the answer about the guillotine in your online archive, you say that "the fatal blow induces immediate unconsciousness." In actuality, the human head does remain conscious fifteen to twenty seconds after decapitation. This was proven when a scientist condemned to the guillotine in the 1700s told his assistant to watch and that he would blink as many times as he could. The assistant counted fifteen to twenty blinks after the head was severed, the blinks coming at intervals of about one second. So the head does remain briefly alive.—Joel Brusk, via AOL

Let's see. In the last few months we've covered crucifixion, kidney theft, and now decapitation. What next, you ask—how to perform your own spinal tap? But bear with me. New facts have come to light.

A lot of people disputed my claim that victims of the guillotine

blacked out immediately. Many had seen a TV show on the Discovery Channel called "The Guillotine" in which a medical expert tells the story above, with the added detail that the scientist was the pioneering French chemist Antoine Lavoisier, who was beheaded during the Reign of Terror in 1794.

Not likely. There is no mention of the blinking incident in the standard biographies of Lavoisier. The expert quoted on the TV show, neurosurgeon Robert Fink, says he heard the story from a colleague. The colleague says he read it in a book but can't remember which. He admits the story may be apocryphal.

But let's return to the original question, appalling though it may be: is a severed head aware of its fate? People have been debating the point since the invention of the guillotine, and not just out of morbid curiosity. Some felt the guillotine, far from being quick and painless, was an instrument of the most profound and horrible torture: to be aware of having been beheaded. Numerous anecdotes and bizarre experiments have been adduced as evidence on either side. After Charlotte Corday was guillotined for murdering Jean-Paul Marat, the executioner slapped her cheek while holding her severed head aloft. Witnesses claimed the cheeks reddened (without blood?) and the face looked indignant. According to another tale, when the heads of two rivals in the National Assembly were placed in a sack following execution, one bit the other so badly the two couldn't be separated.

It doesn't get any better. In one early series of experiments, an anatomist claimed that decapitated heads reacted to stimuli, with one victim turning his eyes toward a speaker 15 minutes after having been beheaded. (Today we know brain death would have occurred long before.) In 1836 the murderer Lacenaire agreed to wink after execution. He didn't. Attempts to elicit a reaction from the head of the murderer Prunier in 1879 were also fruitless. The following year a doctor pumped blood from a living dog into the head of the murderer and rapist Menesclou three hours after execution. The lips trembled, the eyelids twitched, and the head seemed about to speak, although no words emerged. In 1905 another doctor claimed that when he called the name of the murderer Languille just after decapitation, the head opened its eyes and focused on him.

Is it possible? The aforementioned Dr. Fink believed the brain might remain conscious as long as 15 seconds; that's how long cardiac arrest victims last before blacking out. (Dr. Fink's colleague put the window of awareness at five seconds.) He also pointed out that people have remained alert after having had their spinal cords severed. Still, this didn't seem like the sort of question that could ever be conclusively resolved.

Or so I thought. Then I received a note from a U.S. Army veteran who had been stationed in Korea. In June 1989 the taxi he and a friend were riding in collided with a truck. My correspondent was pinned in the wreckage. The friend was decapitated. Here's what happened:

> My friend's head came to rest face up, and (from my angle) upside-down. As I watched, his mouth opened and closed no less than two times. The facial expressions he displayed were first of shock or confusion, followed by terror or grief. I cannot exaggerate and say that he was looking all around, but he did display ocular movement in that his eyes moved from me, to his body, and back to me. He had direct eye contact with me when his eyes took on a hazy, absent expression . . . and he was dead.

I have spoken with the author and am satisfied that the event occurred as described. I repent my previous skepticism on this subject.

From The Straight Dope Message Board

Emergency!!! Help!!! Do Penn and Teller have a Website?

This is an emergency? When was the last time you heard anyone say, "Quick, call a magician"?

Chapter **16**

Etc.

This is something that drives me crazy every time I hear it: "Why is a raven like a writing desk?" Is there really a hilarious answer to this seemingly impossible riddle? Or is the hilarious part that there really isn't an answer? Also, where did this riddle originate?—Mary, via the Internet

This riddle is very famous—so famous that most people have never heard of it, and you can't beat fame like that. It comes from Lewis Carroll's *Alice in Wonderland*. Alice is at the tea party with the March Hare, the Mad Hatter, and the Dormouse, when apropos of pretty much nothing the Hatter pops the question above. Several pages of tomfoolery ensue, and then:

"Have you guessed the riddle yet?" the Hatter said, turning to Alice again.

"No, I give it up," Alice replied. "What's the answer?"

"I haven't the slightest idea," said the Hatter.

"Nor I," said the March Hare.

Alice sighed wearily. "I think you might do something better with the time," she said, "than wasting it in asking riddles that have no answers."

At this point most of us are thinking, Ho-ho, that Lewis Carroll, is he hilarious or what? But inevitably you get a few losers who say, Well, OK, but I still want to know why a raven is like a writing desk. One sighs wearily. Guys! It's a joke! The answer is that there isn't any answer!

Oh, they say. Pause. But why *is* a raven like a . . .

Lewis Carroll himself got bugged about this so much that he was moved to write the following in the preface to the 1896 edition of his book:

Enquiries have been so often addressed to me, as to whether any answer to the Hatter's Riddle can be imagined, that I may as well put on record here what seems to me to be a fairly appropriate answer, viz: "Because it can produce a few notes, tho they are *very* flat; and it is never put with the wrong end in front!" This, however, is merely an afterthought; the Riddle, as originally invented, had no answer at all.

Did this discourage people? No. They figured, That dope Carroll, he's too dumb to figure out his own riddle, setting aside the half-hearted attempt just quoted. So they ventured answers of their own, some of the more notable of which are recorded in Martin Gardner's *The Annotated Alice* and *More Annotated Alice*:

• Because the notes for which they are noted are not noted for being musical notes. (Puzzle maven Sam Loyd, 1914)
• Because Poe wrote on both. (Loyd again)
• Because there is a *B* in both and an *N* in neither. (Get it? Aldous Huxley, 1928)
• Because it slopes with a flap. (Cyril Pearson, undated)

Not bad for amateurs. But the real answer, to which the careers of Poe and Carroll bear ample testimony, is that you can baffle the billions with both.

Postscript: In 1976 Carroll admirer Denis Crutch pointed out that in the 1896 preface quoted above, the author had originally written: "It is nevar put with the wrong end in front." *Nevar*, of course, is raven spelled backward. Big joke! However, said joke did not survive the ministrations of the proofreaders, who, thinking they understood the author's intentions better than the author, changed *nevar* to *never* in subsequent editions. Ain't it always the way? Likewise, if in some book (e.g., this one) you come across a line that really clanks, be assured: it was funny before.

Why A Raven Is Like A Writing Desk, Continued

A comment concerning Lewis Carroll's infamous "Why is a raven like a writing desk?" riddle. The best answer I ever heard—and remember that feather pens were a common writing tool of the day, and that writing desks had inkwells—was, "Because they both come with inky quills."—Connor Freff Cochran, via AOL

I distinctly remember reading in a dumb mid-'80s comic book that one answer is, "Because Poe wrote on both."—Raistlin Wakefield, via the Internet

Back in the 1930s, when I first picked up my mother's dog-eared copy of the works of Lewis Carroll, I asked her why a raven was like a writing desk. She answered with a straight face, "Because you cannot ride either one of them like a bicycle." Since this was true, and it was just as true as saying, "Because neither one of them is made from aluminum," I always thought Mom was right.—Anonymous, via the Internet

So, Mary. (Remember Mary?) You wanted to know whether there was a really hilarious solution to this riddle. Do you have your answer now?

Who exactly were the Aryans? Being Indian, I've heard all about the mythic accomplishments of my forefathers, who were reputedly Aryan. But how much of it is true and how is it that Aryan blood is prized from Calcutta to Berlin? Where exactly did they come from and where did they go? When people make mention of Indo-European languages, cultures, etc., are they referring to Aryans? What did the Aryans look like? I'm pretty sure they weren't the blond-haired, blue-eyed stock of Hitler's wet dreams, but what racial characteristics did they possess? Also, how did the myths of Aryan supremacy come up?—RS

A long strange story, although it began innocently enough. Since ancient times people had noticed that there were a lot of similarities among European languages. But it wasn't until the sixteenth century, when Europeans began studying the Indian language Sanskrit, that scholars realized this similarity extended to several Asian languages as well. The classic example was the word "father," which was echoed by *vater* in German, *pater* in Latin, and *pitar* in Sanskrit.

In 1786 the British orientalist William Jones suggested what today is an accepted fact of science—namely, that all the languages were descended from a common source, of which no trace now remains. In the 1800s the philologist Max Mueller gave this protolanguage a name: Aryan, a name believed to have been used by various peoples living in the vicinity of Persia, modern Iran.

It seemed reasonable that the Aryan language had originated with a single Aryan tribe, or in the parlance of the day, an Aryan race. Language scholars occupied themselves for the next hundred years trying to determine where this tribe had lived and what they had looked like. At first it was assumed that the Aryans were Asians, but nationalistic European scholars found this hard to swallow and began scrounging for evidence that the Aryans had originated in Europe. German scholars were particularly energetic in this regard and persuaded themselves that the Aryans were a tall, blond, "dolichocephalic" (long-headed) people whom today we would call Nordic. The Germans and their supporters believed the blond Aryans had originally lived by the shore of the Baltic Sea and had spread their language and culture throughout the rest of Europe and parts of Asia. The fact that most speakers of Aryan languages did not look at all Nordic they explained away by saying that the original blonds had long since been submerged in the gene pool, and they dug out all sorts of references to fair-haired or fair-complected heroes, heroines, or deities in the Homeric ballads and other ancient texts. These were the now-lost Aryans, they argued, bringing the gift of civilization to the shlubs.

The idea that the blond Aryans were a superior race was first raised explicitly in 1853 by one Joseph Arthur, comte de Gobineau. De Gobineau was a respected ethnologist who argued in all seriousness that the Aryan races would prosper as long as they did not allow themselves to be tainted by mixing with black and yellow peoples. De Gobineau's ideas were widely popular and are said to have influenced Richard Wagner and Friedrich Nietzsche. Stripped of the scholarly trappings, Aryanism soon filtered down to the beer halls and eventually became one of the central tenets of Nazism. By then it had shed any linguistic significance; Hitler justified his persecution of the Slavs on the grounds that they were racially inferior, although they spoke Aryan languages.

After World War II nobody wanted to have anything to do with Aryans and the term was dropped in favor of "Indo-European." But the search for the original Aryans/Indo-Europeans wasn't completely abandoned. The leading candidate at the moment, I gather, is the "Kurgan" people of what is now south Russia, so named because they built mounds called kurgans. From 4000 to 3000 B.C., some researchers believe, they migrated in all directions, bringing their lan-

2-16-96

guage with them. Not much is known about them, although there is
archaeological evidence that they were tall. But blond hair, blue eyes?
Only their hairdressers knew for sure, and they didn't tell.

*I've got a question I hope you can answer quickly. Why is it that we
associate the heart (the organ) with love, affection, relationships? I'm
a writer at an ad agency and I'm working on a Valentine's Day card
project.—Paul Schmelzer, via the Internet*

Damn, late again. Did you have a plan B or are you now on the sup-
pository account?

Folks around the world have regarded the heart as the seat of the
soul and the center of the emotions since ancient times. Even the
most primitive peoples surely noticed that the heart pounded during
times of stress, whether from chasing game or pining for a beloved,
and they also saw that if you took a spear through it you died. It was
only natural to conclude that the heart was the home base of courage,
love, the life essence, and other good stuff. The Bible says, "You shall
love the Lord your God with all your heart and with all your soul," and
similar thoughts can be found in the sacred writings of many religions.
By the sixteenth century B.C. the Egyptians had noticed that the heart
was at the center of a network of blood vessels (actually they thought
the little tubes were blood-spit-semen-and-urine vessels, apparently
never having investigated too closely), and no doubt this reinforced

the source-of-life-and-being concept. Exactly what the heart did in connection with blood circulation remained unclear until the publication of William Harvey's work in 1628, but people have always known it was important.

The real mystery is why the heart got all the glory and not the brain. Today most of us have the sense that our inner being lives behind our eyeballs, and while this is partly because we have the benefit of medical knowledge, given the concentration of sense organs in your head it's hard to understand how anybody could imagine that consciousness resided somewhere else. But some did. The ancient Egyptians thought the center of the intellect, memory, wisdom, and so on was the heart. They attached no special importance to the brain and thought of it mainly as the source of mucus. (Maybe they spent a lot of time vacationing in the Ozarks.) Likewise, some Taoist writings seem to equate heart and mind.

Luckily, the Greeks got things straightened out. The philosopher and physiologist Alcmaeon, a student of Pythagoras who lived around 500 B.C., declared that the brain was the center of the intellect, and mainstream Western thinkers generally followed his lead. Not that anybody forgot about the heart. Instead, the familiar head-heart dichotomy developed, with the former being the intellectual HQ and the latter the home of the emotions and physical virtues such as bravery and endurance.

The idea of the heart as the center of one's being retained its punch surprisingly late in the day. I'm reminded of Catholic veneration of the Sacred Heart of Jesus—and I don't mean metaphorical heart. I mean one with Sacred Atriums and Sacred Ventricles, and I could swear as a kid in parochial school I saw one with a Sacred Aorta. The deluxe model came wrapped in a crown of thorns with drops of blood. Mrs. Adams wonders why I like horror movies. Babe, says I, the nuns started me young.

The spring breeze is blowing, and it's starting to smell like baseball, at least here in Texas. This brings to mind a fundamental question: how do groundskeepers make the checkerboard pattern in the outfield? Alternating types of sod? I've always wondered.—Justin Gaynor, Dallas

For the answer to a classic question, you want a classic source. For my money, you can't do much better than the groundskeepers at Wrigley Field, home of the Chicago Cubs. (I tried Fenway, too, but they didn't answer the phone.) The members of the Wrigley crew take their work seriously, because they know that after a few innings of a typical Cubs game many fans won't be able to bear the sight of the game anymore and will want to turn their gaze to some less exasperating scene, such as a few choice acres of God's green grass. Thus the checkerboard.

Roger Baird, assistant Wrigley GK, says he gets on his 82-inch riding mower and on day one mows east to west and on day two (or the next time he cuts the grass) north to south. He follows precisely the same path every time, mowing east in the east rows and west in the west rows and so on, always taking care that today's rows (swaths, whatever) exactly line up with those from previous days.

If you've ever tried a similar stunt with a vacuum cleaner on a rug, you know what you get: a checkerboard of squares, in this case 82 inches on a side. The grass in a square mowed west and north will catch the light differently from one mowed east and south. It doesn't help the grass grow better, it doesn't align with the earth's magnetic lines of force, but it does look pretty cool on color TV.

how do u do the thing u do?—*Name withheld, via AOL*

ez. no fresh r, no 6, barely time 2 p. y u x?

Why am I seeing pairs of shoes tied together by the laces hung up on power lines?—Lloyd S., via AOL

Been getting this question a lot lately. Lacking a proper way to investigate it, I figured I might as well cast aside the pretense of science and post it to the Net—specifically, the on-line Straight Dope area on AOL and alt.fan.cecil-adams. A sampling of the answers I could read (with a lot of stuff on AOL, you can't tell if what you're seeing is bad spelling or Esperanto):

- I heard tennis shoes hanging over a power line meant you could buy crack there.
- It's a time-honored tradition to throw your sneakers over the power lines on the last day of school.
- When I was a lad of 13 in Nashua, New Hampshire, we used to steal pairs of shoes that had been carelessly left on the sidewalk by kids who had popped open a fireplug. At this point we would play "over the wire keep away" until (a) the kid's mother, brother, father, or a passing police officer put a stop to the game, or (b) shoes went up but didn't come down.
- When I was in the military and guys were getting ready to get out and go back to a "regular" life, they would take their combat boots and paint them up all funky before tying the laces together and throwing them over a wire.
- I agree with the drug theory. I saw a news brief on Amsterdam, and there was a pair of shoes hanging in the ghetto where everyone does drugs. So I assume it means "stop here."

- Either they're meant to increase visibility for low-flying aircraft, frighten rattlesnakes away, or just for the hell of it.
- I read in the newspaper that shoes would be thrown over the power lines to serve as a reminder/warning of a murder that occurred nearby. This seems proven to me: as I was traveling past a home in which a drug-related murder had occurred about three months prior . . . a pair of shoes were hanging from the power lines in front of the home.
- Depending on what part of the country you are from, one shoe from a light post or sign represents the death of a gang member. Usually seen in the inner city.
- When I was a kid (late '60s, early '70s) the boys would tie together (a) their own sneakers that they hated or (b) sneakers of the weak and/or overweight kids and toss them over the telephone wires for fun. It usually took a number of tosses to get them up there, so the boys took this as a challenge.
- The fact about the shoes hanging across the overhead wire is: my wife won't let me bring them into the house after I walked across the barnyard. This is a certified true fact.
- Used to be a gang sign—sneakers hanging over telephone or electrical wires were to designate gang turf.
- I'll admit to being a former shoe thrower. After getting a new pair of sneakers, it was a common ritual in my neighborhood to tie the shoelaces of your old pair together and throw them up on the telephone wires. What else are you going to do with your old pair of sneakers?
- I used to teach inner-city youths in Washington, D.C., and witnessed older children throwing the shoes of younger children over tree branches and telephone lines, or a gang of children would take a single child's shoes and toss them. This was, as far as I could tell, an exclusively male pastime. The kids did this to be mean and make a difficult time of life even more difficult. One fun part about this type of kid is that if an adult tells them to stop, the adult is "disrespecting" their right to do whatever they want. The other fun part about some of these kids is that they are armed. I am not restricting my criticisms to children in inner-city Washington, either.

- There is no solid cause-effect going on here. Just your everyday kid high jinks. I suppose you could say it's a way of marking territory. Shoes can be seen hanging all over the beach area here in San Diego, over lampposts, power lines, trees, etc. It's as pointless as jamming gum in water fountains or throwing water balloons at cars. Just one of the things kids do.

So there you have it. It's either a harmless prank, a rite of passage, or a sign of the end of civilization. You figure it out.

From The Straight Dope Message Board

Subject: DOG CRAPPING IN YOUR YARD
From: rpfpa
What can I do about neighborhood coming into my yard and doing their business on my plants and such?

From: AskNott
You have several options. You can learn to accept dog poop as a natural part of your lawn-care program. You can perplex the dogs by pouring your own urine along the edge of your lawn. You can build a fence. Now that I reread your question, though, I notice you did not mention dogs. If your "neighborhood" is coming into your yard and doing their business, you may have material for an "America's Weirdest Videos" winner.

Flame Mail Generator

(For use on the Straight Dope Message Board on America Online and where otherwise appropriate. Reprinted with kind permission of OpalCat and Bermuda999.)

Dear (choose one):
- [ ] Clueless newbie
- [ ] Loser
- [ ] Pervert
- [ ] Fanatic
- [ ] Me tooer
- [ ] Incomprehensible ranter
- [ ] Adolescent twit
- [ ] Elvis
- [ ] Spammer
- [ ] Doofus
- [ ] Amateur flamer
- [ ] Unbearably self-righteous person

You are being flamed because (check all that apply):
- [ ] You posted the "gry" question
- [ ] You posted a lame "____ sucks" message
- [ ] You continued a long, stupid thread
- [ ] You started a redundant thread

☐ You posted the "driveway/parkway" question
☐ You posted anything from a Gallagher routine
☐ You act like you're five and then call everyone "ageist" for treating you like an infant
☐ You posted a "YOU ALL SUCK" message
☐ You said "me too" to something
☐ You don't know which board to post in
☐ You're an unattractive middle-aged man and your homepage has pictures of you in your underwear
☐ You brag about things that never happened or have no meaning
☐ You made a comment that had it been said in the presence of an actual human being it would have gotten you beaten up
☐ Your signature/screen name is inane
☐ You posted a sex ad
☐ You posted something totally uninteresting
☐ YOU POSTED A MESSAGE ALL WRITTEN IN CAPS
☐ You didn't Copy & Paste what you were responding to
☐ I don't like your tone of voice
☐ I think you might be a fed
☐ No reason, I'm just feeling ornery today

Your post was (check all that apply):
☐ lame
☐ stupid
☐ apparently not in English
☐ longer than any worthwhile thought of which you are capable

My attention was drawn to the fact that (check all that apply):
☐ Your question or comment has been posted before
☐ Your question or comment has been posted earlier THIS FRIGGIN WEEK
☐ Not only that, it was done better the last time
☐ The process of placing one word after another until a coherent thought has been formed has obviously eluded you
☐ Your answer was readily available in your nearest dictionary

- [ ] You posted a blatantly obvious troll
- [ ] You responded to a blatantly obvious troll
- [ ] You used the word "proactive" or "paradigm"
- [ ] You posted to a long-dead thread
- [ ] You posted an incorrect answer to a long-dead thread
- [ ] You posted an answer before reading the rest of the thread
- [ ] It was barely funny in English
- [ ] No, you didn't understand it in Latin without translating it to English
- [ ] Non satis scire
- [ ] Your post contained numerous spelling errors that did not appear to be typos
- [ ] Your post contained multiple grammatical errors that did not appear to be typos
- [ ] Your "post" contained: "excessive" punctuations!!!!!!!!!!!!!!!!
- [ ] Your post was such a scrambled mess that I am wondering if lightning struck the telephone pole outside your house
- [ ] The colors or fonts you used were distressing and could cause seizures
- [ ] Your joke was much funnier when my grandfather told it, although he probably ripped it off too
- [ ] You asked for replies via E-mail because you "don't read this board"
- [ ] Gallagher is dead, or should be
- [ ] Posts that contain the phrase "I hope this helps" almost never do
- [ ] It was obvious to all that you were laughing when you posted that war story
- [ ] Humorous, interesting flaming is an art, and you ain't Art
- [ ] The Information Please almanac is not usually used for constitutional interpretation
- [ ] You failed to lurk and get a feel for the tone of the board before posting

Furthermore (check all that apply):

- ☐ You may have greatly misunderstood the purpose of The Straight Dope MB
- ☐ You are too stupid to live, yet somehow you operate a computer
- ☐ This has been pointed out to you before
- ☐ All the regulars on this board are pagans, and if you insist on "witnessing" again we are going to come to your house and sacrifice small animals

To repent, you must (check all that apply):

- ☐ Die
- ☐ Die REALLY SLOWLY. And we all get to watch
- ☐ Give up your AOL account
- ☐ Give up your bank account
- ☐ Give up
- ☐ Change your name and move to another country and live in a cave and never speak to another human being
- ☐ Bust up your modem with a hammer and eat it
- ☐ Promise never again to post on a day when you haven't taken your meds
- ☐ Let us tattoo all over your body
- ☐ Read every single message ever posted to this board in hopes that eventually you'll get it
- ☐ Actually post something relevant
- ☐ Find all the other people who think like you do and kill them
- ☐ Personally apologize to everybody on this board. And their mom and dad too. And buy them a little present
- ☐ Take a long hike off a short pier
- ☐ Get a life
- ☐ Return to your home planet
- ☐ And destroy it
- ☐ Be really, really nice to us because we have traced the wire to your computer and we know where you live
- ☐ Repeat what you posted on this board to your mother
- ☐ Repeat what you posted on this board to Mike Tyson
- ☐ Be the guest of honor in all posts for a month

- ☐ Locate your Shift key and your dictionary
- ☐ Go to the district attorney's office and confess

In closing, I'd like to say (check all that apply):
- ☐ Bite me
- ☐ I believe that every person is basically good but you are forcing me to reconsider
- ☐ Never post again
- ☐ I console myself with the thought that you and I don't live in the same town
- ☐ I console myself with the thought that you and I don't live in the same dimension
- ☐ At least there isn't much chance of your reproducing yourself
- ☐ Although the possibility of cloning has got me worried
- ☐ Go to hell
- ☐ If God had known you were going to come along he might have rested on the sixth day, too
- ☐ Take your smut somewhere else
- ☐ You are probably the least popular person on the entire message board, and you ought to see the people you beat out
- ☐ Nyaah nyaah nyaah nyaah
- ☐ All of the above

#2

Online Interview Of Ed Zotti By *Bizarre* Magazine, London, May 1998

Q. How did this interest in esoteric information start?

A. Oh, you wrote esoteric. Initially I thought you wrote something else, and I was going to say, "I think it was the hormones kicking in." Actually, this would be better addressed to the Teeming Millions, since they're the ones who ask the esoteric questions. We'd be perfectly happy to answer questions about lawn care or Gwyneth Paltrow or . . . gawd, I'm about to barf. How do I know how this interest in esoteric information started? I guess we just found it more interesting than the non-esoteric kind.

Q. What does your job as Cecil's assistant entail?

A. Well, my co-assistant, Jane, now handles Cecil's more exotic requests. Anything involving farm animals, for example.

As for me, I do pretty much what you'd expect. I assist. I edit. I post bail. Whatever it takes.

Q. What's the strangest thing Cecil's ever been asked?

A. This is like asking what's the world's ugliest insect. Possibilities crowd the mind. Our bosses at the *Chicago Reader* newspaper, which syndicates the column, used to answer all inquiries from potential subscribers with a copy of Cecil's answer to the question "Why is [doodoo] brown?" They figured this might chase off the weak-stomached types, but that anybody who stuck with it was Our Kind. Or at least was in no position to beef later.

A question that is perhaps more frightening is: has there ever been a question that Cecil refused to answer? After all, we did expound once on what an exhumed body would look like, not to mention gerbils, pig reproductive geometry, etc. I will say we drew the line at exploring whether there was any way to keep a severed head alive. We felt, and I don't mean to imply anything by this, that that was hitting a bit close to home.

Q. Are there any questions which keep recurring no matter how often they're answered?

A. One shudders. Yes, quite a few. One of the appendices to *The Straight Dope Tells All* was a list of questions we never wanted to hear again, most along the lines of "Why do we park in the driveway and drive in the parkway?" When someone submits one of these questions now, we have a macro that automatically sends 10,000 volts through their keyboard. This has cut down on the problem a lot. Of course, it was a shame about Mom.

Q. Are there any great unanswerable questions—barring the "Why don't sheep shrink in the rain?" dumb ones, of course?

A. You think that's dumb, eh? That's because you're English. We Americans have been blazing new trails in the dumbness department. The one TV interviewers used to think was clever was "When the snow melts, where does the white go?" Just thinking about it gives me the shivers. I can honestly say that no question we have seriously pursued has ultimately resisted . . . I take that back. We never got a satisfactory answer on the cause of, um, piss shiver. You know, that little frisson that occurs after one has watered the flowers. Science has been content to leave this field of inquiry wholly unexplored, so far as I know. However, it occurs to me that this interview will be appearing in England, that land of storied eccentrics, and perhaps someone has made a study of the matter. If so, sir or madam, I implore you. Stop what you are doing. Call us (our dime). Worldwide recognition awaits.

Q. How is the column researched?

A. Well, of course you understand that Cecil knows everything, having been imprinted with perfect world knowledge at the moment of conception. However, the lawyers insist that we fact-check everything, which is where I come in. My main tools are the library, the telephone, a computer (see below). Although as I have said in the past, there are times when you can't beat the persuasiveness of good bourbon and a roll of twenties.

Q. Has the Internet made your job easier or more difficult?

A. On the whole, vastly easier. One drawback is that it has rather lowered the bar in terms of stupid questions, since previously you had to find a stamp and an envelope, and spell the address more or less right, and perform other tasks indicative of a certain baseline level of mental organization, whereas now all you have to do is find the "send" button on Dad's E-mail program.

On the other hand, we now have access to resources of astonishing depth and breadth, making it possible to answer questions previously impervious to inquiry. The theory of general relativity, now . . . anyone can explain that. But try walking down the street and see if you can find someone who can give a convincing account of the purpose of a merkin—i.e., a pubic wig. Not that we got a definitive answer using Usenet, but we did amass a fine collection of barmy theories, the best undoubtedly being that a merkin is somebody who lives in Merika.

Q. Has Cecil ever been forced to back down and admit to being wrong?

A. Cecil is genetically incapable of error. His assistants, however, occasionally screw up. The Monty Hall three doors fiasco, for example . . . that was me. Also, the sorry contretemps over "the exception proves the rule." A few others I hope you've forgotten and certainly don't plan to remind you of. After each such incident, well, let's just say I know how the sorcerer's apprentice felt.

Q. How do you respond to people who allege that you are, in fact, Cecil Adams?

A. With ill-concealed delight. It is difficult to object strenuously to being mistaken for the world's most intelligent human being. If Cecil gets a little miffed, well, he has no one to blame but himself. Of course, I am contractually bound to tell the truth, but one meets these eager young reporters who do so want to believe that they have uncovered one's dirty little secret, and who am I to disappoint them? I remember one fellow . . . yes, he believed I was Cecil, all right. Two more beers and I'd have had him believing I was Amelia Earhart.

People often ask me if Slug Signorino, infamous illustrator of the Straight Dope, is real. I am obliged to reply: real in what sense? Just now I was speaking with an editor on the Straight Dope copy desk, who told me Slug was upset because one of his illustrations had appeared in the newspaper backward. I asked: Who could tell? (I am reminded of a comment attributed to the late Timothy Leary by Robert Anton Wilson: "I don't like any painting you can't turn upside down.") But Slug knew, because his signature was backward. We puzzled about that for a moment, because the illustrations are scanned electronically, and ought to be immune to such mishaps. Finally I said, "Maybe he just drew it backwards. He has those days, you know." It tells you something about Slug that for a moment both of us seriously considered this possibility.

Not to be mysterious, but I have often thought it interesting that people accept unquestioningly that my name is Ed Zotti.

Index

A

Abagnale, Frank (counterfeiting consultant), 32

Absorbine Jr., whether there is an Absorbine Sr. counterpart to, 227–229

Ack-Ti Lining company, 219

Age of Aquarius, starting date of, 55–56

airspace, above one's home, rights to, 136–139

Alice in Wonderland, 266–267

Alka-Seltzer, whether seagulls will explode if fed, 84–86

aluminum cans, why Coca-Cola fails to dissolve, 222

aluminum foil, whether shiny side should be in or out when wrapping with, 172–174

Alzheimer's disease, prevention of, by smoking, 96–98

Amherst, Lord Jeffrey, 67–68

Anslinger, Harry, 133, 135–136

antibacterial soap, 88

Aquarius, Age of, starting date of, 55–56

arthritis, and ability to predict changes in weather, 57–59

Aryans, evolving views regarding, 269–271

astrologers, and Age of Aquarius, 56

Atlantis, location of, 69–71

Aughty-Aught, Class of (pronunciation of Class of '00), 160–161

Auschwitz, 79

Azoff, Irving, 3

B

Backster, Cleve, 47, 48

Baird, Roger, 273

Barbet, Pierre (crucifixion researcher), 241

Barlett, Donald, 141

Barton, William (Great Seal of U.S. co-designer), 23

baseball. *See* checkerboard pattern in baseball outfield

bathroom, why women go in groups to, 36–37

Beatles, connection of "Helter Skelter" song by, to Manson murders, 3–4

bee: alleged mystery regarding flight by, 45–46; whether honey is really vomit of, 40–41

beheading, whether one can remain briefly conscious following, 262–264

Bennett, Charles, 198–199

Berry, Chuck, and "Johnny B. Goode," 8–9

bezoars (calcified hair balls), use of, for aesthetic and medicinal purposes, 104–105

Bible, 63, 271; jokes in, 244–247

Bird, Christopher, 47

birds, alleged explosions of,
following rice consumption,
81–87
black doctor, death of, after alleged
refusal of hospital to admit
following injury, 73–74
"black Irish," origin of term, 77–78
"Blinded by the Light," correct lyrics
for, 148–149
Block, Keith, 99
blood test, premarital, purpose of,
193–196
Bluto, vs. Brutus, as main Popeye
nemesis, 216–217
boiling water, why pioneer childbirth
apparently required, 190–111
bones, aching, as sign of change in
weather, 57–59
Boniface VIII (pope), 247–248
"book, bell, and candle" ceremony
for excommunication, 243–244
Bounce (antistatic dryer sheet),
explanation of, 175–176
Bouquet, Henry, 68
Braun company, alleged construction
of Nazi crematoria by,
78–79
bridges, covered, reason for,
174–175
Britain, why "Great" appended to,
153
Brown, Glenn, 72
Bruse, Rev. James, 238, 239, 242
Brutus, vs. Bluto, as main Popeye
nemesis, 216–217
Bugliosi, Vincent (Manson
prosecutor), 4
bullet, whether dropped will hit
ground faster than shot, 201
bulls, whether nose rings really worn
by, 213–214
bumblebee, alleged mystery
regarding flying ability of,
45–46

C

Caen, Herb, 151
call letters, broadcast, why W used
east of Mississippi and K used
west in, 176–177
Campbell, Joseph, 23
Canal, Panama, whether sea would
pour through after locks blown
on, 46–47
cannibalism, whether love of Spam is
related to prior practice of,
232–235
cans, aluminum, why Coca-Cola fails
to dissolve, 222
Carroll, Lewis: and suspicious
interest in little girls, 185–186;
and why raven is like a writing
desk, 266–268
cartoons. See Looney Tunes;
"8-Man"; Popeye
cataracts, whether fluorescent lights
can cause, 102–103
Catholic Church, how to get
excommunicated from, 242–244.
See also Christianity; Holy Door
cats, alleged ability of, to fall
unlimited distances and survive,
190–193
ceiling, how close fly gets to, before
flipping over to land on, 43–44
checkerboard pattern in baseball
outfield, explanation for, 272–273
chicken gun (jet engine testing
device), 170–172
childbirth, why boiling water needed
for, 109–111
Chinese, use of computers by,
despite pictogrammic language,
177–180
chocolate, toxicity to dogs of,
211–212
Christianity, explanation for

drowning, danger of, from swimming immediately after eating, 87–88

drug test, whether consumption of poppy seed rolls can make you fail, 116–118

Drummond, Jan, 188

drums, talking, whether really such a thing as, 158–160

dryer antistatic sheets, explanation of, 175–176

du Pont corporation, alleged suppression of hemp at behest of, 133, 135

duck's quack, inability of, to echo, 71–73

E

Eagles (rock group), 1–3, 14

ear candles, efficacy of, 98–100

ears: ringing in, causes of, 94–96; whether insects can get stuck in, 111–113

earwax: purpose and removal of, 111–112; removal of, by ear candles, 98–100

earwigs, lodging of, in ears, 113

eating: of clay and other unusual substances, 90–92; whether you will drown if you swim immediately after, 87–88

Eberhardt, Aubrey, 147

echo, whether duck's quack will, 71–73

Egyptians, ancient, views of, regarding heart and brain, 271–272

"8-Man" (cartoon), use of cigarettes to recharge super powers in, 49–51

Ellis, Bill, 259

ESP (extrasensory perception), and plants, 47–48

"esquire," how one obtains title, 121–122

excommunication from Catholic Church, how to arrange for, 242–244

eyes, whether excessively close viewing of TV will ruin, 105–107

F

falls, alleged ability of cats to survive, regardless of height, 190–193

Federer, Clark, 99

"feed a cold, starve a fever," proper way to say, 154–156

fever, advisability of starving, while feeding cold, 154–156

fifty-cent pieces, what happened to, 24–26

Fink, Robert, 263, 264

first decade of century, what to call, 161–164

Fitzsimmons, Scott (Zegrahm Space Voyages VP), 202–203

flat tax, stupidity of proposals for, 140–144

flight: alleged mystery about bumblebees' ability regarding, 45–46; independent evolution of, in various species, 216. See also space flight

fluorescent lights, whether cataracts can be caused by, 102–103

fly, proximity of, to ceiling before turning to land on, 43–44

Flynn, Errol, whether "in like Flynn" refers to sexual exploits of, 156–158

foil, aluminum, whether shiny side should be in or out when wrapping, 172–174

Foley artists (movie sound effects creators), secrets of, 12–14

Forbes, Jr., Malcolm, 142

I

IBM, legitimacy of teleportation claims in ad by, 198–199

ibuprofen, susceptibility of dogs to poisoning by, 211–212

Illuminati, and symbols on dollar bill, 24

"in like Flynn," origin of phrase, 156–158

income tax: alleged invalidity of, due to improper ratification, 127–131; whether rich pay very little, 139–142

Indians, alleged intentional infection of, with smallpox by whites, 66–68

intestines, whether suction toilet sucked out someone's, 260–262

Irish, "black," origin of term, 77–78

Ising, Rudolph, 7

Itard, Jean-Marc-Gaspard, 95

J

Japanese, use of computers by, despite pictogrammic language, 177–180

Jesus, explanation for popularity of, 248–250. See also Bible; stigmata

jet engines, and testing by chicken gun, 170–172

John 3:16 man (Rock'n Rollen Stewart), crime spree by, 18–21

"Johnny B. Goode" (Chuck Berry song), what tunes were more popular than, on Billboard charts, 8–9

joints, aching, as sign of change in weather, 57–59

jokes in Bible, 244–247

Jones, Marc Edward, 55–56

Judas Priest, meaning of, 150–151

K

K, why broadcast call letters west of Mississippi begin with, 176–177

Kaufman, Phil, 15–16

Kelly, Kitty, 12

kidney theft: in India, 258; veracity of stories regarding, 255–258

King Features, 216–217

knee jerk reflex, medical significance of, 100–102

kraut juice, inexplicable marketability of, 227

Krupp munition works, use of World War II slave laborers by, 79

Krups company, alleged construction of Nazi crematoria by, 78–79

L

Lake, Leonard, 260

Lateau, Louise, 238, 239

Lavoisier, Antoine, 263

left-handedness, and death, 92–94

Liddell, Alice, 185

life spans, whether trees and plants have limited, 42–43

light, why moths attracted to, 38–40

Looney Tunes (cartoon series), difference between Merrie Melodies and, 6–8

love, how heart came to be associated with, 271–272

Lowell, Percival, 197

M

MacKinnon, Catharine, 259

magnetic strips in dollar bills, purpose of, 30–32

Manfred Mann's Earth Band, 148–149

mano a mano, meaning of term, 164

Manson, Charles, significance of

About The Author

Cecil Adams is still the author. If anything changes, we'll let you know.